DEADPOOL

WRITERS

GERRY DUGGAN & BRIAN POSEHN

ARTIST
TONY MOORE

COLOR ARTIST
VAL STAPLES

COVER ART
GEOF DARROW & PETER DOHERTY (#1-5) AND ZACH BALDUS (#6)

LETTERERS
VC'S JOE SABINO (#1-5) & CLAYTON COWLES (#6)

EDITOR
JORDAN D. WHITE

SENIOR EDITOR
NICK LOWE

DEADPOOL CREATED BY ROB LIEFELD AND FABIAN NICIEZA

Collection Editor: Jennifer Grünwald • Assistant Editors: Alex Starbuck & Nelson Ribeiro • Editor, Special Projects: Mark D. Beazley
Senior Editor, Special Projects: Jeff Youngquist • SVP of Print & Digital Publishing Sales: David Gabriel • Book Design: Jeff Powell

Editor in Chief: Axel Alonso • Chief Creative Officer: Joe Quesada • Publisher: Dan Buckley • Executive Producer: Alan Fine

DEADPOOL VOL. 1: DEAD PRESIDENTS. Contains material original… ISBN# 978-0-7851-6680-1. Published by MARVEL WORLDWIDE, INC., a subsidiary of MARVEL ENTERTAINMENT, LLC, OFFICE OF PUBLICATION: 135 West 50th Street, New York, NY 10020. Copyright … el Characters, Inc. All rights reserved. All characters featured in this issue and the distinctive names and likenesses thereof, and all related indicia are trademarks of Marvel Characters, Inc. No similarity between any of the names, characters, persons, and/or institutions in this magazine with those of any living or dead person or institution is intended, and any such similarity which may exist is purely coincidental. Printed in the U.S.A. ALAN FINE, EVP - Office of the President, Marvel Worldwide, Inc. and EVP & CMO Marvel Characters B.V.; DAN BUCKLEY, Publisher & President - Print, Animation & Digital Divisions; JOE QUESADA, Chief Creative Officer; TOM BREVOORT, SVP of Publishing; DAVID BOGART, SVP of Operations & Procurement, Publishing; C.B. CEBULSKI, SVP of Creator & Content Development; DAVID GABRIEL, SVP of Print & Digital Publishing Sales; JIM O'KEEFE, VP of Operations & Logistics; DAN CARR, Executive Director of Publishing Technology; SUSAN CRESPI, Editorial Operations Manager; ALEX MORALES, Publishing Operations Manager; STAN LEE, Chairman Emeritus. For information regarding advertising in Marvel Comics or on Marvel.com, please contact Niza …isla, Director of Marvel Partnerships, at ndisla@marvel.com. For Marvel subscription inquiries, please call 800-217-9158. Manufactured between 4/10/2013 and 5/13/2013 by QUAD/GRAPHICS, VERSAILLES, KY, USA.

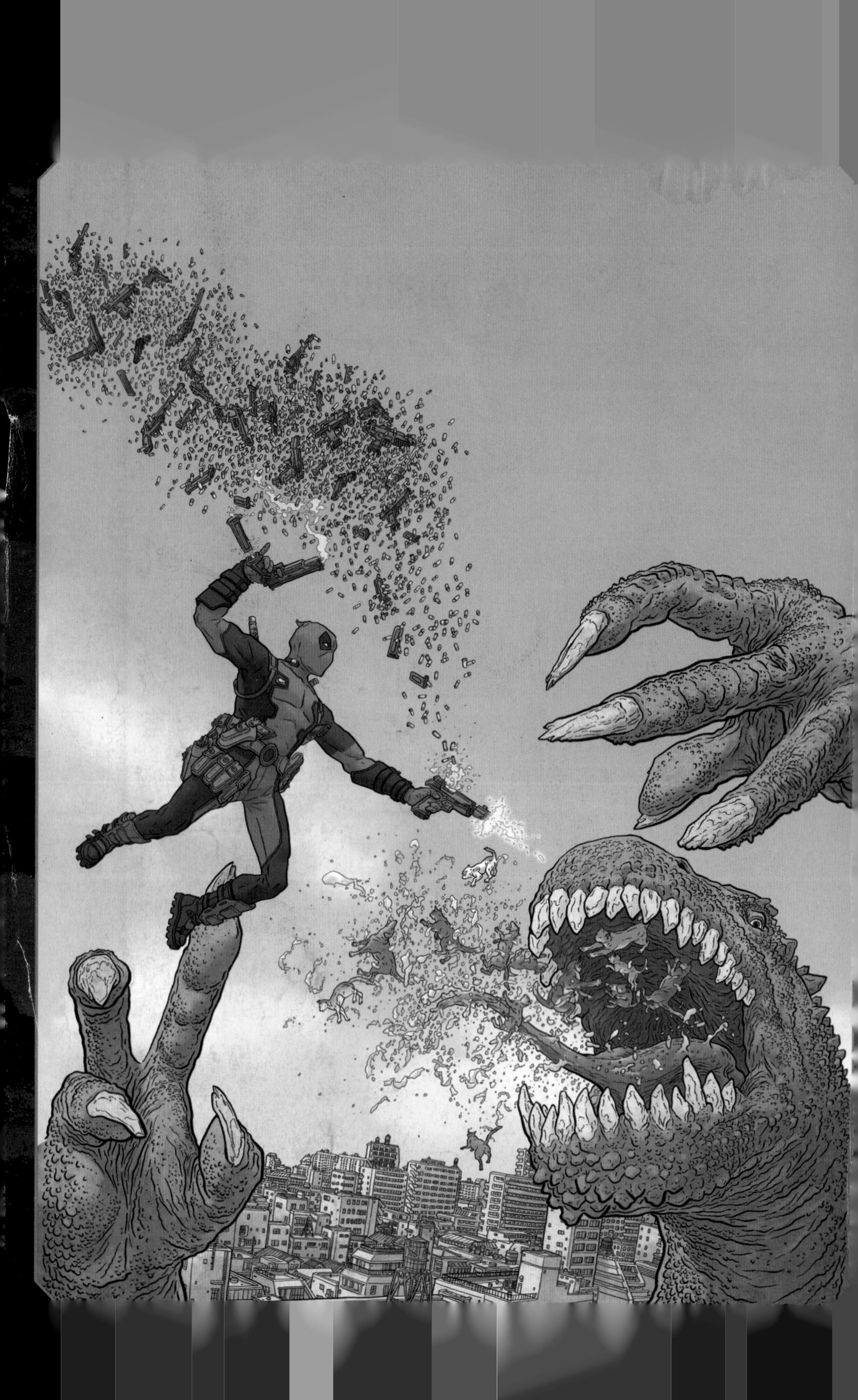

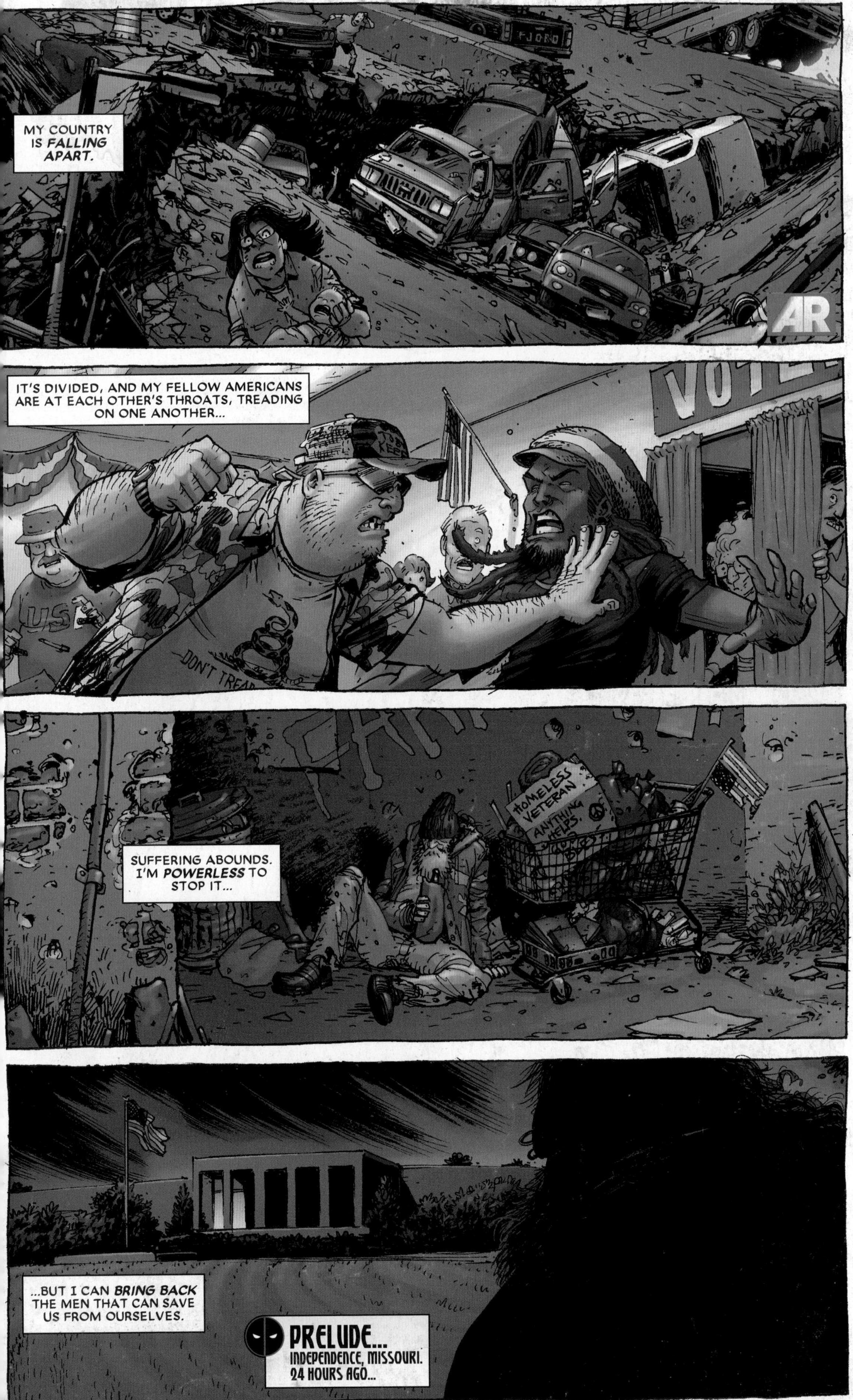
MY COUNTRY IS *FALLING APART.*
IT'S DIVIDED, AND MY FELLOW AMERICANS ARE AT EACH OTHER'S THROATS, TREADING ON ONE ANOTHER...
SUFFERING ABOUNDS. I'M *POWERLESS* TO STOP IT...
HOMELESS VETERAN
ANYTHING HELPS.
...BUT I CAN *BRING BACK* THE MEN THAT CAN SAVE US FROM OURSELVES.
PRELUDE...
INDEPENDENCE, MISSOURI.
24 HOURS AGO...

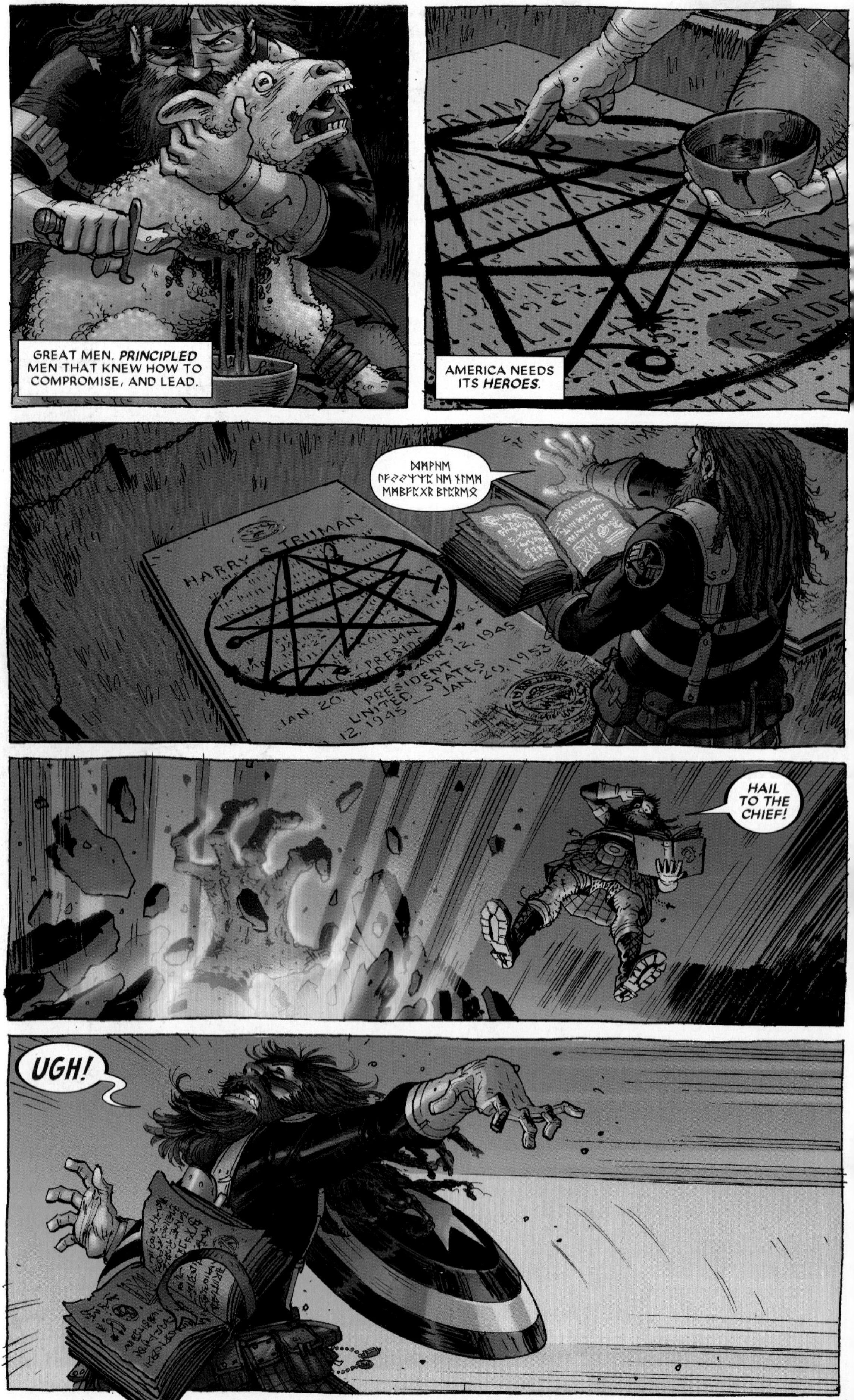
GREAT MEN. PRINCIPLED MEN THAT KNEW HOW TO COMPROMISE, AND LEAD.
AMERICA NEEDS ITS HEROES.
HAIL TO THE CHIEF!
UGH!

THIS STOPS NOW, MADMAN.

YOU SHOULD BE HELPING ME! NO ONE LOVES THE COUNTRY MORE THAN CAPTAIN AMERICA!

I KNOW WHAT YOU'RE TRYING TO DO. NO GOOD CAN COME FROM BRINGING THEM BACK.

RRRAAARRGH

WHO DARES VETO THE ETERNAL REST OF HARRY S. TRUMAN?

MR. PRESIDENT, I BROUGHT YOU BACK SO YOU CAN HELP US FIX THIS COUNTRY!

FIX...THIS COUNTRY?

I'LL DESTROY IT!

SEND HIM BACK!

I CAN'T--IT DOESN'T WORK LIKE THAT!

ᛏᛁᚾᛗ ᛗᚱᛒᚤᚲᚨ ᛈᚨᛒᛏᚤᚤᚲ ᚾᛗ ᛏᛗᛗ ᛗᛗᛒᚠᛒᚲᚱ ᛒᛁᛒᚱᛗ!

DON'T DISAPPEAR ON ME, YOU COWARD!

DAMN.

LAST TIME I WAS HERE YOU WERE DEAD. I THINK I LIKED IT BETTER THAT WAY...

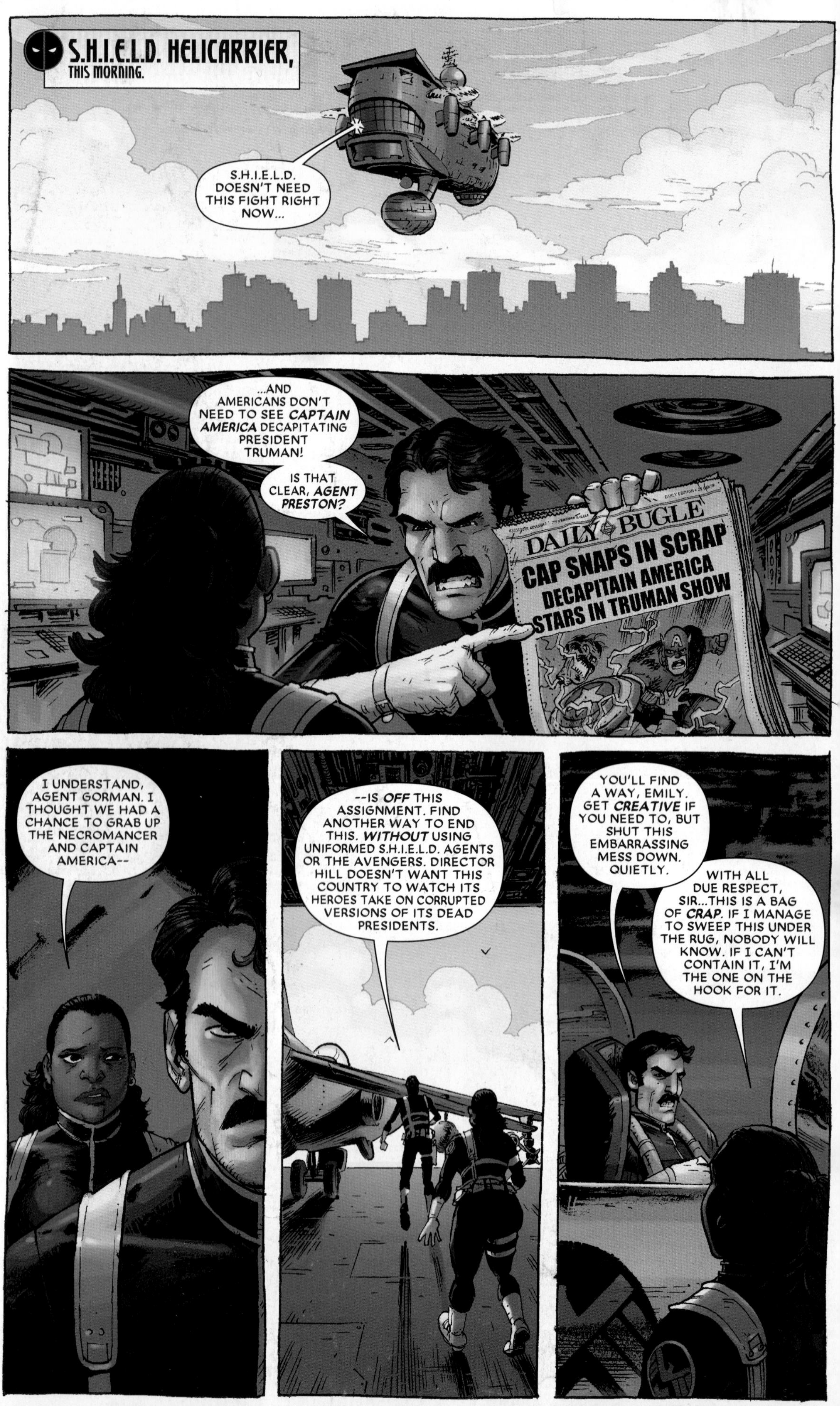
S.H.I.E.L.D. HELICARRIER, THIS MORNING.
S.H.I.E.L.D. DOESN'T NEED THIS FIGHT RIGHT NOW...
...AND AMERICANS DON'T NEED TO SEE CAPTAIN AMERICA DECAPITATING PRESIDENT TRUMAN!
IS THAT CLEAR, AGENT PRESTON?
DAILY BUGLE
CAP SNAPS IN SCRAP
DECAPITAIN AMERICA STARS IN TRUMAN SHOW
I UNDERSTAND, AGENT GORMAN. I THOUGHT WE HAD A CHANCE TO GRAB UP THE NECROMANCER AND CAPTAIN AMERICA--
--IS OFF THIS ASSIGNMENT. FIND ANOTHER WAY TO END THIS. WITHOUT USING UNIFORMED S.H.I.E.L.D. AGENTS OR THE AVENGERS. DIRECTOR HILL DOESN'T WANT THIS COUNTRY TO WATCH ITS HEROES TAKE ON CORRUPTED VERSIONS OF ITS DEAD PRESIDENTS.
YOU'LL FIND A WAY, EMILY. GET CREATIVE IF YOU NEED TO, BUT SHUT THIS EMBARRASSING MESS DOWN. QUIETLY.
WITH ALL DUE RESPECT, SIR...THIS IS A BAG OF CRAP. IF I MANAGE TO SWEEP THIS UNDER THE RUG, NOBODY WILL KNOW. IF I CAN'T CONTAIN IT, I'M THE ONE ON THE HOOK FOR IT.

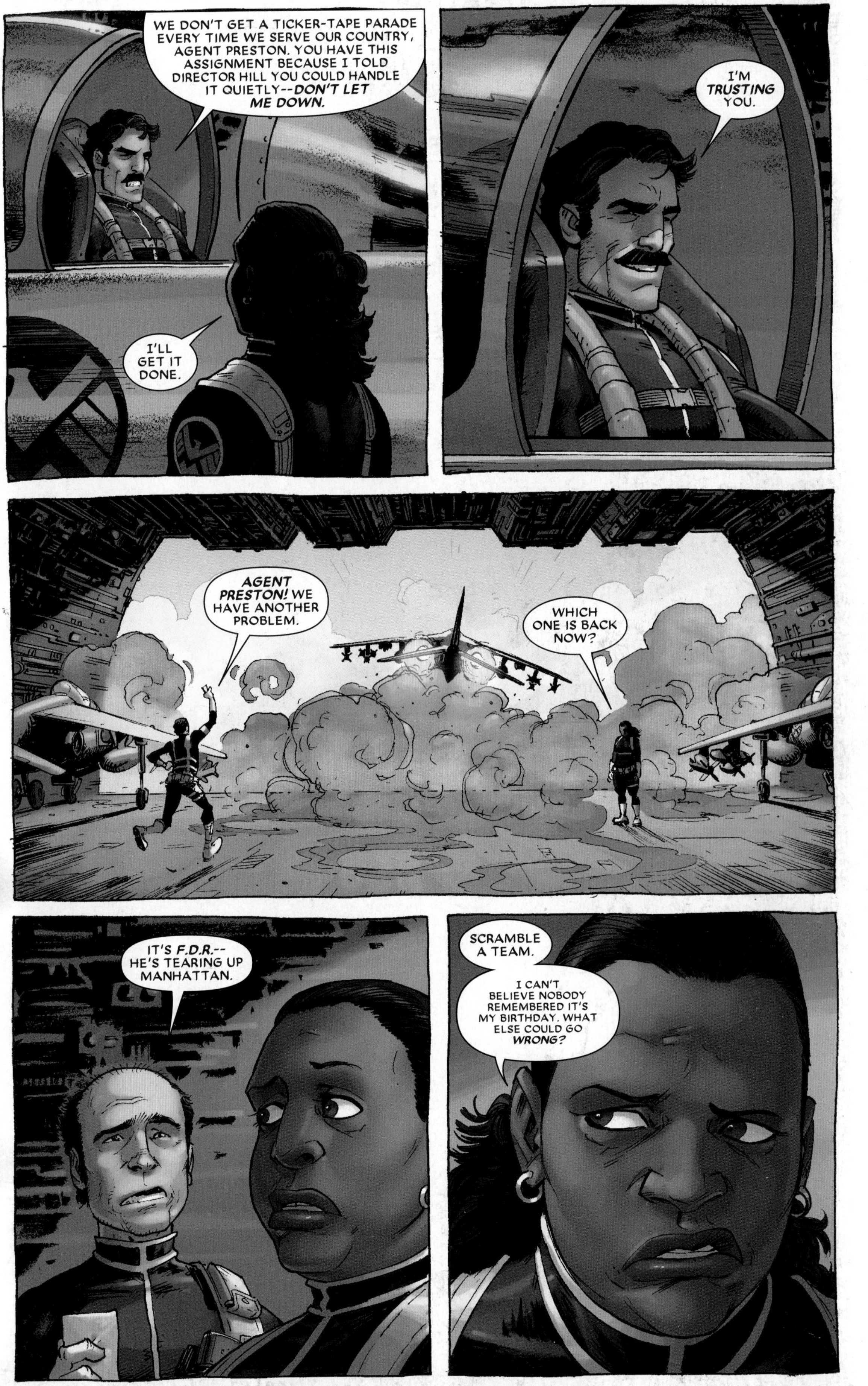
WE DON'T GET A TICKER-TAPE PARADE EVERY TIME WE SERVE OUR COUNTRY, AGENT PRESTON. YOU HAVE THIS ASSIGNMENT BECAUSE I TOLD DIRECTOR HILL YOU COULD HANDLE IT QUIETLY--DON'T LET ME DOWN.
I'LL GET IT DONE.
I'M TRUSTING YOU.
AGENT PRESTON! WE HAVE ANOTHER PROBLEM.
WHICH ONE IS BACK NOW?
IT'S F.D.R.-- HE'S TEARING UP MANHATTAN.
SCRAMBLE A TEAM.
I CAN'T BELIEVE NOBODY REMEMBERED IT'S MY BIRTHDAY. WHAT ELSE COULD GO WRONG?

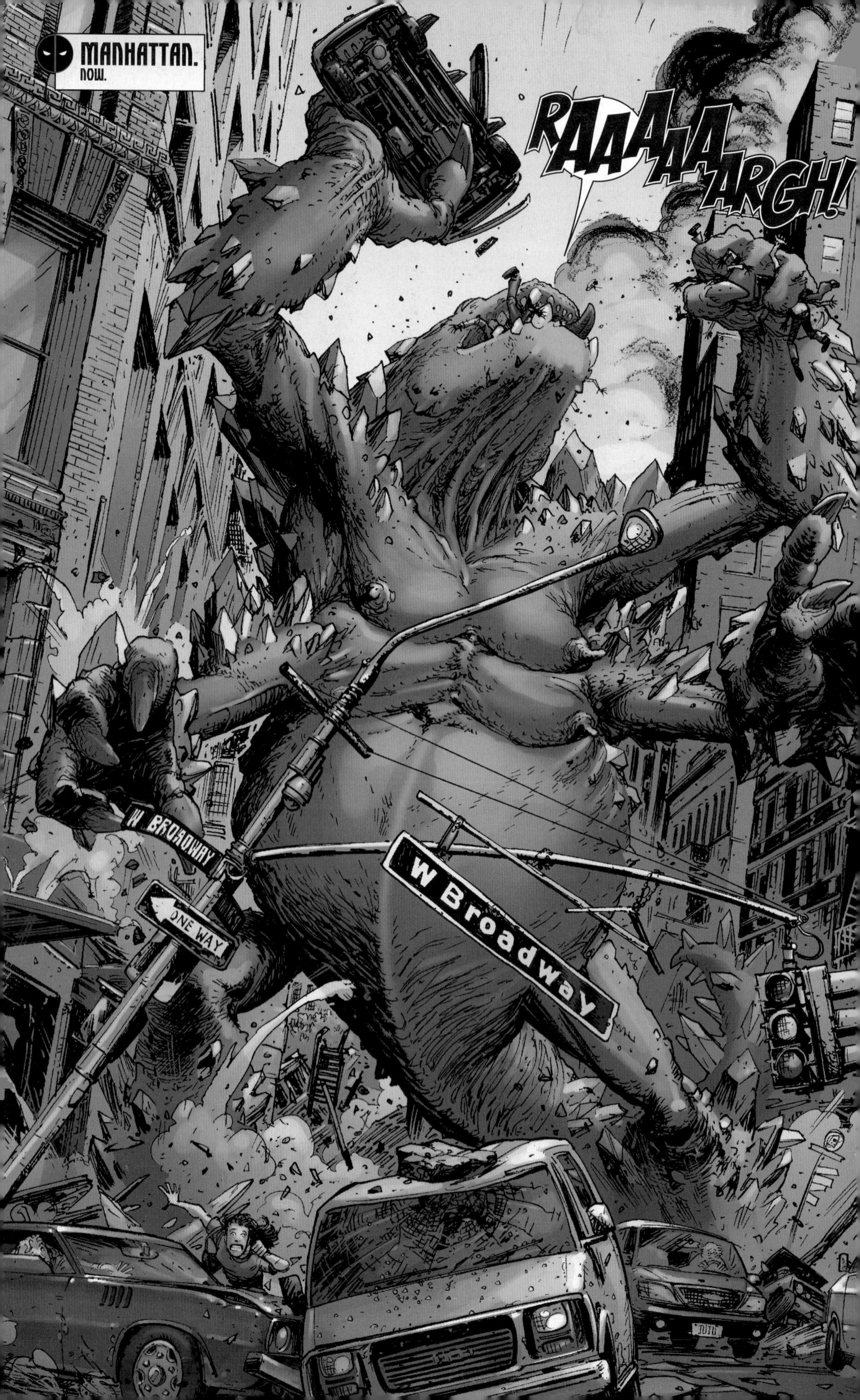
MANHATTAN.
NOW.
RAAAAAAARGH!
W BROADWAY
ONE WAY
W Broadway

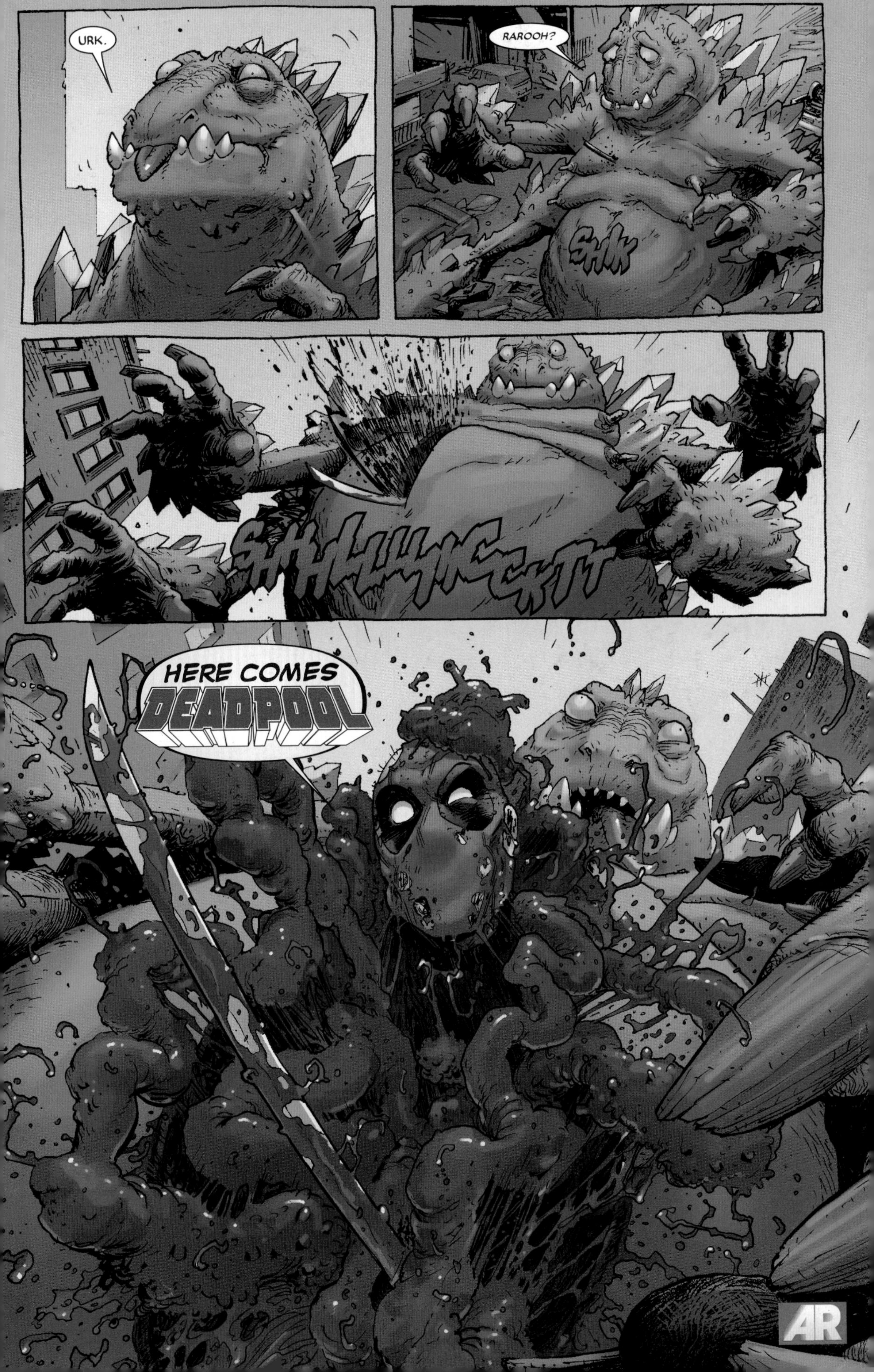
URK.
RAROOH?
SHK
SHLLUKCHTT
HERE COMES
DEADPOOL

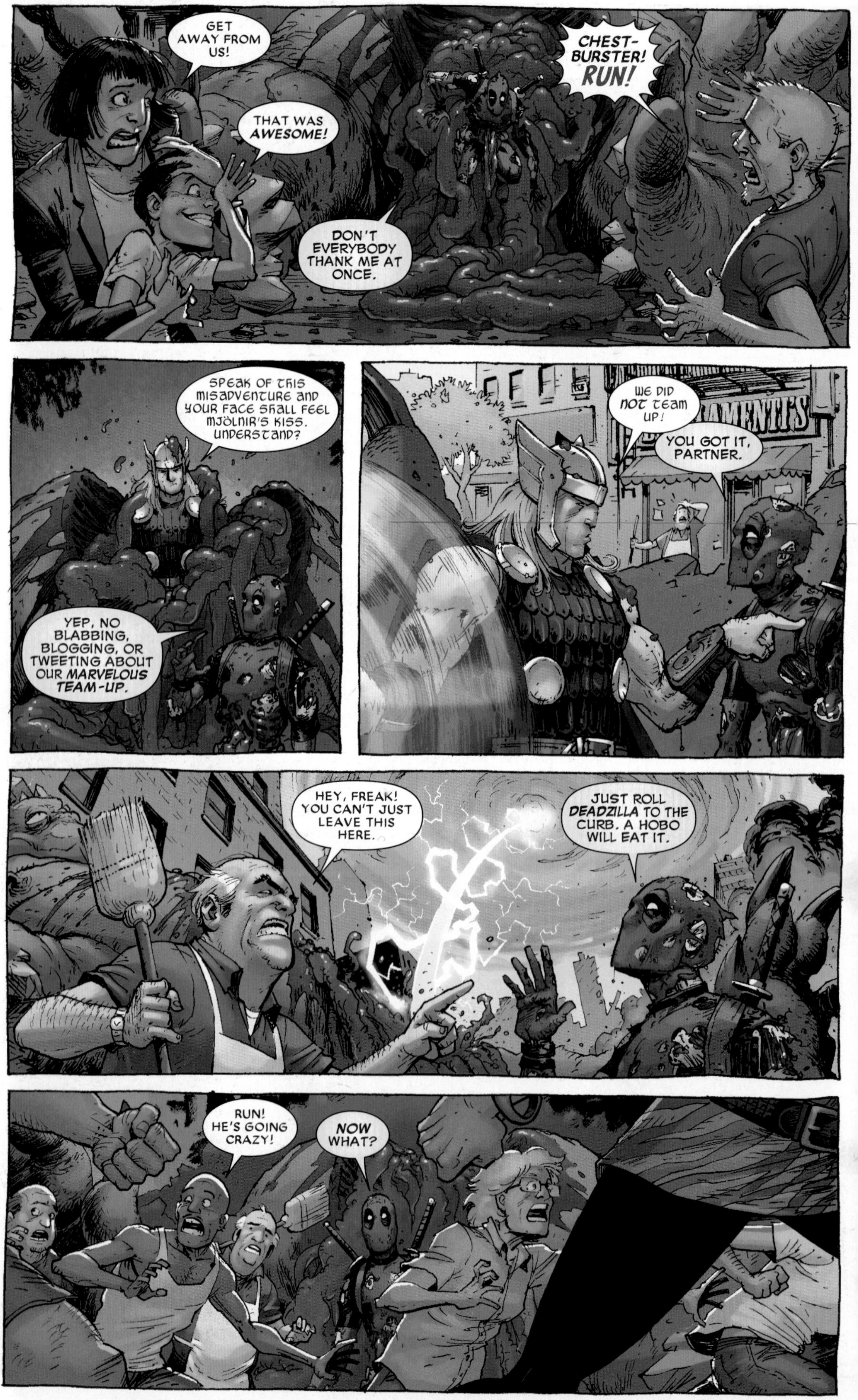
GET AWAY FROM US!
THAT WAS *AWESOME!*
CHEST-BURSTER! *RUN!*
DON'T EVERYBODY THANK ME AT ONCE.
SPEAK OF THIS MISADVENTURE AND YOUR FACE SHALL FEEL MJÖLNIR'S KISS. UNDERSTAND?
YEP, NO BLABBING, BLOGGING, OR TWEETING ABOUT OUR *MARVELOUS TEAM-UP.*
WE DID *NOT* TEAM UP!
YOU GOT IT, PARTNER.
HEY, FREAK! YOU CAN'T JUST LEAVE THIS HERE.
JUST ROLL *DEADZILLA* TO THE CURB. A HOBO WILL EAT IT.
RUN! HE'S GOING CRAZY!
NOW WHAT?

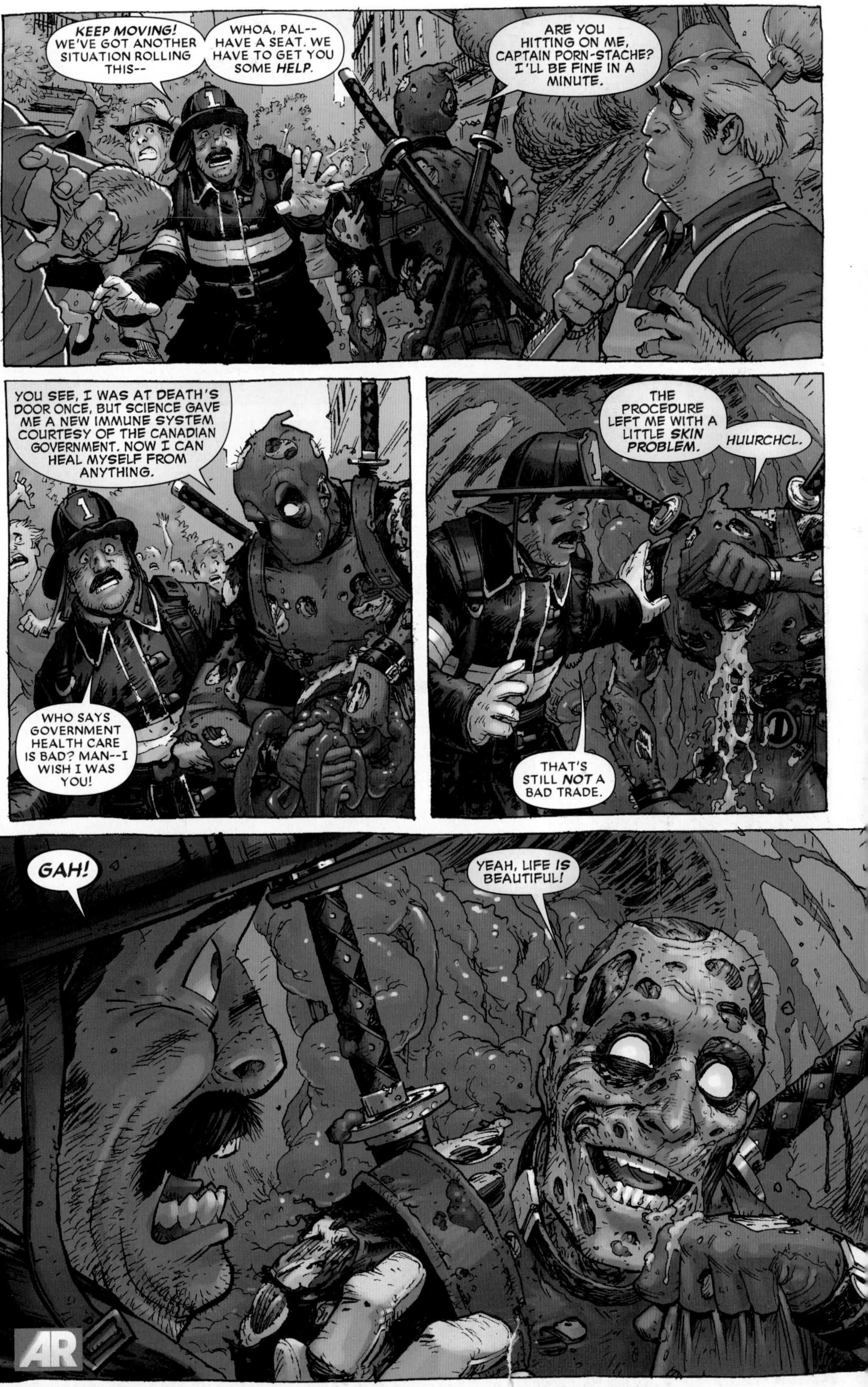
KEEP MOVING! WE'VE GOT ANOTHER SITUATION ROLLING THIS--
WHOA, PAL-- HAVE A SEAT. WE HAVE TO GET YOU SOME HELP.
ARE YOU HITTING ON ME, CAPTAIN PORN-STACHE? I'LL BE FINE IN A MINUTE.
YOU SEE, I WAS AT DEATH'S DOOR ONCE, BUT SCIENCE GAVE ME A NEW IMMUNE SYSTEM COURTESY OF THE CANADIAN GOVERNMENT. NOW I CAN HEAL MYSELF FROM ANYTHING.
WHO SAYS GOVERNMENT HEALTH CARE IS BAD? MAN--I WISH I WAS YOU!
THE PROCEDURE LEFT ME WITH A LITTLE SKIN PROBLEM.
HUURCHCL.
THAT'S STILL NOT A BAD TRADE.
GAH!
YEAH, LIFE IS BEAUTIFUL!
AR

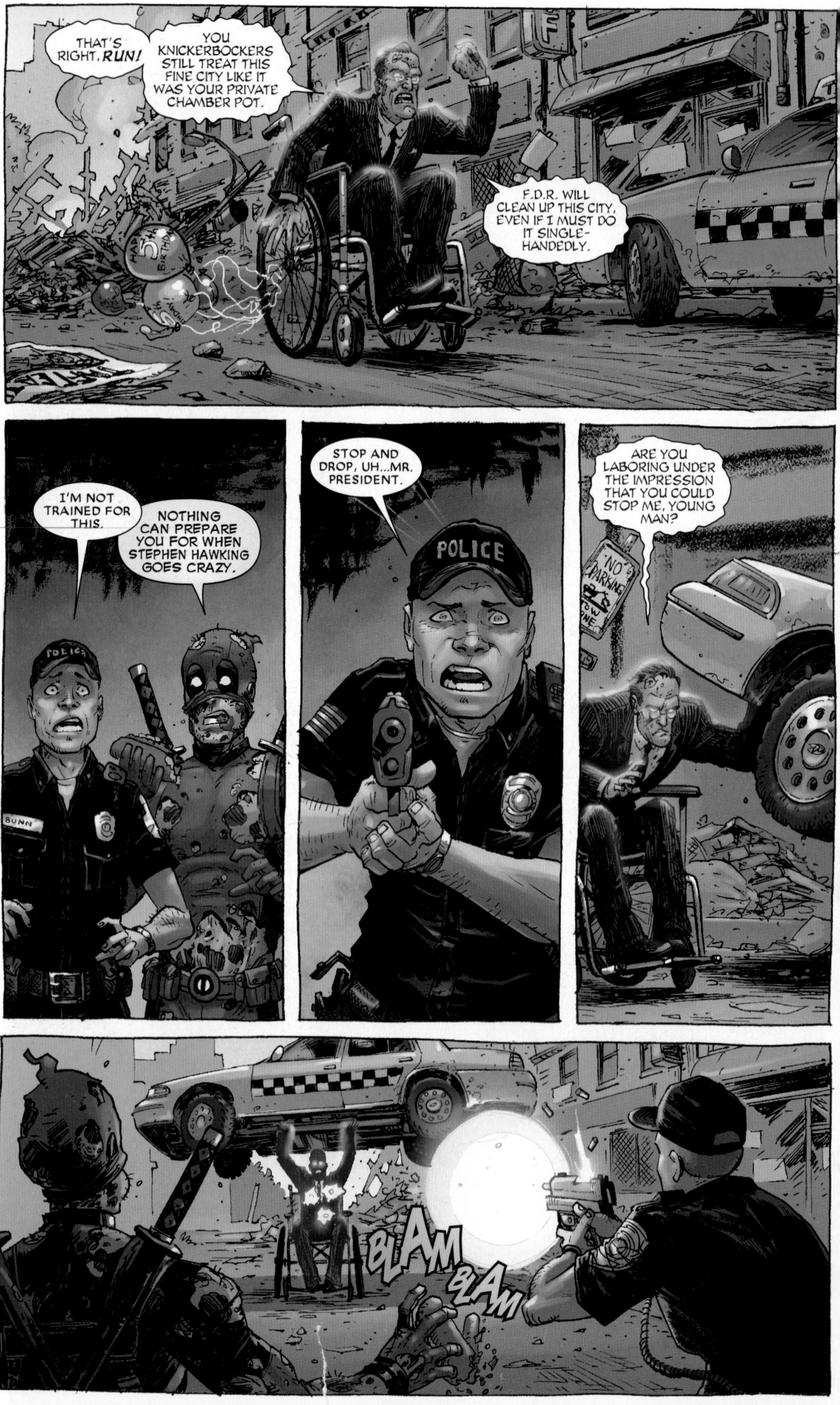
THAT'S RIGHT, RUN!
YOU KNICKERBOCKERS STILL TREAT THIS FINE CITY LIKE IT WAS YOUR PRIVATE CHAMBER POT.
F.D.R. WILL CLEAN UP THIS CITY, EVEN IF I MUST DO IT SINGLE-HANDEDLY.
I'M NOT TRAINED FOR THIS.
NOTHING CAN PREPARE YOU FOR WHEN STEPHEN HAWKING GOES CRAZY.
STOP AND DROP, UH...MR. PRESIDENT.
POLICE
ARE YOU LABORING UNDER THE IMPRESSION THAT YOU COULD STOP ME, YOUNG MAN?
"NO" PARKING
BLAM
BLAM

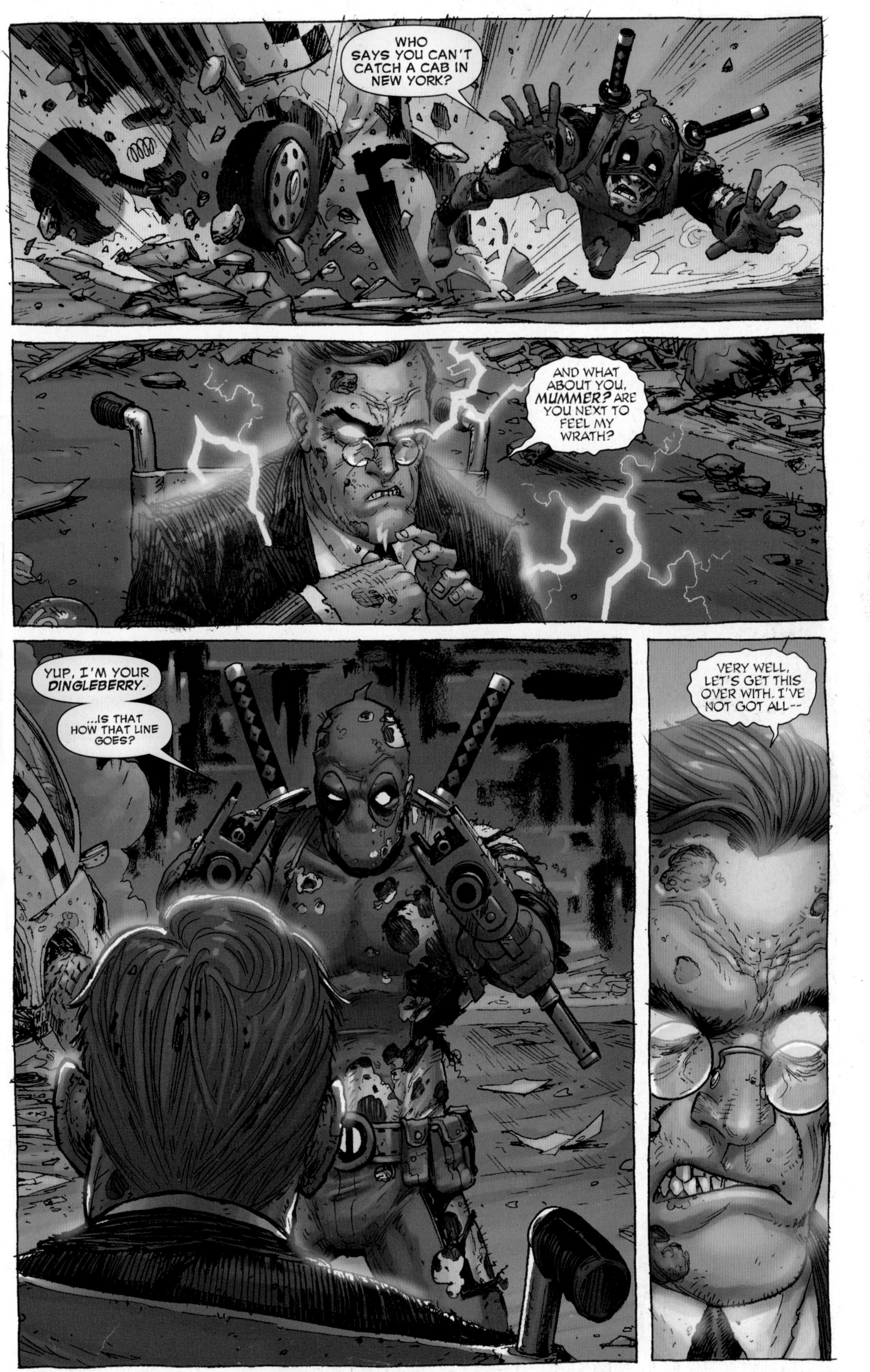
WHO SAYS YOU CAN'T CATCH A CAB IN NEW YORK?
AND WHAT ABOUT YOU, MUMMER? ARE YOU NEXT TO FEEL MY WRATH?
YUP, I'M YOUR DINGLEBERRY.
...IS THAT HOW THAT LINE GOES?
VERY WELL, LET'S GET THIS OVER WITH. I'VE NOT GOT ALL--

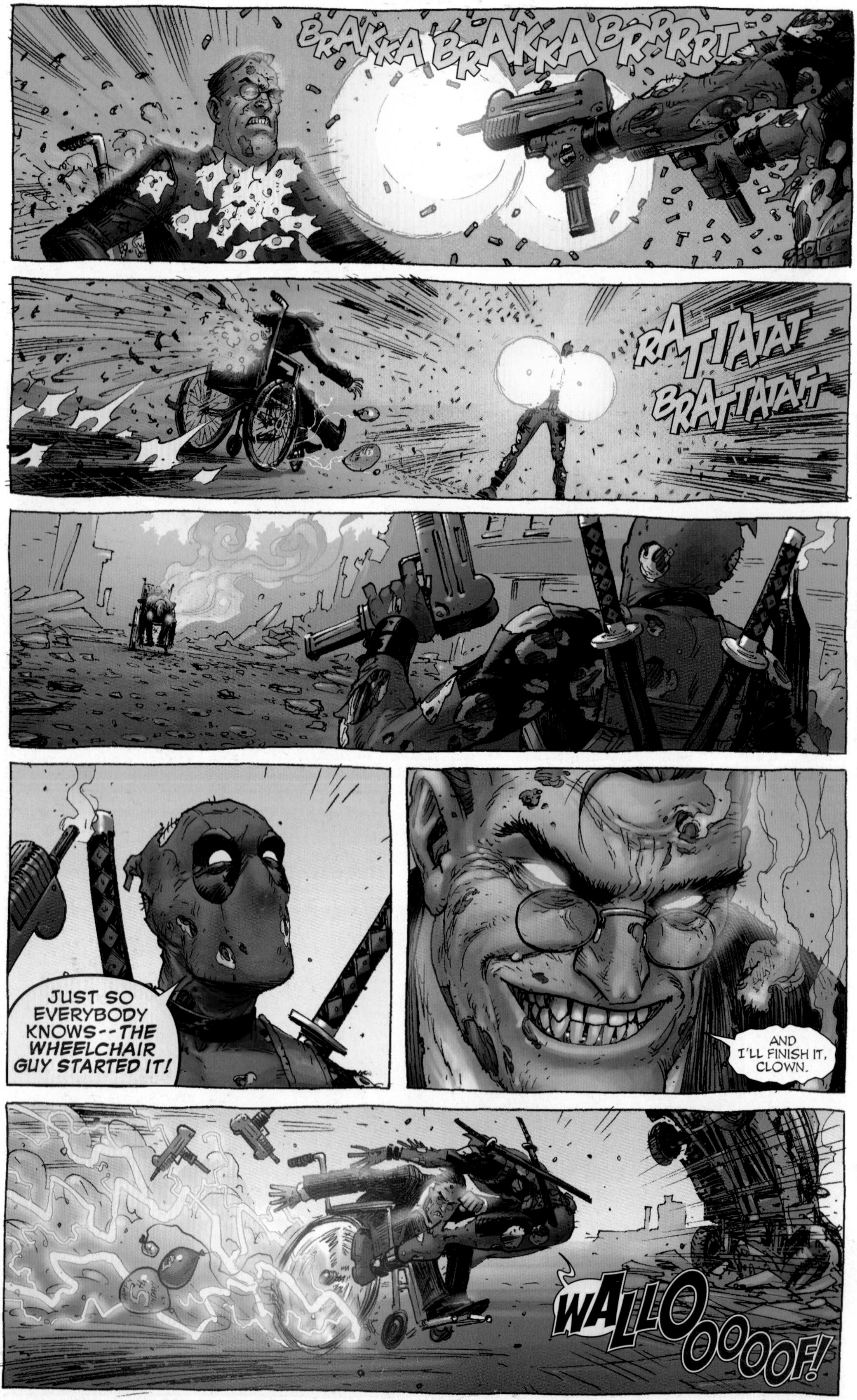
BRAKKA BRAKKA BRRRRT
RATTATAT BRATTATATT
JUST SO EVERYBODY KNOWS--THE WHEELCHAIR GUY STARTED IT!
AND I'LL FINISH IT, CLOWN.
WALLOOOOOF!

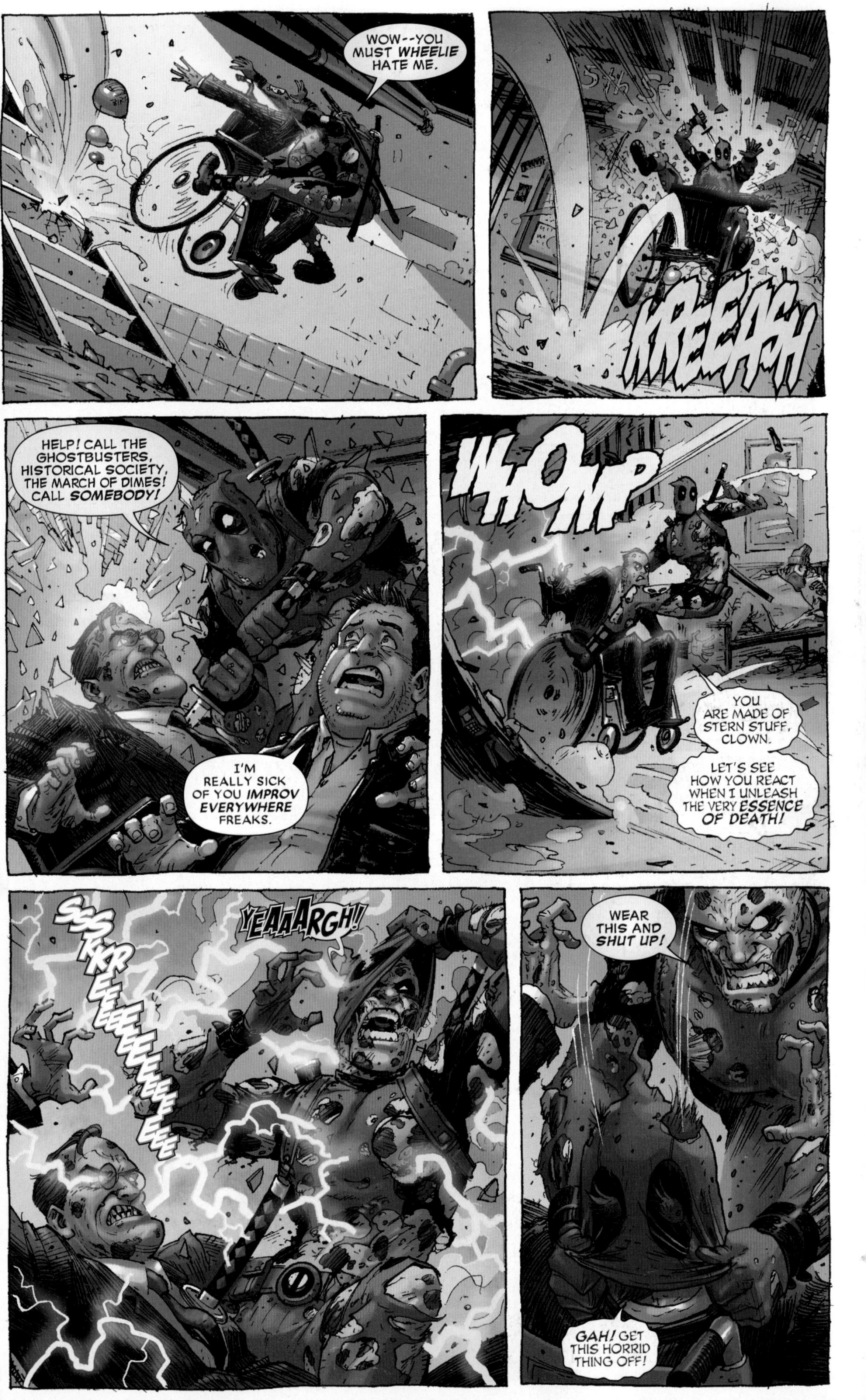
WOW--YOU MUST WHEELIE HATE ME.
KREEASH
HELP! CALL THE GHOSTBUSTERS, HISTORICAL SOCIETY, THE MARCH OF DIMES! CALL SOMEBODY!
I'M REALLY SICK OF YOU IMPROV EVERYWHERE FREAKS.
WHOMP
YOU ARE MADE OF STERN STUFF, CLOWN.
LET'S SEE HOW YOU REACT WHEN I UNLEASH THE VERY ESSENCE OF DEATH!
SSSKKREEEEEEEEEEEE
YEAAAARGH!
WEAR THIS AND SHUT UP!
GAH! GET THIS HORRID THING OFF!

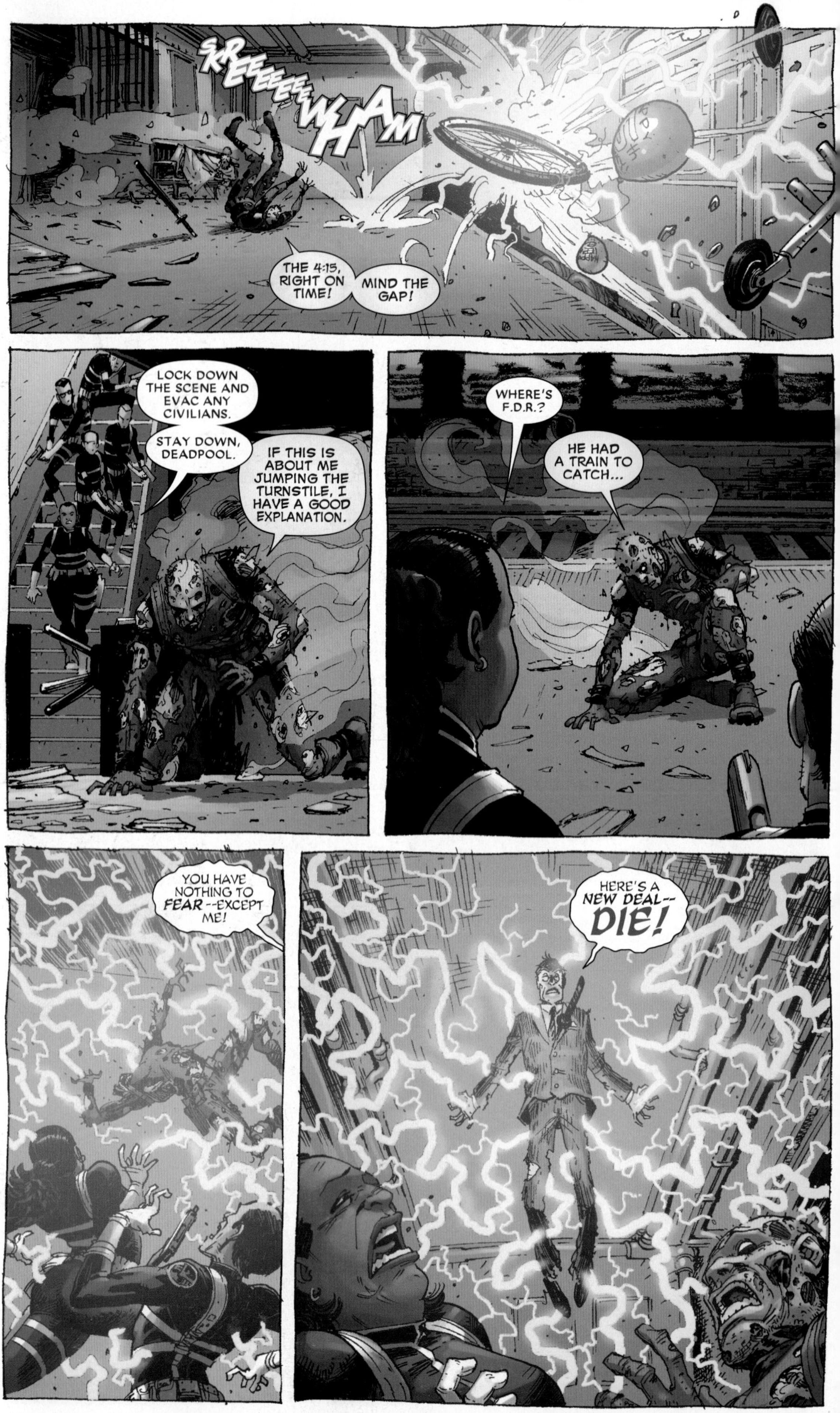
SKREEEEEEWHAM
THE 4:15, RIGHT ON TIME!
MIND THE GAP!
LOCK DOWN THE SCENE AND EVAC ANY CIVILIANS.
STAY DOWN, DEADPOOL.
IF THIS IS ABOUT ME JUMPING THE TURNSTILE, I HAVE A GOOD EXPLANATION.
WHERE'S F.D.R.?
HE HAD A TRAIN TO CATCH...
YOU HAVE NOTHING TO FEAR--EXCEPT ME!
HERE'S A NEW DEAL--DIE!

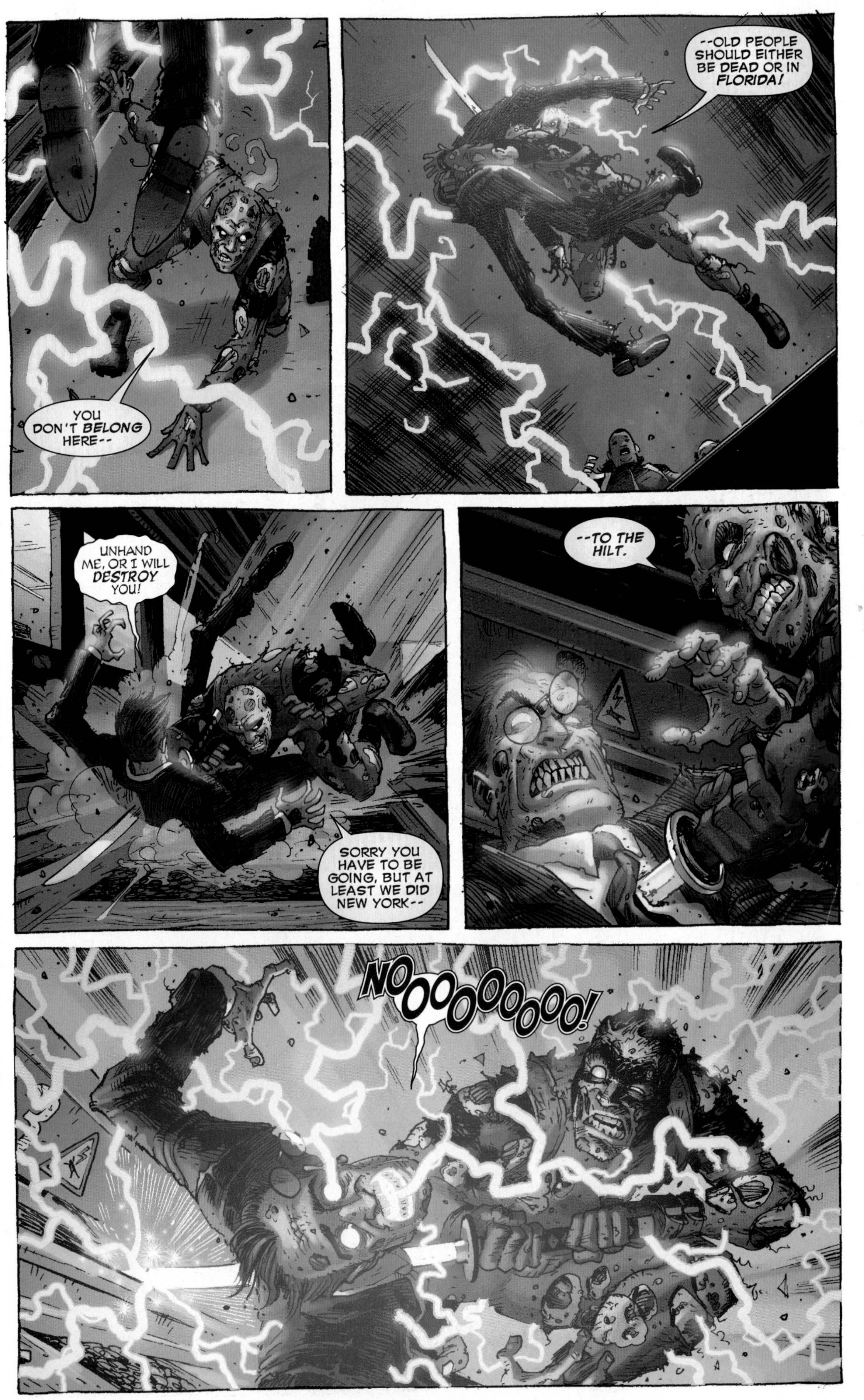
YOU DON'T BELONG HERE--
--OLD PEOPLE SHOULD EITHER BE DEAD OR IN FLORIDA!
UNHAND ME, OR I WILL DESTROY YOU!
SORRY YOU HAVE TO BE GOING, BUT AT LEAST WE DID NEW YORK--
--TO THE HILT.
NOOOOOOOOOO!

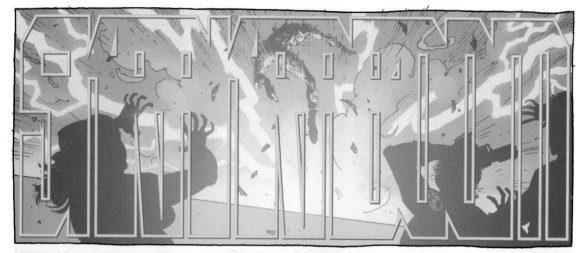

HE *DID* IT!

HOW WOULD YOU LIKE A JOB, DEADPOOL?

LADY, I'M TAKING SOME *TIME OFF*, THANK YOU VERY MUCH.

I'LL MAKE IT WORTH YOUR WHILE. THERE'S MORE OF THESE CORRUPTED PRESIDENTS OUT THERE.

I THINK I BETTER JUST LIE HERE FOR A LITTLE WHILE.

WE'LL GET YOU BACK TO THE HELICARRIER.

I'M HONORED THAT YOU TRUST ME TO SERVE *AMERICA*, THE COUNTRY THAT I DO THE MOST *DAMAGE* IN.

ARE YOU KIDDING? AMERICA'S *REAL* HEROES CAN'T BE SEEN FIGHTING OUR DEAD PRESIDENTS. NO, *WADE*-- YOU'RE NOT THE HERO WE *WANT*, YOU'RE THE SCUMBAG WE *NEED*.

STILL HAPPY TO BE PART OF THE TEAM!

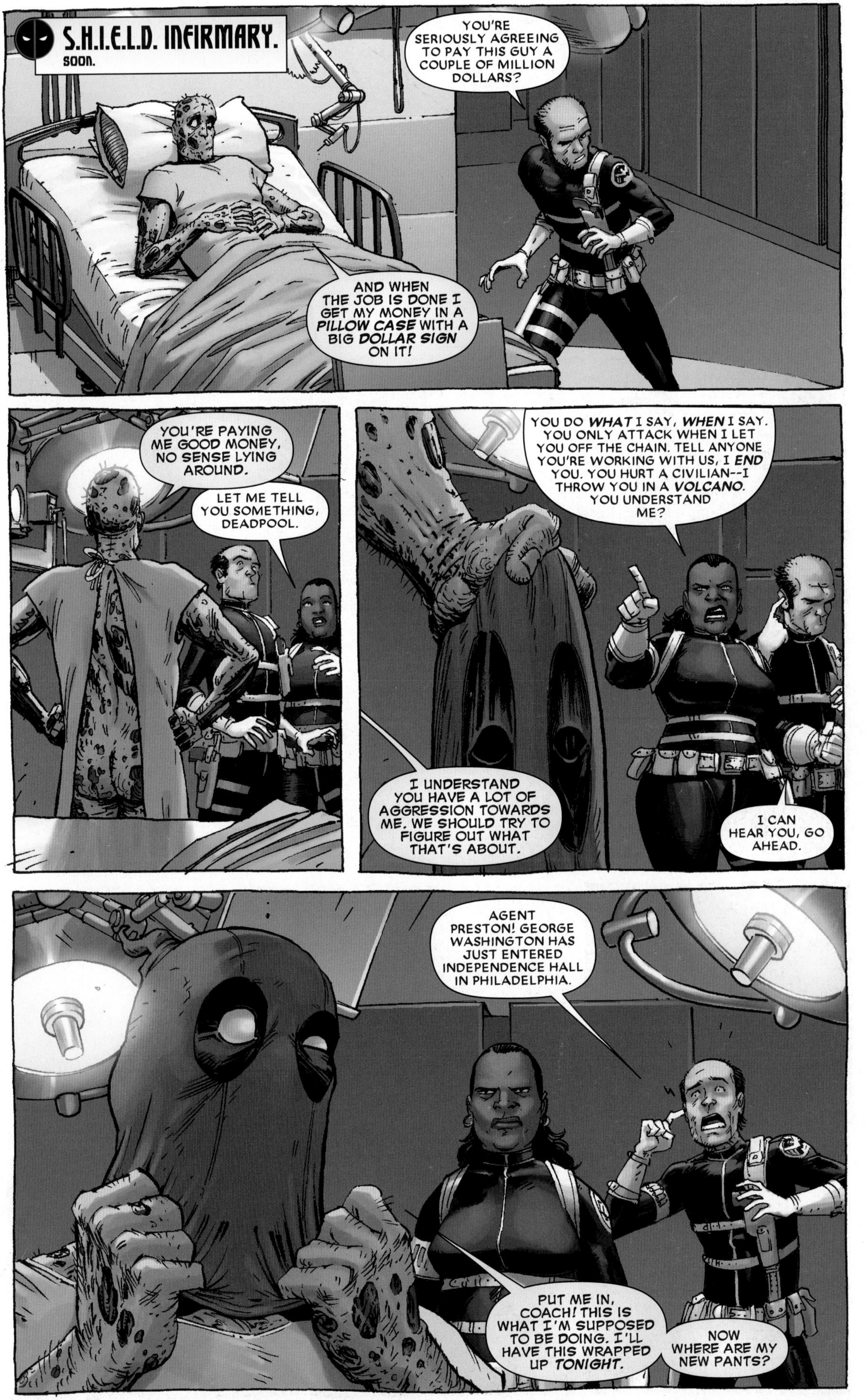
S.H.I.E.L.D. INFIRMARY.
SOON.
YOU'RE SERIOUSLY AGREEING TO PAY THIS GUY A COUPLE OF MILLION DOLLARS?
AND WHEN THE JOB IS DONE I GET MY MONEY IN A PILLOW CASE WITH A BIG DOLLAR SIGN ON IT!
YOU'RE PAYING ME GOOD MONEY, NO SENSE LYING AROUND.
LET ME TELL YOU SOMETHING, DEADPOOL.
YOU DO WHAT I SAY, WHEN I SAY. YOU ONLY ATTACK WHEN I LET YOU OFF THE CHAIN. TELL ANYONE YOU'RE WORKING WITH US, I END YOU. YOU HURT A CIVILIAN--I THROW YOU IN A VOLCANO. YOU UNDERSTAND ME?
I UNDERSTAND YOU HAVE A LOT OF AGGRESSION TOWARDS ME. WE SHOULD TRY TO FIGURE OUT WHAT THAT'S ABOUT.
I CAN HEAR YOU, GO AHEAD.
AGENT PRESTON! GEORGE WASHINGTON HAS JUST ENTERED INDEPENDENCE HALL IN PHILADELPHIA.
PUT ME IN, COACH! THIS IS WHAT I'M SUPPOSED TO BE DOING. I'LL HAVE THIS WRAPPED UP TONIGHT.
NOW WHERE ARE MY NEW PANTS?

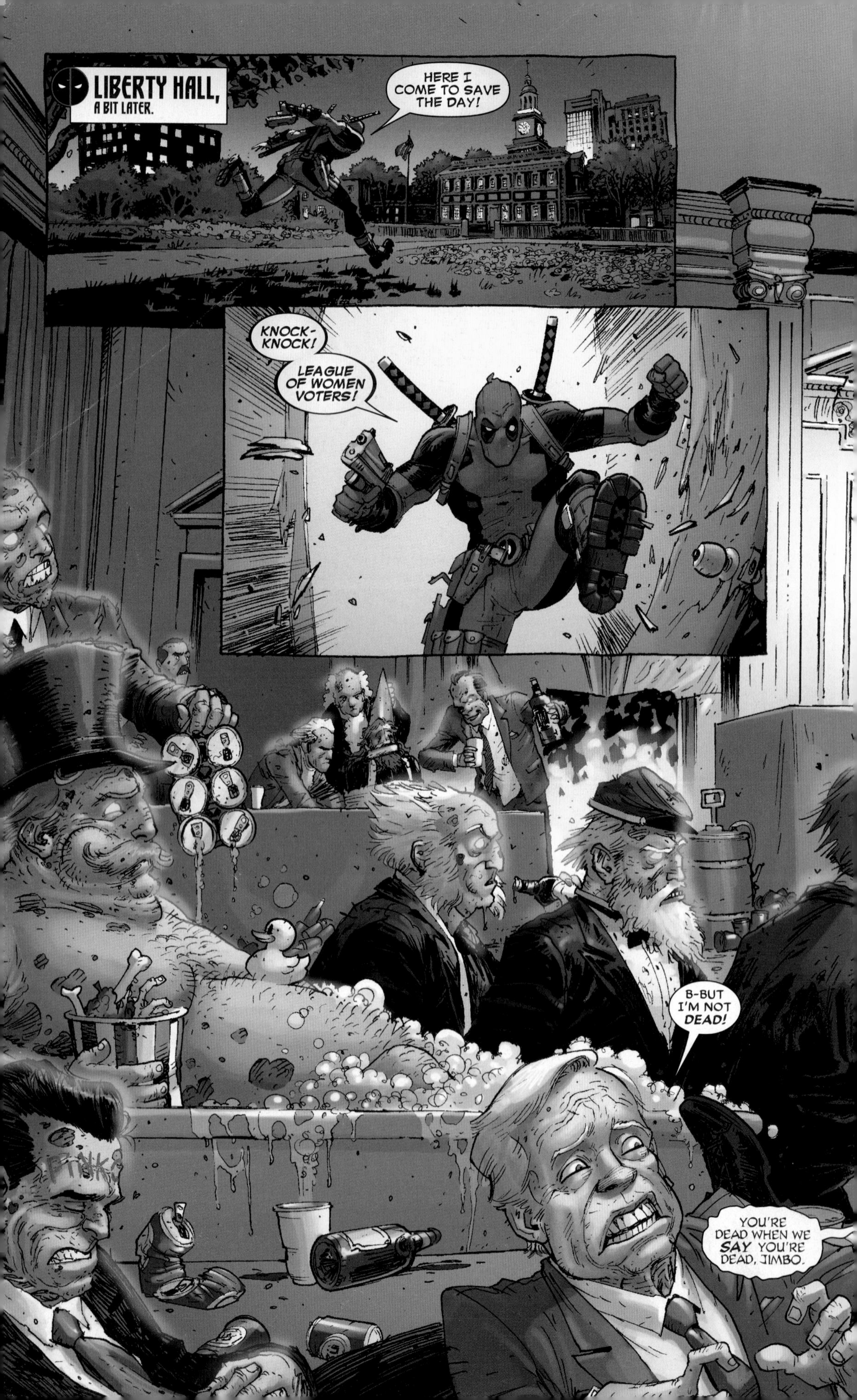
LIBERTY HALL,
A BIT LATER.
HERE I COME TO SAVE THE DAY!
KNOCK-KNOCK!
LEAGUE OF WOMEN VOTERS!
B-BUT I'M NOT *DEAD!*
YOU'RE DEAD WHEN WE **SAY** YOU'RE DEAD, JIMBO.

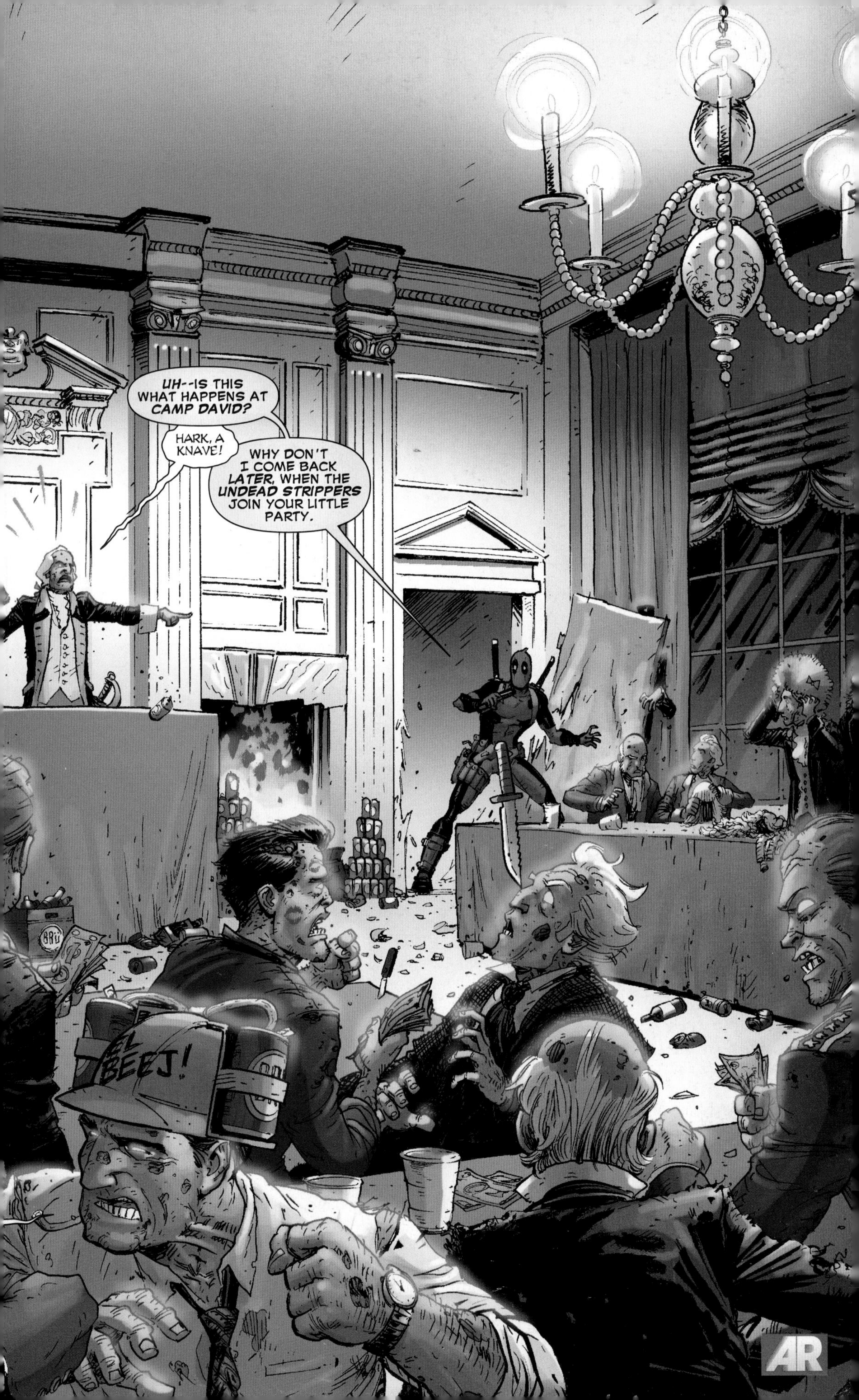
UH--IS THIS WHAT HAPPENS AT CAMP DAVID?
HARK, A KNAVE!
WHY DON'T I COME BACK LATER, WHEN THE UNDEAD STRIPPERS JOIN YOUR LITTLE PARTY.
EL BEEJ!

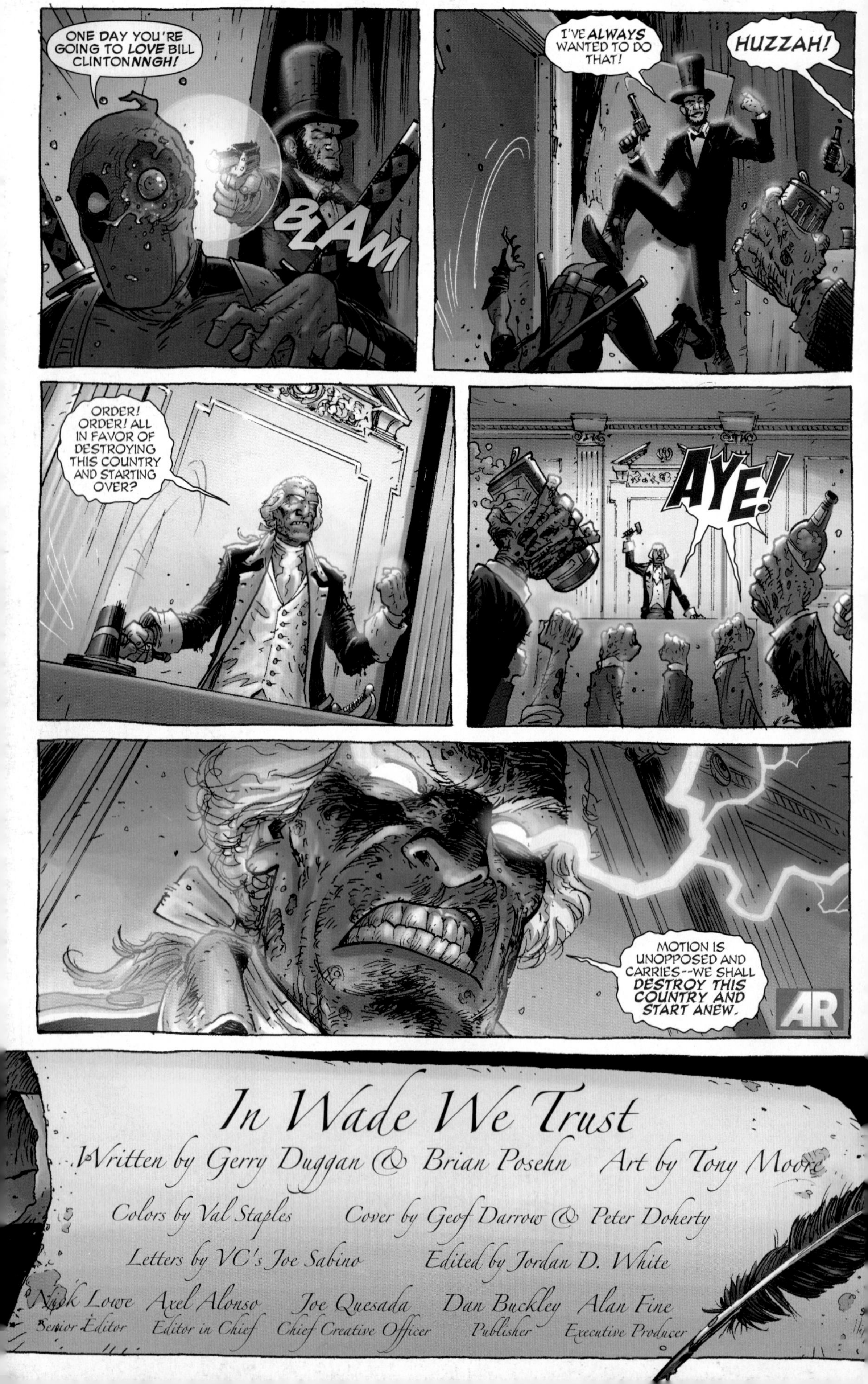

ONE DAY YOU'RE GOING TO LOVE BILL CLINTONNNGH!
BLAM
I'VE ALWAYS WANTED TO DO THAT!
HUZZAH!
ORDER! ORDER! ALL IN FAVOR OF DESTROYING THIS COUNTRY AND STARTING OVER?
AYE!
MOTION IS UNOPPOSED AND CARRIES--WE SHALL DESTROY THIS COUNTRY AND START ANEW.

In Wade We Trust

Written by Gerry Duggan & Brian Posehn Art by Tony Moore

Colors by Val Staples Cover by Geof Darrow & Peter Doherty

Letters by VC's Joe Sabino Edited by Jordan D. White

Nick Lowe, Senior Editor; Axel Alonso, Editor in Chief; Joe Quesada, Chief Creative Officer; Dan Buckley, Publisher; Alan Fine, Executive Producer

2

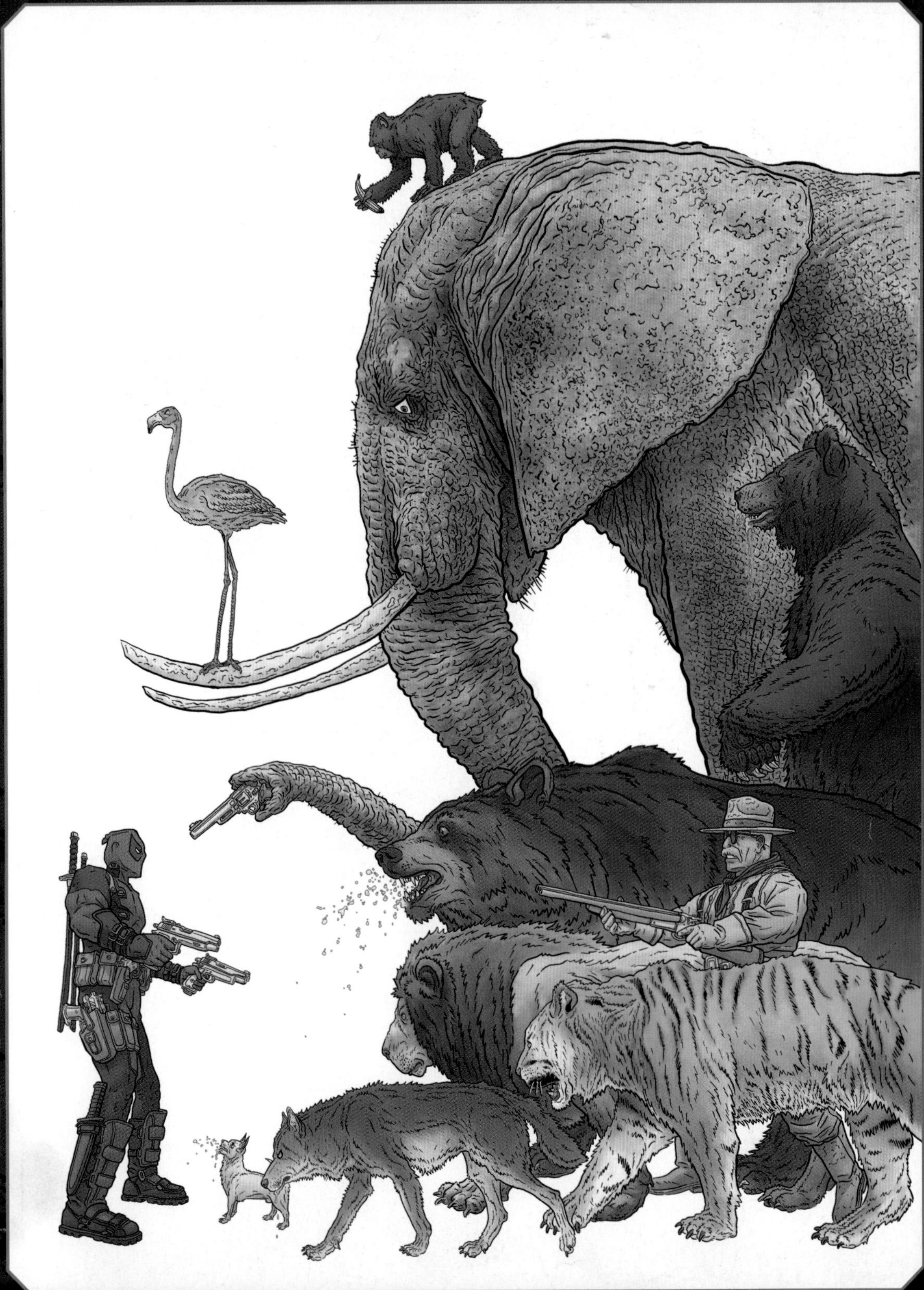

WE FOUGHT A ZOO

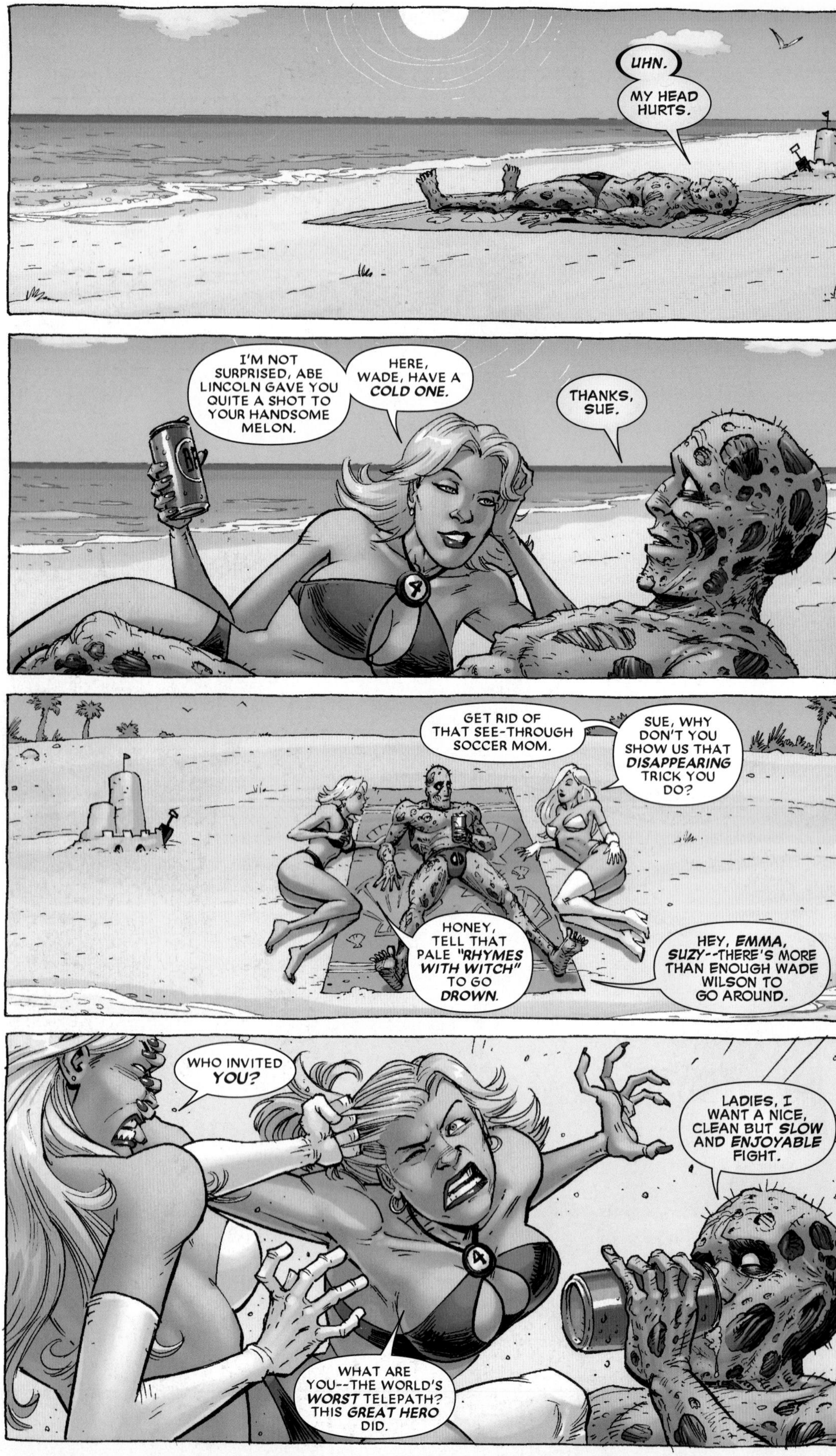
UHN.
MY HEAD HURTS.
I'M NOT SURPRISED, ABE LINCOLN GAVE YOU QUITE A SHOT TO YOUR HANDSOME MELON.
HERE, WADE, HAVE A COLD ONE.
THANKS, SUE.
GET RID OF THAT SEE-THROUGH SOCCER MOM.
SUE, WHY DON'T YOU SHOW US THAT DISAPPEARING TRICK YOU DO?
HONEY, TELL THAT PALE "RHYMES WITH WITCH" TO GO DROWN.
HEY, EMMA, SUZY--THERE'S MORE THAN ENOUGH WADE WILSON TO GO AROUND.
WHO INVITED YOU?
WHAT ARE YOU--THE WORLD'S WORST TELEPATH? THIS GREAT HERO DID.
LADIES, I WANT A NICE, CLEAN BUT SLOW AND ENJOYABLE FIGHT.

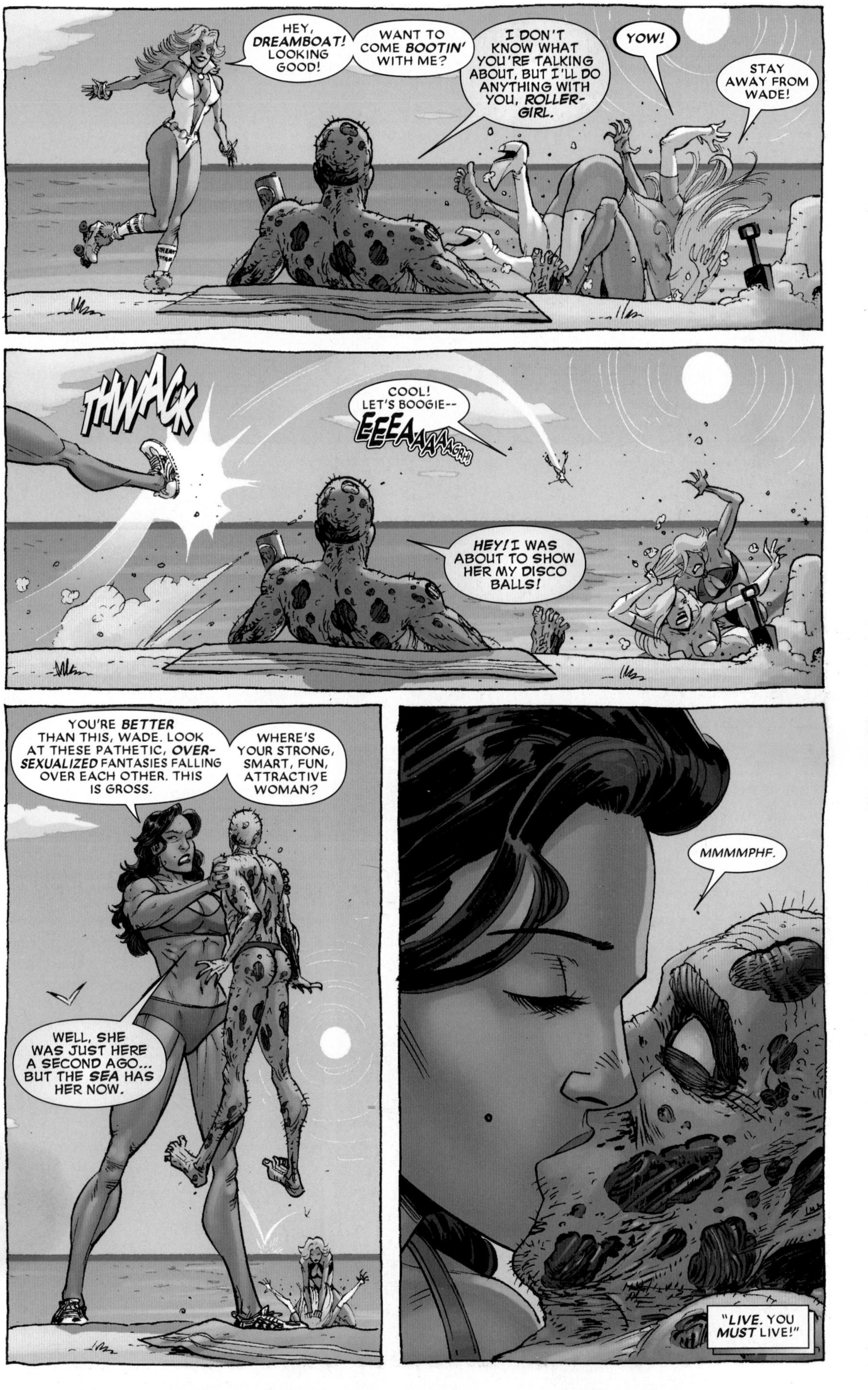
HEY, DREAMBOAT! LOOKING GOOD!
WANT TO COME BOOTIN' WITH ME?
I DON'T KNOW WHAT YOU'RE TALKING ABOUT, BUT I'LL DO ANYTHING WITH YOU, ROLLER-GIRL.
YOW!
STAY AWAY FROM WADE!
THWACK
COOL! LET'S BOOGIE--
EEEAAAAAAGH!
HEY! I WAS ABOUT TO SHOW HER MY DISCO BALLS!
YOU'RE BETTER THAN THIS, WADE. LOOK AT THESE PATHETIC, OVER-SEXUALIZED FANTASIES FALLING OVER EACH OTHER. THIS IS GROSS.
WHERE'S YOUR STRONG, SMART, FUN, ATTRACTIVE WOMAN?
WELL, SHE WAS JUST HERE A SECOND AGO... BUT THE SEA HAS HER NOW.
MMMMPHF.
"LIVE. YOU MUST LIVE!"

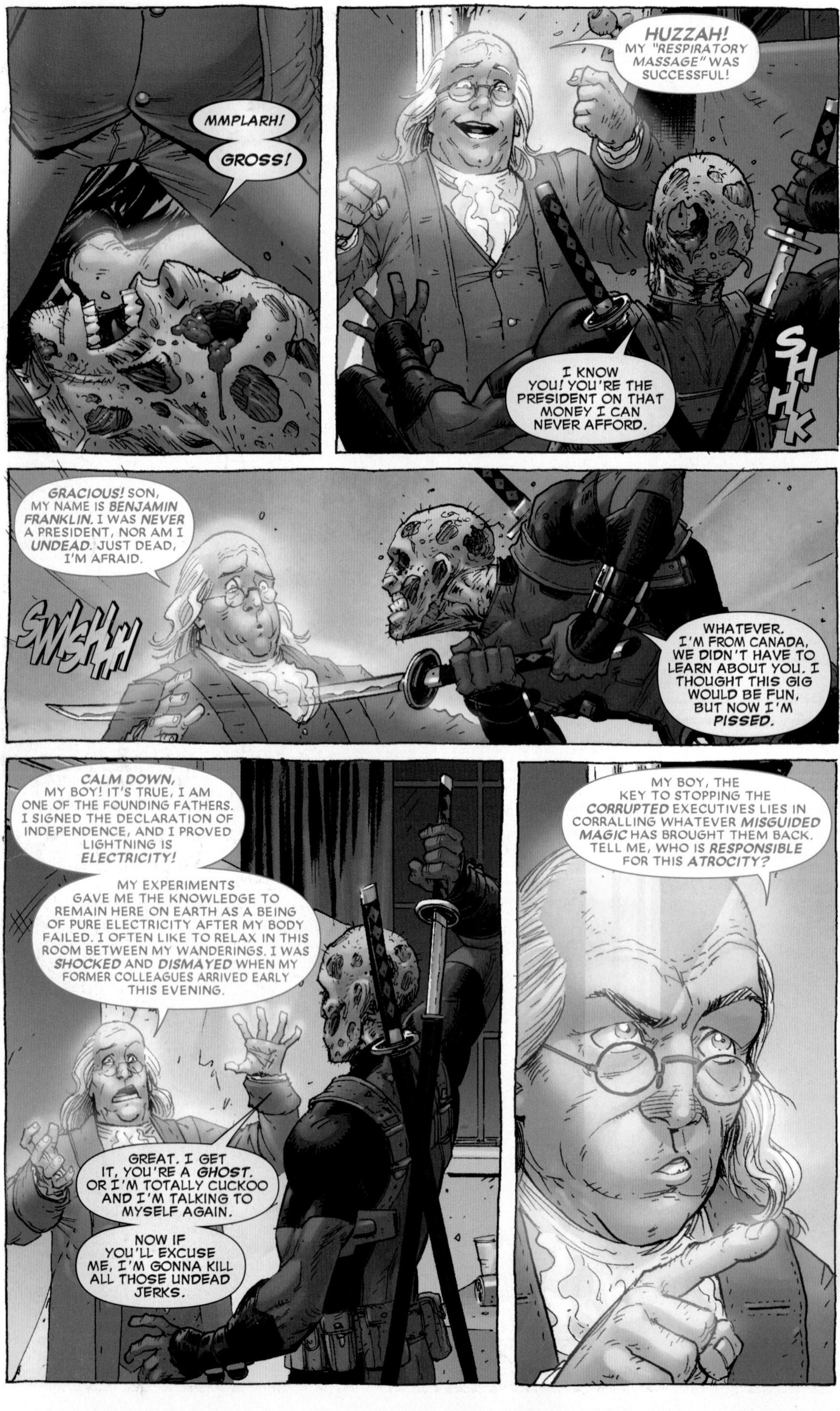

MMPLARH!
GROSS!
HUZZAH! MY "RESPIRATORY MASSAGE" WAS SUCCESSFUL!
I KNOW YOU! YOU'RE THE PRESIDENT ON THAT MONEY I CAN NEVER AFFORD.
SHHK
GRACIOUS! SON, MY NAME IS BENJAMIN FRANKLIN. I WAS NEVER A PRESIDENT, NOR AM I UNDEAD. JUST DEAD, I'M AFRAID.
SWISHHH
WHATEVER. I'M FROM CANADA, WE DIDN'T HAVE TO LEARN ABOUT YOU. I THOUGHT THIS GIG WOULD BE FUN, BUT NOW I'M PISSED.
CALM DOWN, MY BOY! IT'S TRUE, I AM ONE OF THE FOUNDING FATHERS. I SIGNED THE DECLARATION OF INDEPENDENCE, AND I PROVED LIGHTNING IS ELECTRICITY!
MY EXPERIMENTS GAVE ME THE KNOWLEDGE TO REMAIN HERE ON EARTH AS A BEING OF PURE ELECTRICITY AFTER MY BODY FAILED. I OFTEN LIKE TO RELAX IN THIS ROOM BETWEEN MY WANDERINGS. I WAS SHOCKED AND DISMAYED WHEN MY FORMER COLLEAGUES ARRIVED EARLY THIS EVENING.
GREAT. I GET IT, YOU'RE A GHOST. OR I'M TOTALLY CUCKOO AND I'M TALKING TO MYSELF AGAIN.
NOW IF YOU'LL EXCUSE ME, I'M GONNA KILL ALL THOSE UNDEAD JERKS.
MY BOY, THE KEY TO STOPPING THE CORRUPTED EXECUTIVES LIES IN CORRALLING WHATEVER MISGUIDED MAGIC HAS BROUGHT THEM BACK. TELL ME, WHO IS RESPONSIBLE FOR THIS ATROCITY?

RAISE MY ARMY, MAGICIAN.

NO. ENOUGH. I THOUGHT YOU WOULD SERVE THIS GREAT COUNTRY, BUT YOU'RE A SLAVE TO DEATH.

YOU EH... YOU *HEARD* THE GENERAL.

AR

MAKE WITH THE, AH...*HOCUS-POCUS.*

NO! NO MORE!

RAISING YOU GUYS IS PROBABLY THE *WORST* MISTAKE I'VE EVER MADE-- AFTER MARRYING *BRENDA.*

I DATED A BRENDA ONNNNN*HEY!*

ᛗᛗᛗᛒᚠᚲᚱ ᛒᚾᚲᛗ ᛈᚱᛒᚱᛉ ᛈᚠᛒᛁᚾᚲᚷ ᛁᛋ ᛗᛈᚱ ᛗᛋᚱᛉᛉ ᚺᚲ ᛗᛈᚱ ᛋᚠᚲᚱᛉᛉ

DAMN YOU, KENNEDY! FOCUS!

FWOOOSH

BRAAAP!

DAMN YOU!

MY TEEF ARE WOOD!

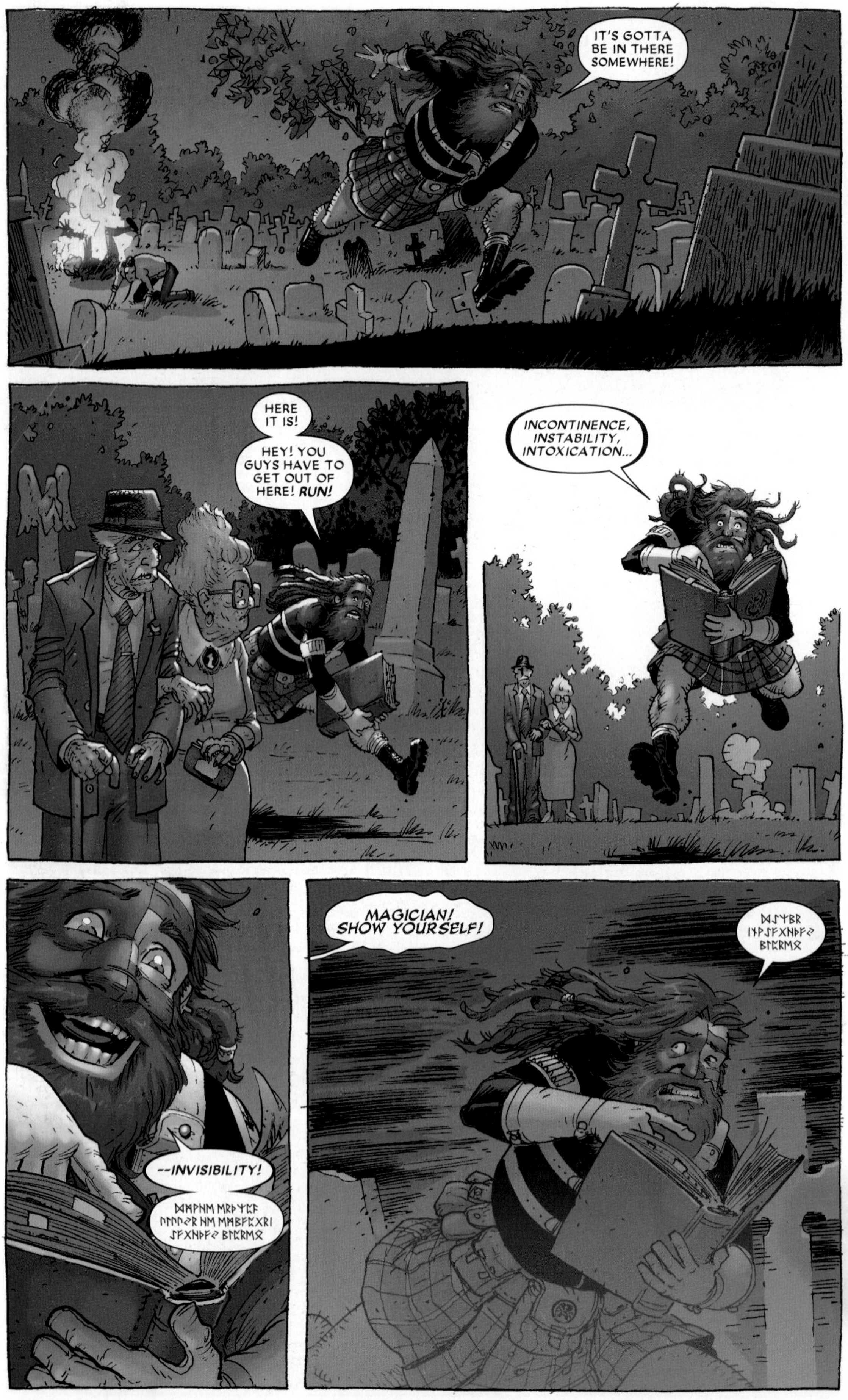
IT'S GOTTA BE IN THERE SOMEWHERE!
HERE IT IS!
HEY! YOU GUYS HAVE TO GET OUT OF HERE! RUN!
INCONTINENCE, INSTABILITY, INTOXICATION...
--INVISIBILITY!
MAGICIAN! SHOW YOURSELF!

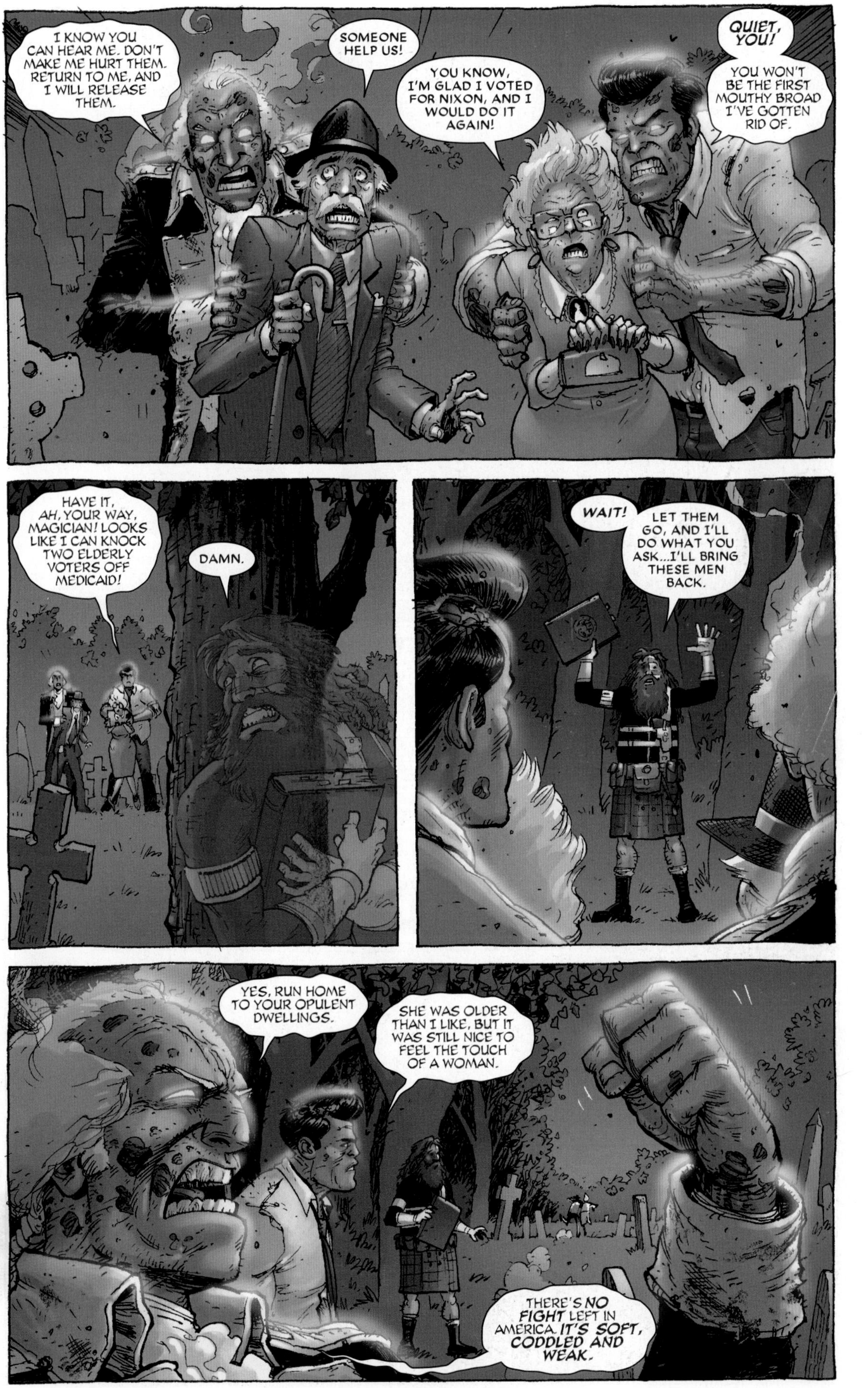

I KNOW YOU CAN HEAR ME. DON'T MAKE ME HURT THEM. RETURN TO ME, AND I WILL RELEASE THEM.
SOMEONE HELP US!
YOU KNOW, I'M GLAD I VOTED FOR NIXON, AND I WOULD DO IT AGAIN!
QUIET, YOU!
YOU WON'T BE THE FIRST MOUTHY BROAD I'VE GOTTEN RID OF.
HAVE IT, AH, YOUR WAY, MAGICIAN! LOOKS LIKE I CAN KNOCK TWO ELDERLY VOTERS OFF MEDICAID!
DAMN.
WAIT!
LET THEM GO, AND I'LL DO WHAT YOU ASK...I'LL BRING THESE MEN BACK.
YES, RUN HOME TO YOUR OPULENT DWELLINGS.
SHE WAS OLDER THAN I LIKE, BUT IT WAS STILL NICE TO FEEL THE TOUCH OF A WOMAN.
THERE'S NO FIGHT LEFT IN AMERICA. IT'S SOFT, CODDLED AND WEAK.

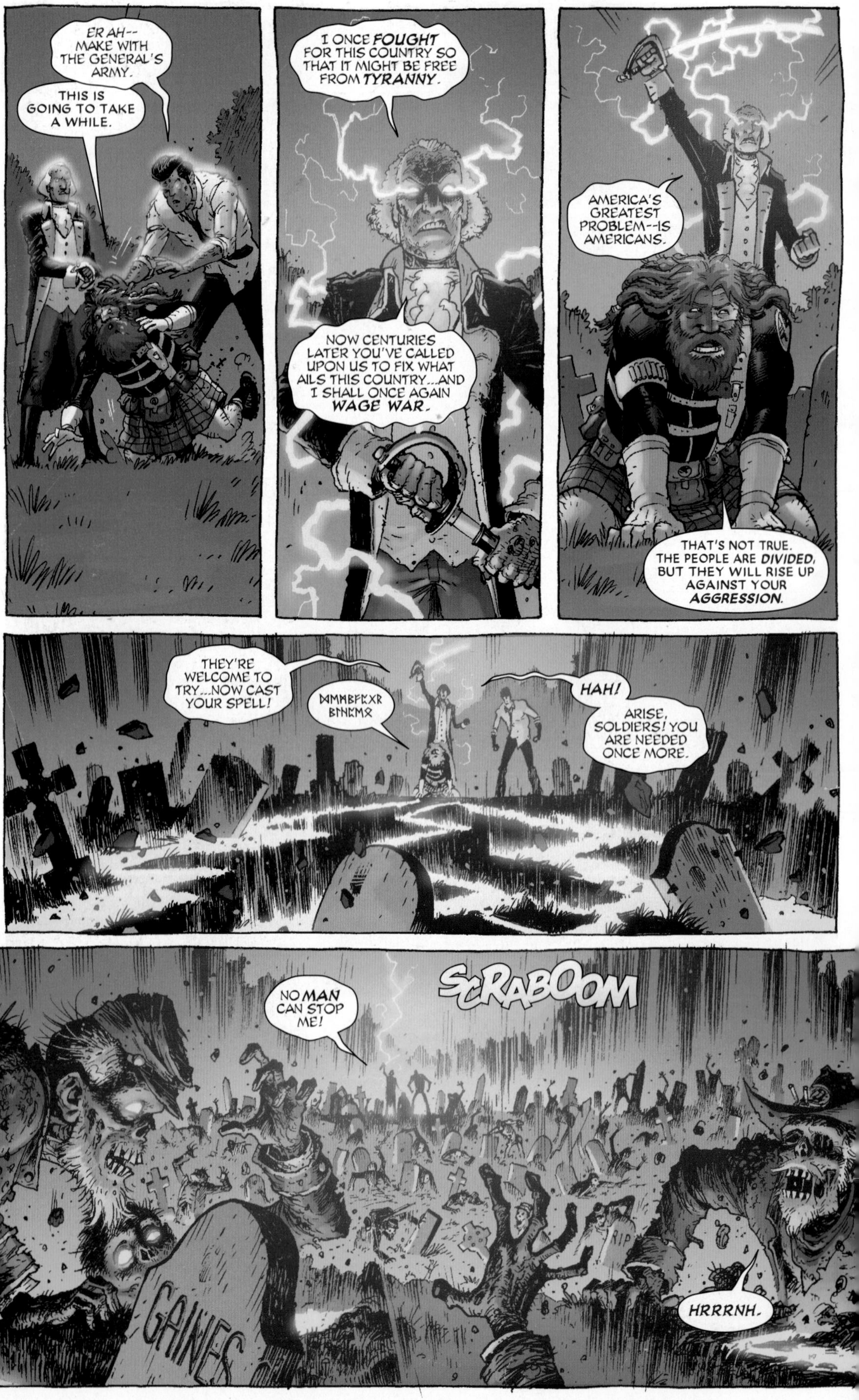
ER AH--
MAKE WITH THE GENERAL'S ARMY.
THIS IS GOING TO TAKE A WHILE.
I ONCE FOUGHT FOR THIS COUNTRY SO THAT IT MIGHT BE FREE FROM TYRANNY.
NOW CENTURIES LATER YOU'VE CALLED UPON US TO FIX WHAT AILS THIS COUNTRY...AND I SHALL ONCE AGAIN WAGE WAR.
AMERICA'S GREATEST PROBLEM--IS AMERICANS.
THAT'S NOT TRUE. THE PEOPLE ARE DIVIDED, BUT THEY WILL RISE UP AGAINST YOUR AGGRESSION.
THEY'RE WELCOME TO TRY...NOW CAST YOUR SPELL!
HAH!
ARISE, SOLDIERS! YOU ARE NEEDED ONCE MORE.
SCRABOOM
NO MAN CAN STOP ME!
GAINES
RIP
HRRRNH.

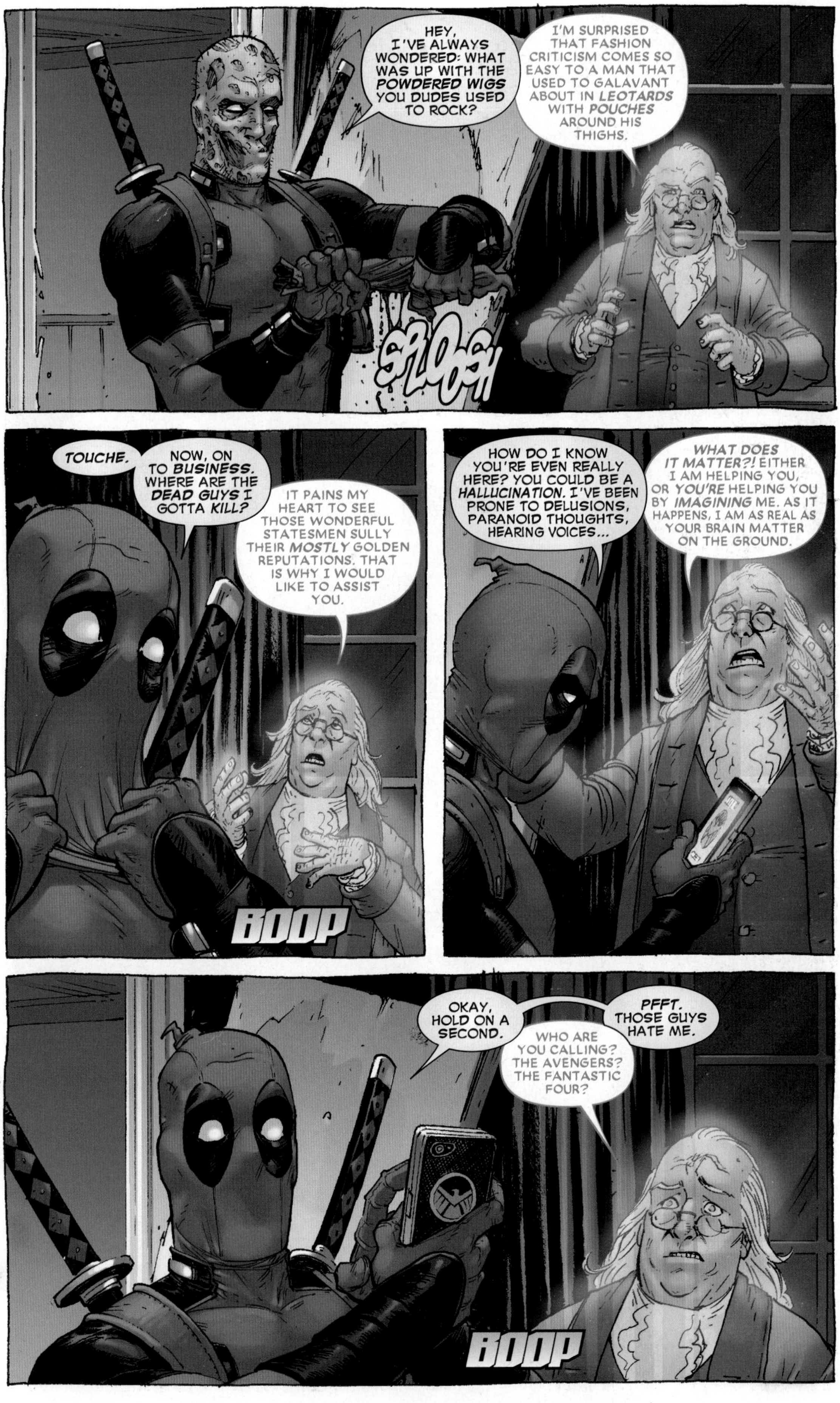

HEY, I'VE ALWAYS WONDERED: WHAT WAS UP WITH THE POWDERED WIGS YOU DUDES USED TO ROCK?
I'M SURPRISED THAT FASHION CRITICISM COMES SO EASY TO A MAN THAT USED TO GALAVANT ABOUT IN LEOTARDS WITH POUCHES AROUND HIS THIGHS.
SPLOOSH
TOUCHE.
NOW, ON TO BUSINESS. WHERE ARE THE DEAD GUYS I GOTTA KILL?
IT PAINS MY HEART TO SEE THOSE WONDERFUL STATESMEN SULLY THEIR MOSTLY GOLDEN REPUTATIONS. THAT IS WHY I WOULD LIKE TO ASSIST YOU.
BOOP
HOW DO I KNOW YOU'RE EVEN REALLY HERE? YOU COULD BE A HALLUCINATION. I'VE BEEN PRONE TO DELUSIONS, PARANOID THOUGHTS, HEARING VOICES...
WHAT DOES IT MATTER?! EITHER I AM HELPING YOU, OR YOU'RE HELPING YOU BY IMAGINING ME. AS IT HAPPENS, I AM AS REAL AS YOUR BRAIN MATTER ON THE GROUND.
OKAY, HOLD ON A SECOND.
WHO ARE YOU CALLING? THE AVENGERS? THE FANTASTIC FOUR?
PFFT. THOSE GUYS HATE ME.
BOOP

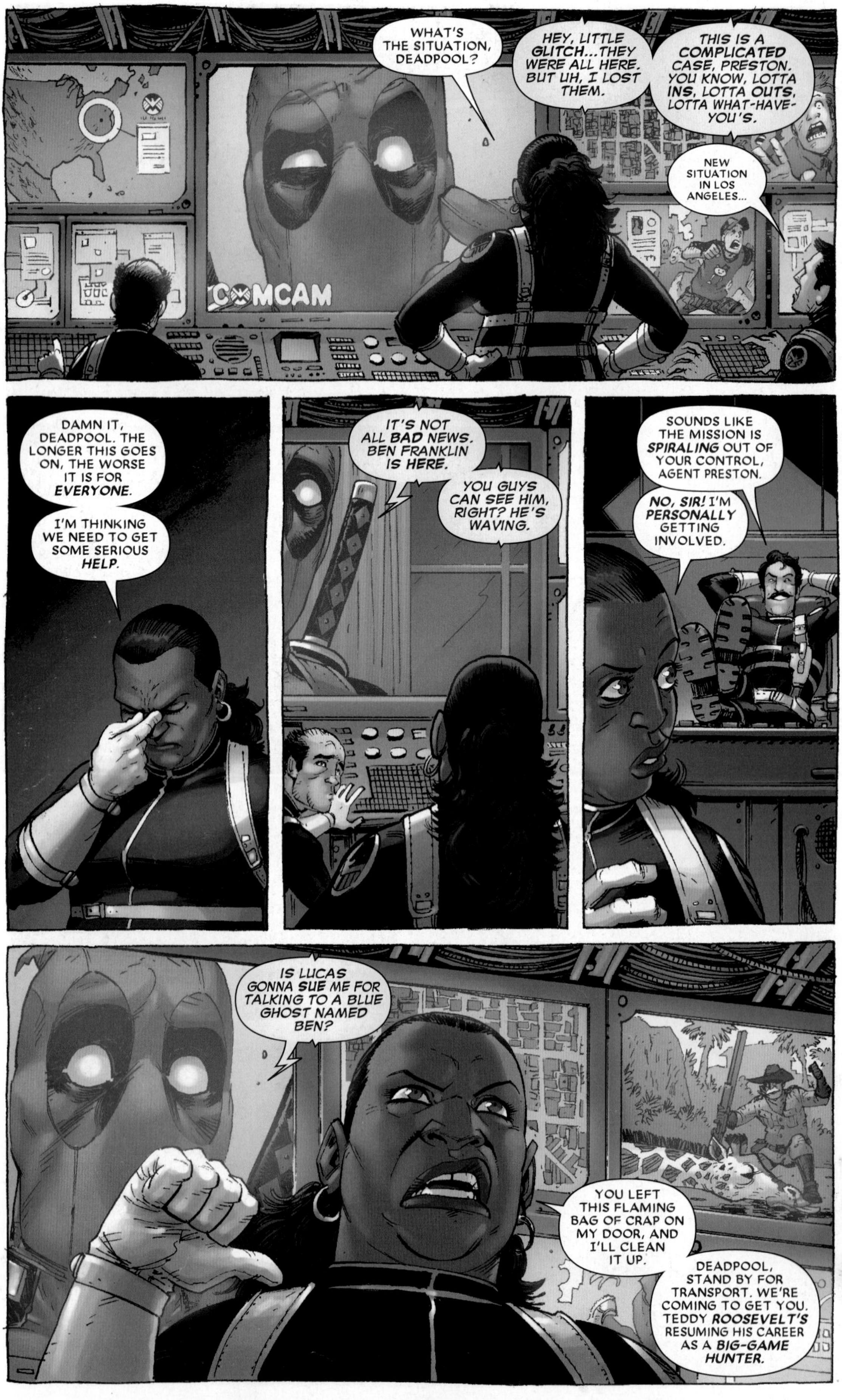
WHAT'S THE SITUATION, DEADPOOL?
HEY, LITTLE GLITCH...THEY WERE ALL HERE. BUT UH, I LOST THEM.
THIS IS A COMPLICATED CASE, PRESTON. YOU KNOW, LOTTA INS, LOTTA OUTS, LOTTA WHAT-HAVE-YOU'S.
NEW SITUATION IN LOS ANGELES...
COMCAM
DAMN IT, DEADPOOL. THE LONGER THIS GOES ON, THE WORSE IT IS FOR EVERYONE.
I'M THINKING WE NEED TO GET SOME SERIOUS HELP.
IT'S NOT ALL BAD NEWS. BEN FRANKLIN IS HERE.
YOU GUYS CAN SEE HIM, RIGHT? HE'S WAVING.
SOUNDS LIKE THE MISSION IS SPIRALING OUT OF YOUR CONTROL, AGENT PRESTON.
NO, SIR! I'M PERSONALLY GETTING INVOLVED.
IS LUCAS GONNA SUE ME FOR TALKING TO A BLUE GHOST NAMED BEN?
YOU LEFT THIS FLAMING BAG OF CRAP ON MY DOOR, AND I'LL CLEAN IT UP.
DEADPOOL, STAND BY FOR TRANSPORT. WE'RE COMING TO GET YOU. TEDDY ROOSEVELT'S RESUMING HIS CAREER AS A BIG-GAME HUNTER.

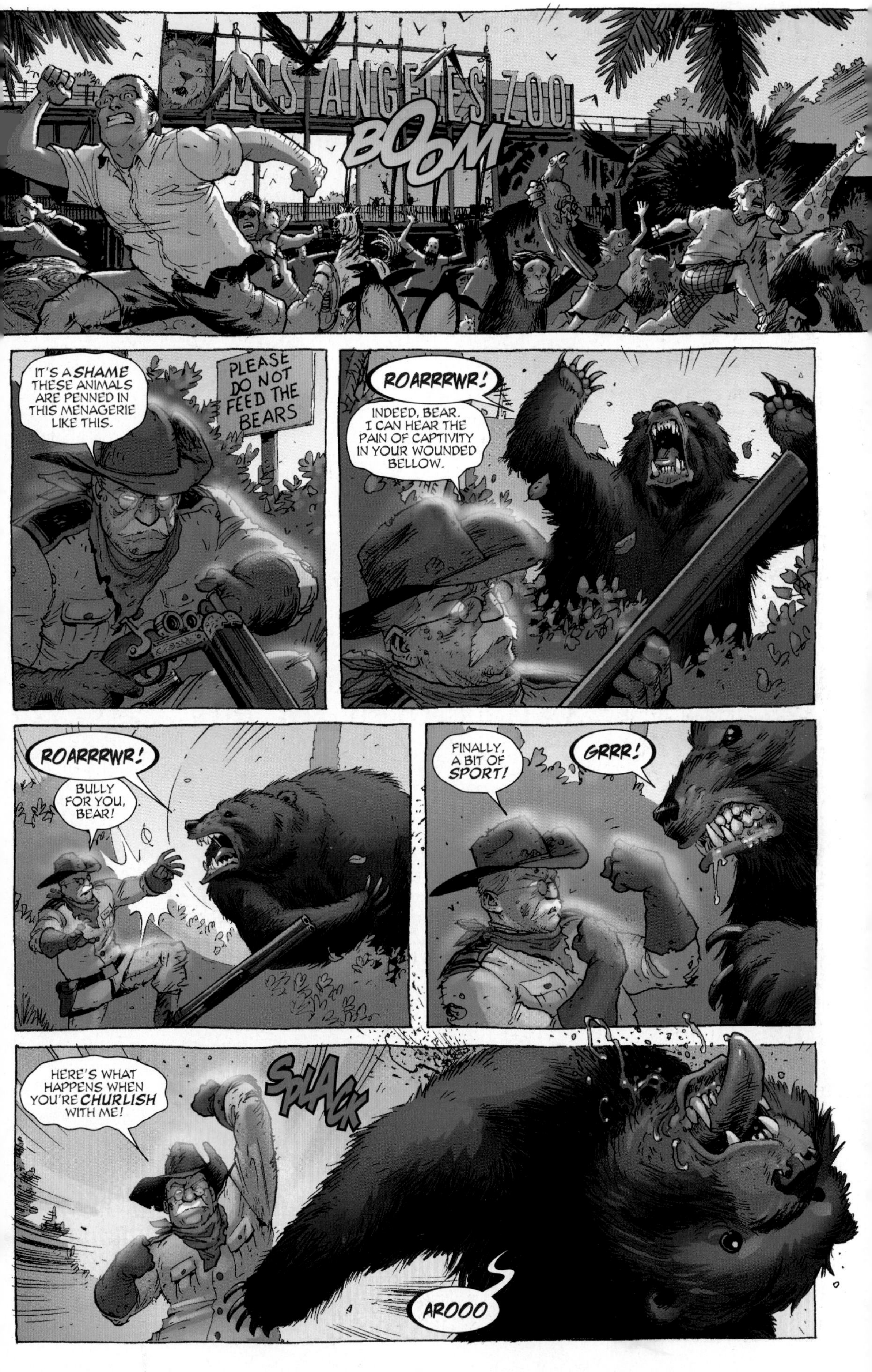
LOS ANGELES ZOO
BOOM
IT'S A SHAME THESE ANIMALS ARE PENNED IN THIS MENAGERIE LIKE THIS.
PLEASE DO NOT FEED THE BEARS
ROARRRWR!
INDEED, BEAR. I CAN HEAR THE PAIN OF CAPTIVITY IN YOUR WOUNDED BELLOW.
ROARRRWR!
BULLY FOR YOU, BEAR!
FINALLY, A BIT OF SPORT!
GRRR!
HERE'S WHAT HAPPENS WHEN YOU'RE CHURLISH WITH ME!
SPLACK
AROOO

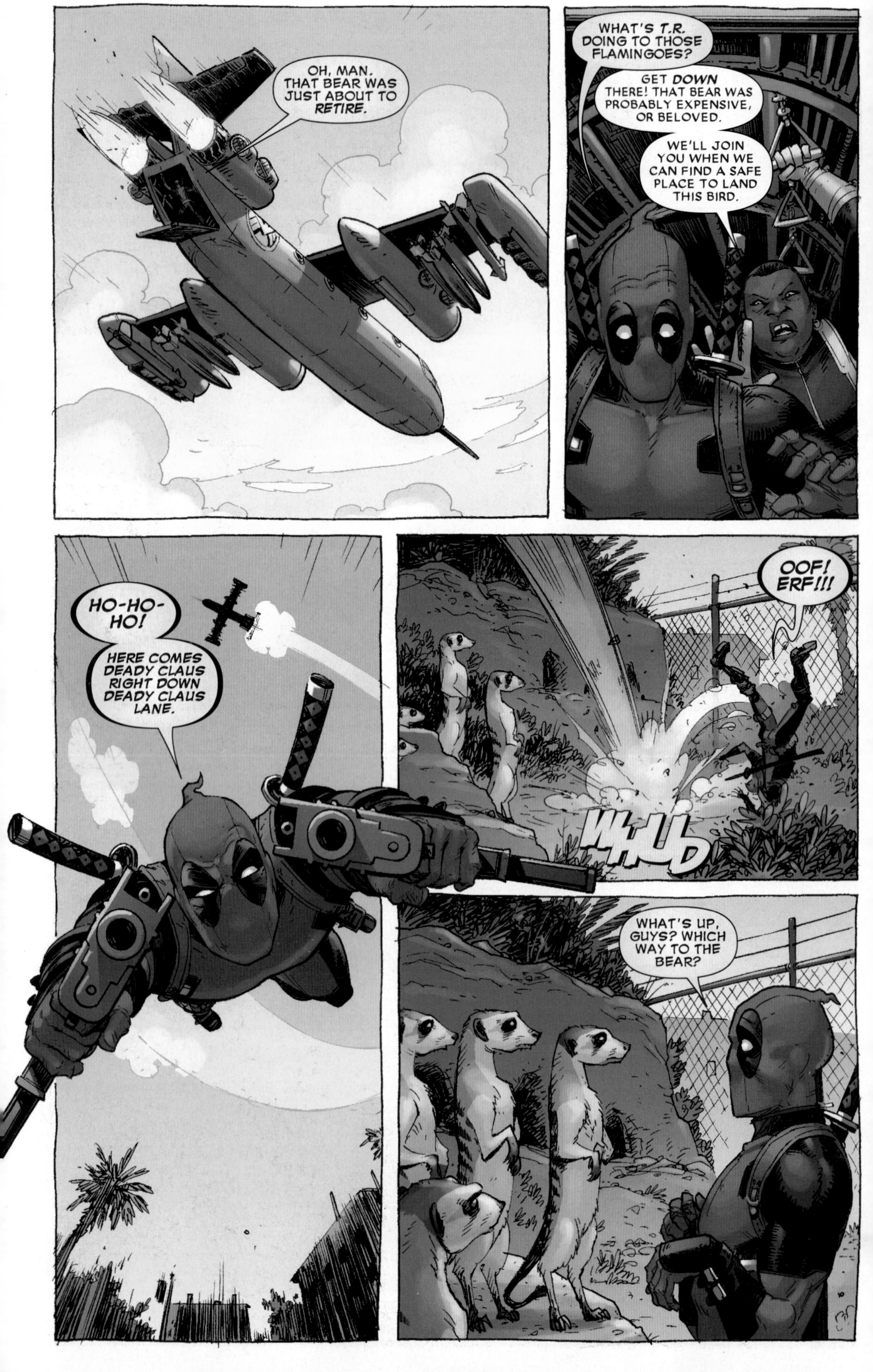
OH, MAN. THAT BEAR WAS JUST ABOUT TO RETIRE.
WHAT'S T.R. DOING TO THOSE FLAMINGOES?
GET DOWN THERE! THAT BEAR WAS PROBABLY EXPENSIVE, OR BELOVED.
WE'LL JOIN YOU WHEN WE CAN FIND A SAFE PLACE TO LAND THIS BIRD.
HO-HO-HO!
HERE COMES DEADY CLAUS RIGHT DOWN DEADY CLAUS LANE.
OOF! ERF!!!
WHUD
WHAT'S UP, GUYS? WHICH WAY TO THE BEAR?

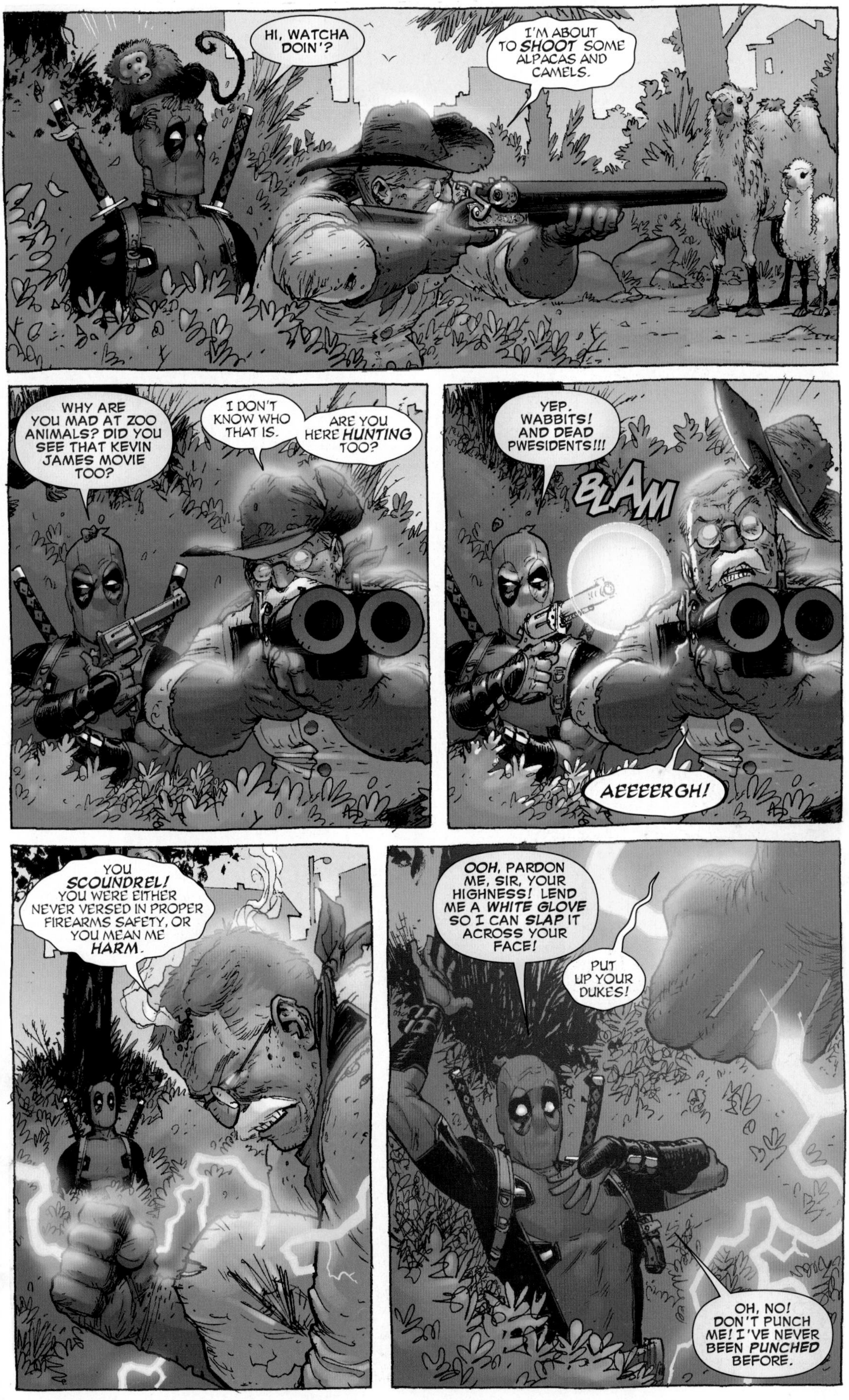
HI, WATCHA DOIN'?
I'M ABOUT TO SHOOT SOME ALPACAS AND CAMELS.
WHY ARE YOU MAD AT ZOO ANIMALS? DID YOU SEE THAT KEVIN JAMES MOVIE TOO?
I DON'T KNOW WHO THAT IS.
ARE YOU HERE HUNTING TOO?
YEP. WABBITS! AND DEAD PWESIDENTS!!!
BLAM
AEEEERGH!
YOU SCOUNDREL! YOU WERE EITHER NEVER VERSED IN PROPER FIREARMS SAFETY, OR YOU MEAN ME HARM.
OOH, PARDON ME, SIR, YOUR HIGHNESS! LEND ME A WHITE GLOVE SO I CAN SLAP IT ACROSS YOUR FACE!
PUT UP YOUR DUKES!
OH, NO! DON'T PUNCH ME! I'VE NEVER BEEN PUNCHED BEFORE.

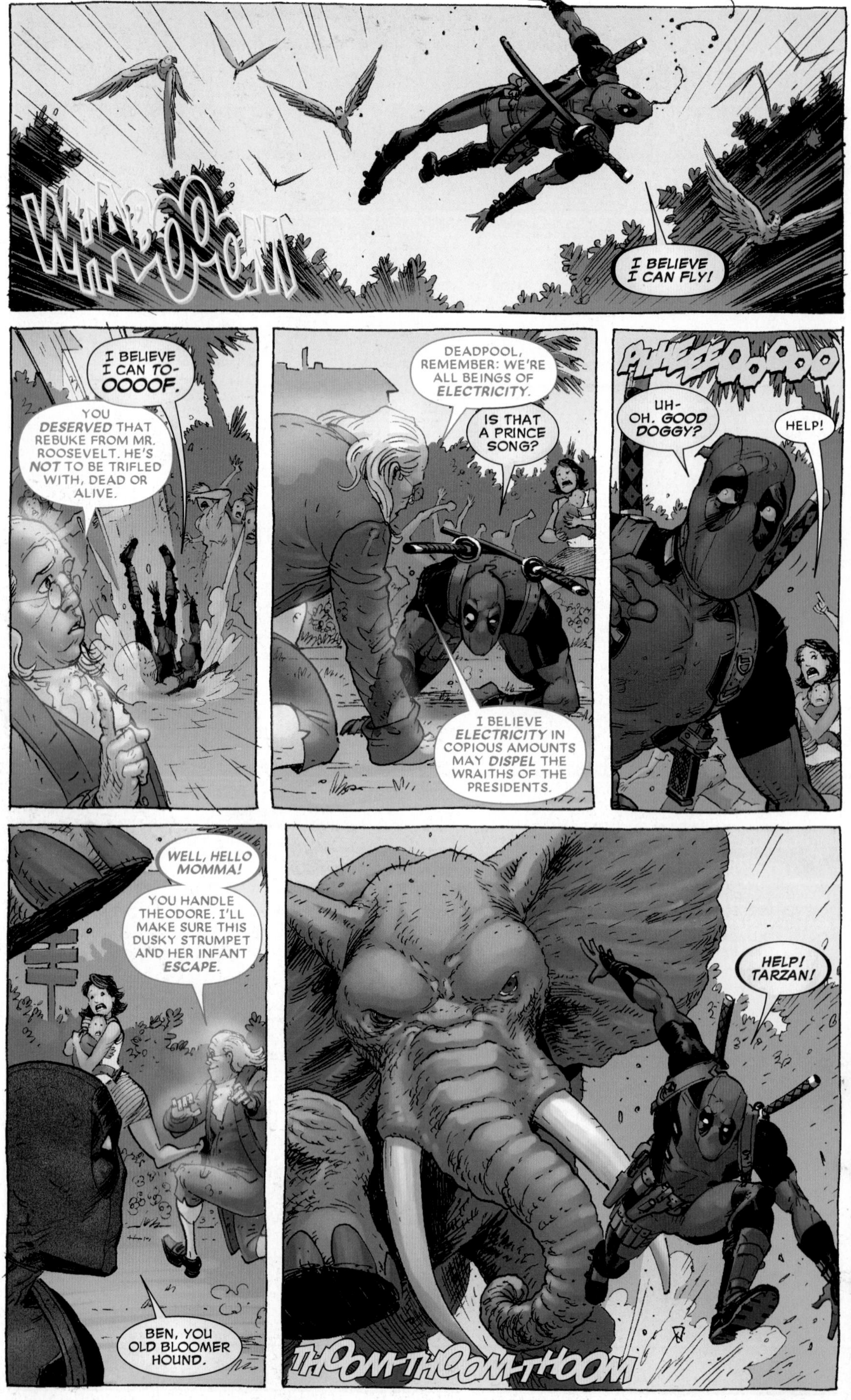
WHOOOM
I BELIEVE I CAN FLY!
I BELIEVE I CAN TO-OOOOF.
YOU DESERVED THAT REBUKE FROM MR. ROOSEVELT. HE'S NOT TO BE TRIFLED WITH, DEAD OR ALIVE.
DEADPOOL, REMEMBER: WE'RE ALL BEINGS OF ELECTRICITY.
IS THAT A PRINCE SONG?
I BELIEVE ELECTRICITY IN COPIOUS AMOUNTS MAY DISPEL THE WRAITHS OF THE PRESIDENTS.
PHHEEOOOOOO
UH-OH. GOOD DOGGY?
HELP!
WELL, HELLO MOMMA!
YOU HANDLE THEODORE. I'LL MAKE SURE THIS DUSKY STRUMPET AND HER INFANT ESCAPE.
BEN, YOU OLD BLOOMER HOUND.
HELP! TARZAN!
THOOM-THOOM-THOOM

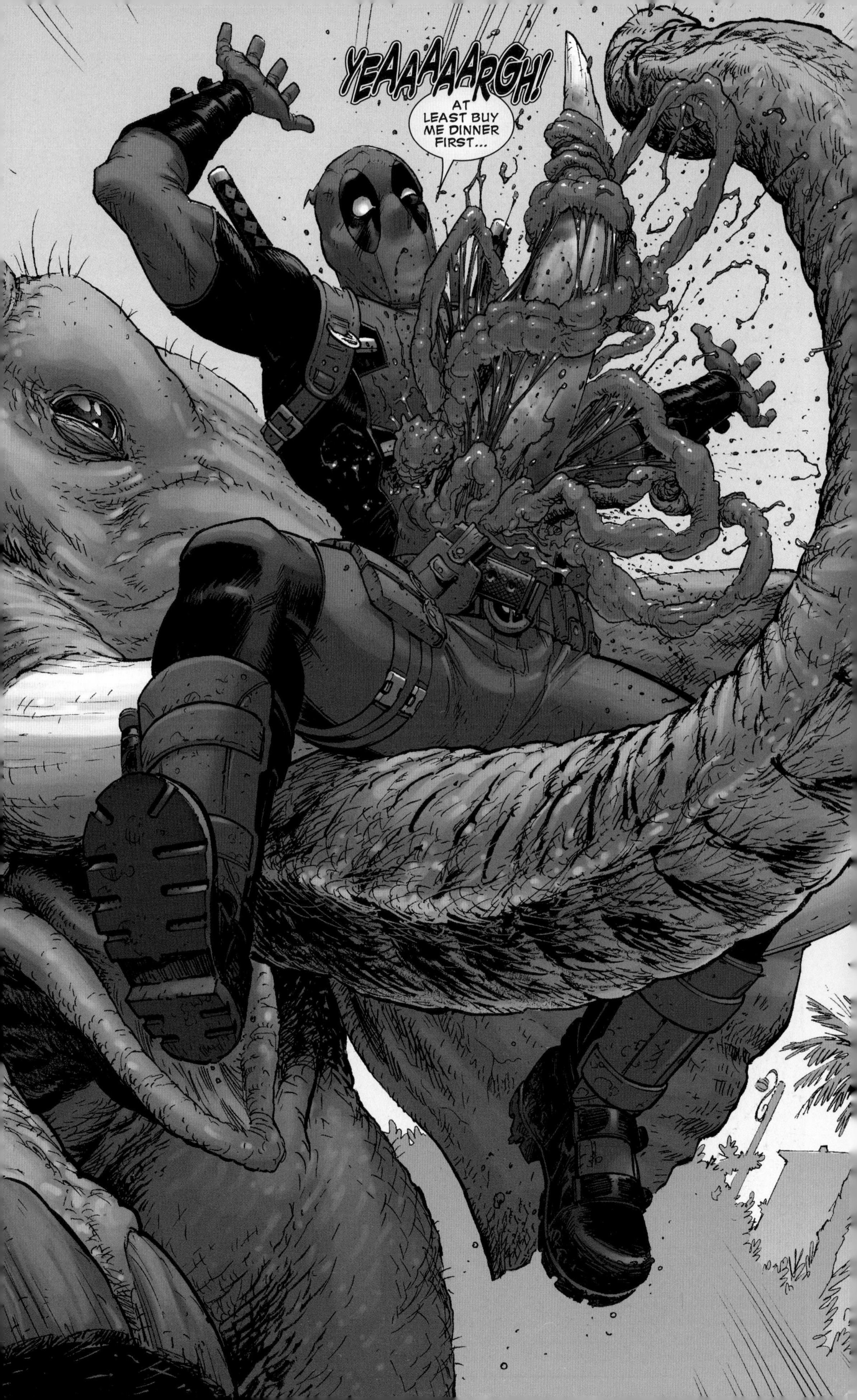
YEAAAAAARGH!
AT LEAST BUY ME DINNER FIRST...

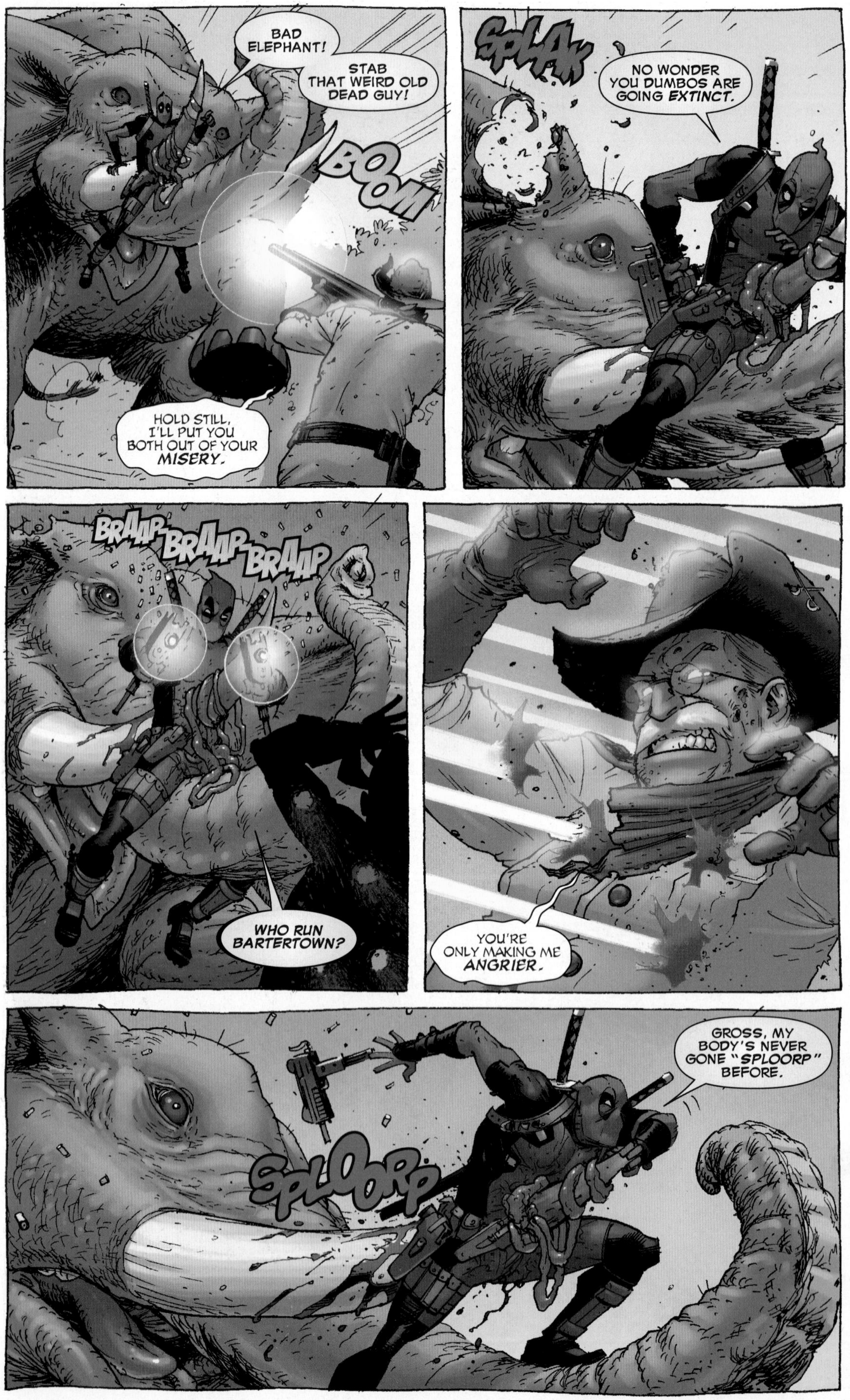
BAD ELEPHANT!
STAB THAT WEIRD OLD DEAD GUY!
BOOM
HOLD STILL, I'LL PUT YOU BOTH OUT OF YOUR MISERY.
SPLAK
NO WONDER YOU DUMBOS ARE GOING EXTINCT.
BRAAP BRAAP BRAAP
WHO RUN BARTERTOWN?
YOU'RE ONLY MAKING ME ANGRIER.
GROSS, MY BODY'S NEVER GONE "SPLOORP" BEFORE.
SPLOORP

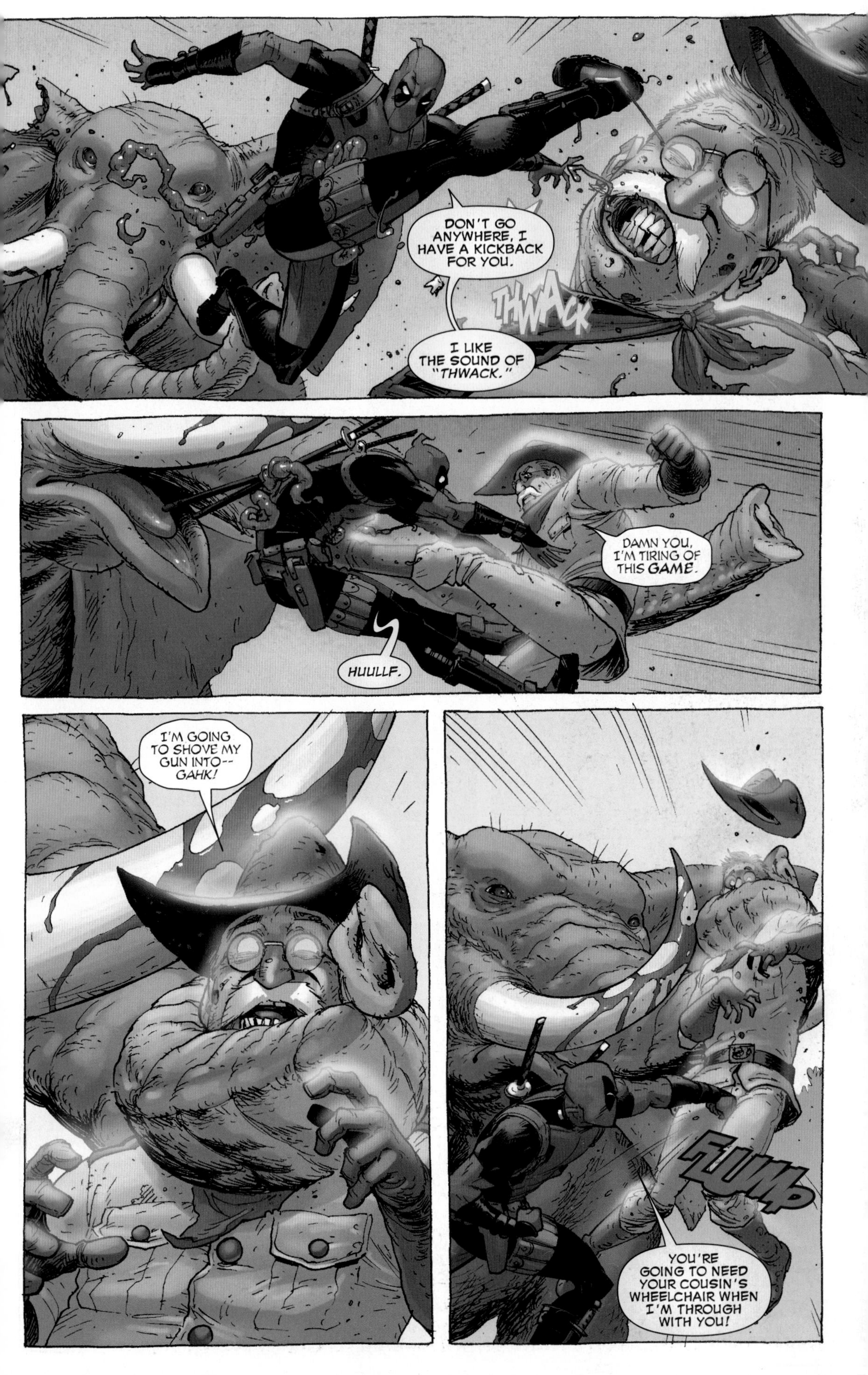
DON'T GO ANYWHERE, I HAVE A KICKBACK FOR YOU.
THWACK
I LIKE THE SOUND OF "THWACK."
DAMN YOU, I'M TIRING OF THIS GAME.
HUULLF.
I'M GOING TO SHOVE MY GUN INTO-- GAHK!
FLUMP
YOU'RE GOING TO NEED YOUR COUSIN'S WHEELCHAIR WHEN I'M THROUGH WITH YOU!

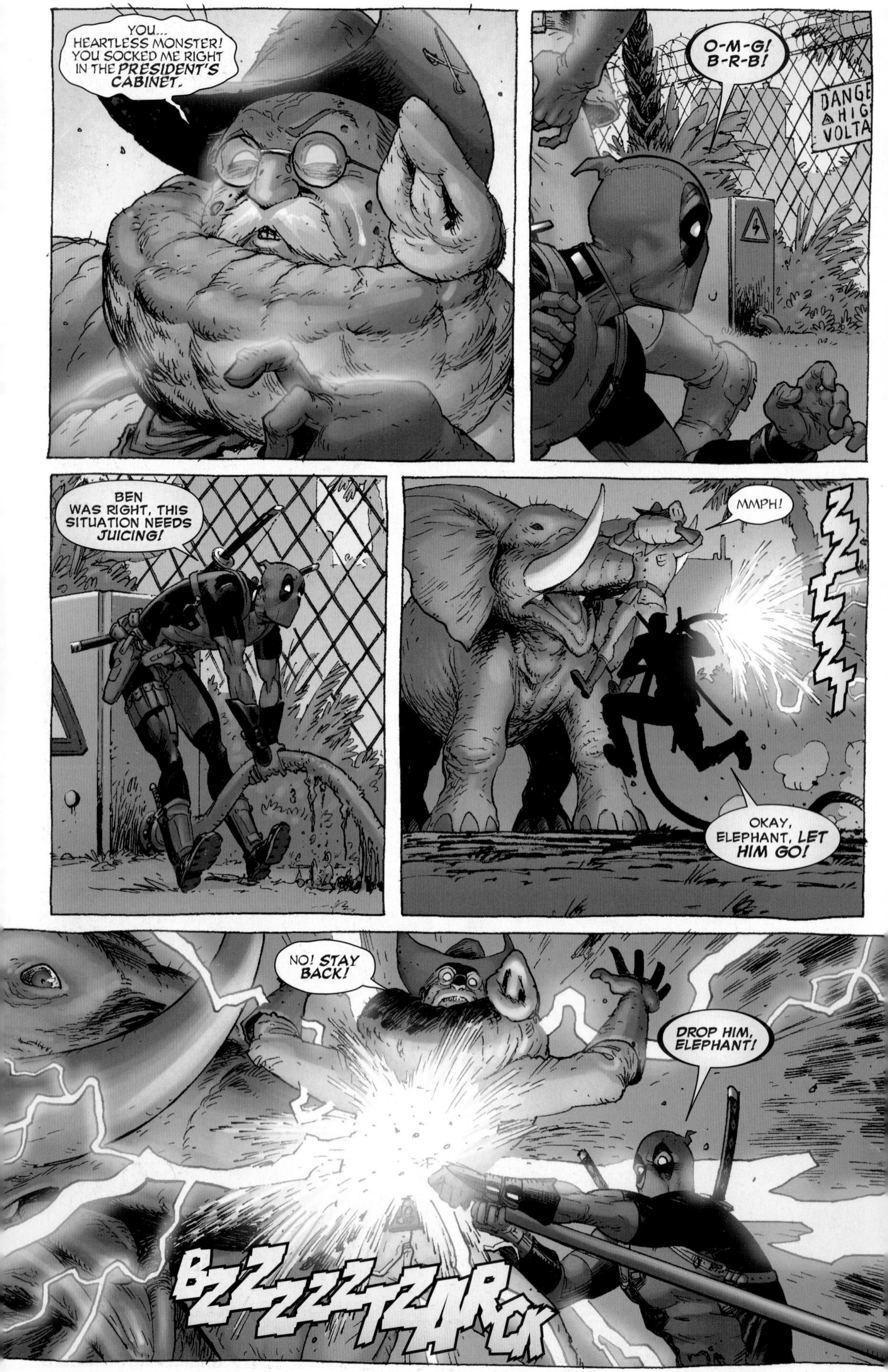
YOU... HEARTLESS MONSTER! YOU SOCKED ME RIGHT IN THE PRESIDENT'S CABINET.
O-M-G! B-R-B!
DANGE
HIG
VOLTA
BEN WAS RIGHT, THIS SITUATION NEEDS JUICING!
MMPH!
ZZZZZZ
OKAY, ELEPHANT, LET HIM GO!
NO! STAY BACK!
DROP HIM, ELEPHANT!
BZZZZZZTZARCK

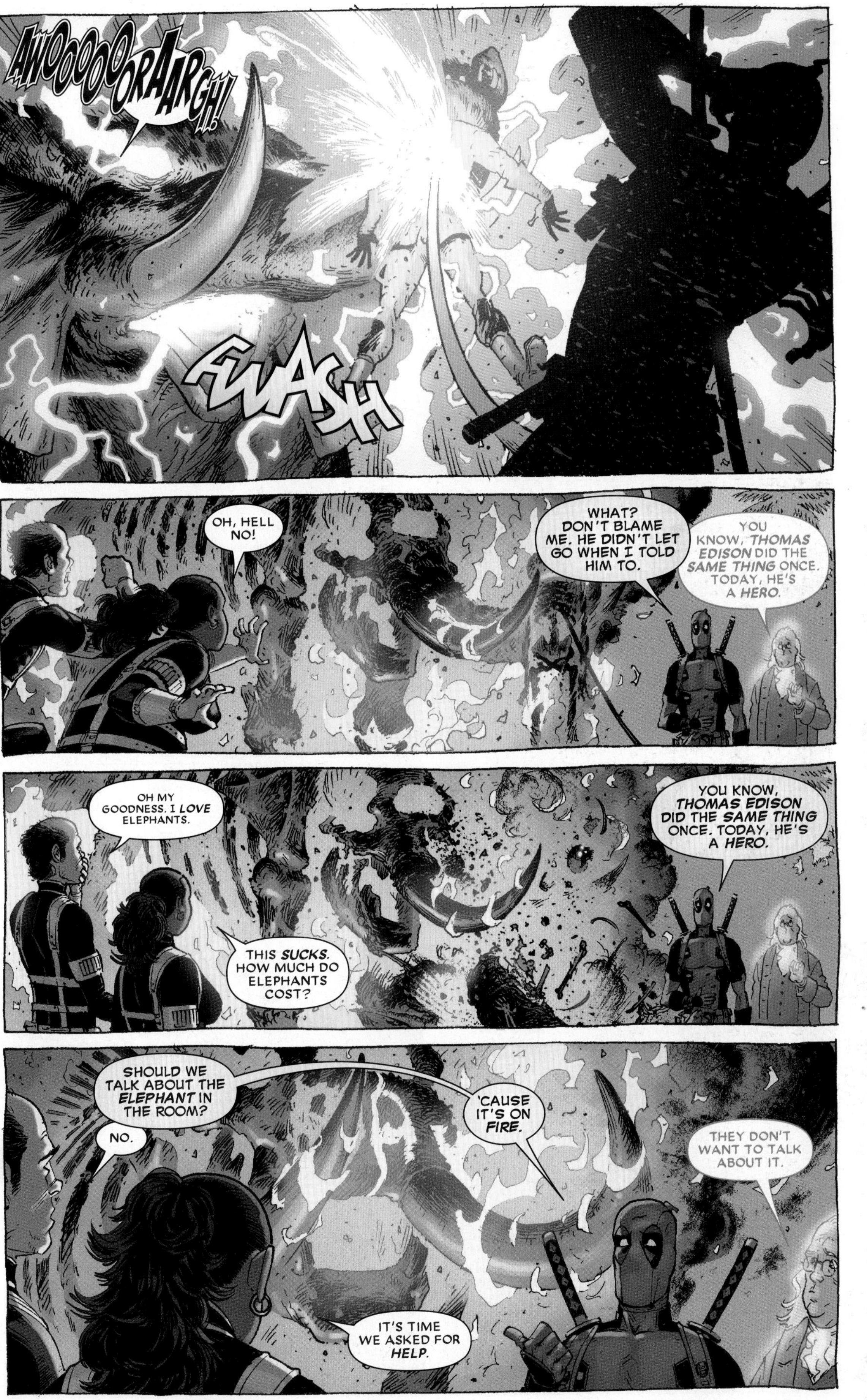
AWOOOOOORAARGH!
FWASH
OH, HELL NO!
WHAT? DON'T BLAME ME. HE DIDN'T LET GO WHEN I TOLD HIM TO.
YOU KNOW, THOMAS EDISON DID THE SAME THING ONCE. TODAY, HE'S A HERO.
OH MY GOODNESS. I LOVE ELEPHANTS.
THIS SUCKS. HOW MUCH DO ELEPHANTS COST?
YOU KNOW, THOMAS EDISON DID THE SAME THING ONCE. TODAY, HE'S A HERO.
SHOULD WE TALK ABOUT THE ELEPHANT IN THE ROOM?
NO.
'CAUSE IT'S ON FIRE.
THEY DON'T WANT TO TALK ABOUT IT.
IT'S TIME WE ASKED FOR HELP.

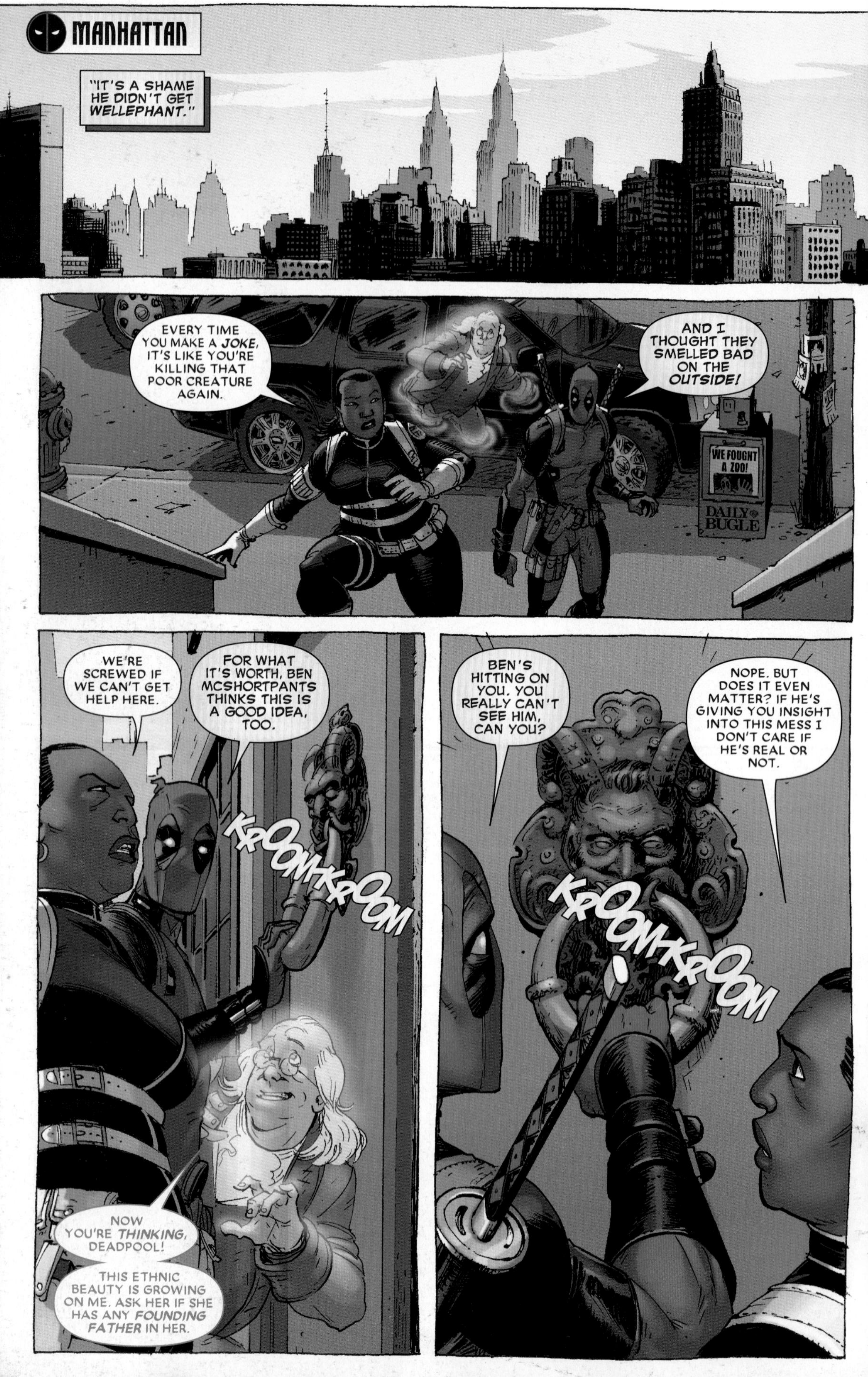
MANHATTAN
"IT'S A SHAME HE DIDN'T GET WELLEPHANT."
EVERY TIME YOU MAKE A JOKE, IT'S LIKE YOU'RE KILLING THAT POOR CREATURE AGAIN.
AND I THOUGHT THEY SMELLED BAD ON THE OUTSIDE!
WE FOUGHT A ZOO!
DAILY BUGLE
WE'RE SCREWED IF WE CAN'T GET HELP HERE.
FOR WHAT IT'S WORTH, BEN MCSHORTPANTS THINKS THIS IS A GOOD IDEA, TOO.
KROOM-KROOM
NOW YOU'RE THINKING, DEADPOOL!
THIS ETHNIC BEAUTY IS GROWING ON ME. ASK HER IF SHE HAS ANY FOUNDING FATHER IN HER.
BEN'S HITTING ON YOU. YOU REALLY CAN'T SEE HIM, CAN YOU?
NOPE. BUT DOES IT EVEN MATTER? IF HE'S GIVING YOU INSIGHT INTO THIS MESS I DON'T CARE IF HE'S REAL OR NOT.
KROOM-KROOM

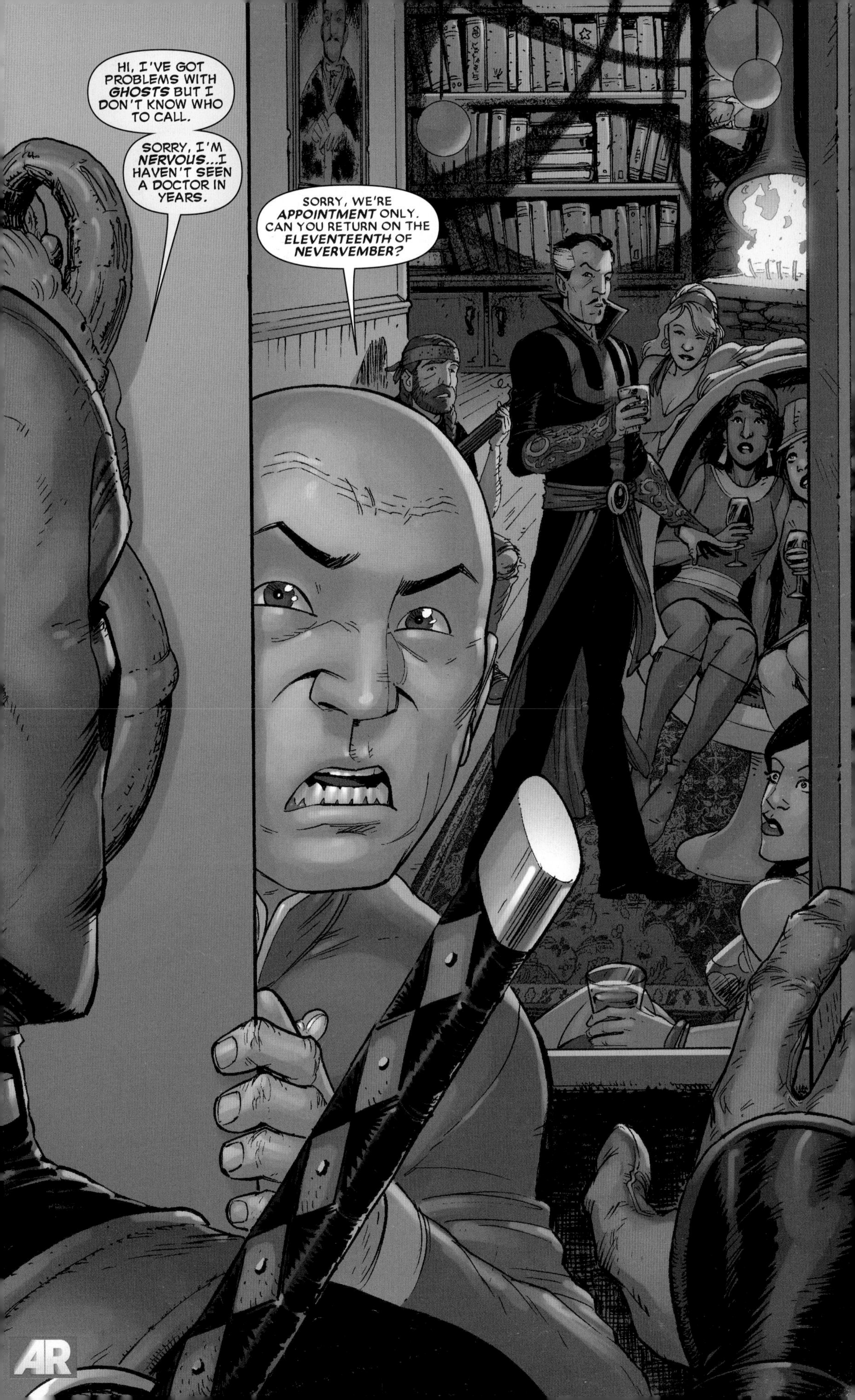
HI, I'VE GOT PROBLEMS WITH GHOSTS BUT I DON'T KNOW WHO TO CALL.
SORRY, I'M NERVOUS...I HAVEN'T SEEN A DOCTOR IN YEARS.
SORRY, WE'RE APPOINTMENT ONLY. CAN YOU RETURN ON THE ELEVENTEENTH OF NEVERVEMBER?

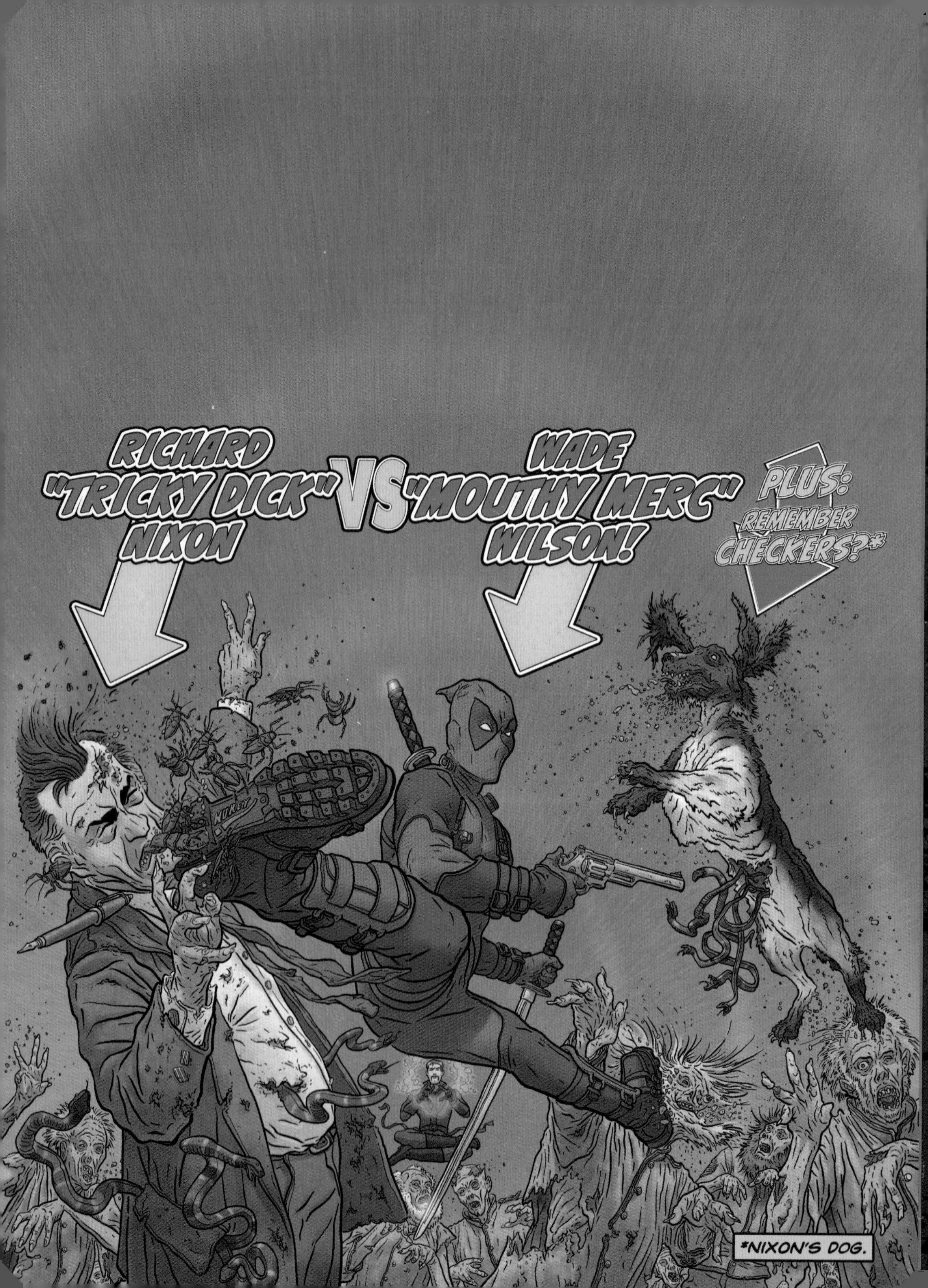
RICHARD "TRICKY DICK" NIXON
VS
WADE "MOUTHY MERC" WILSON!
PLUS: REMEMBER CHECKERS?*
*NIXON'S DOG.

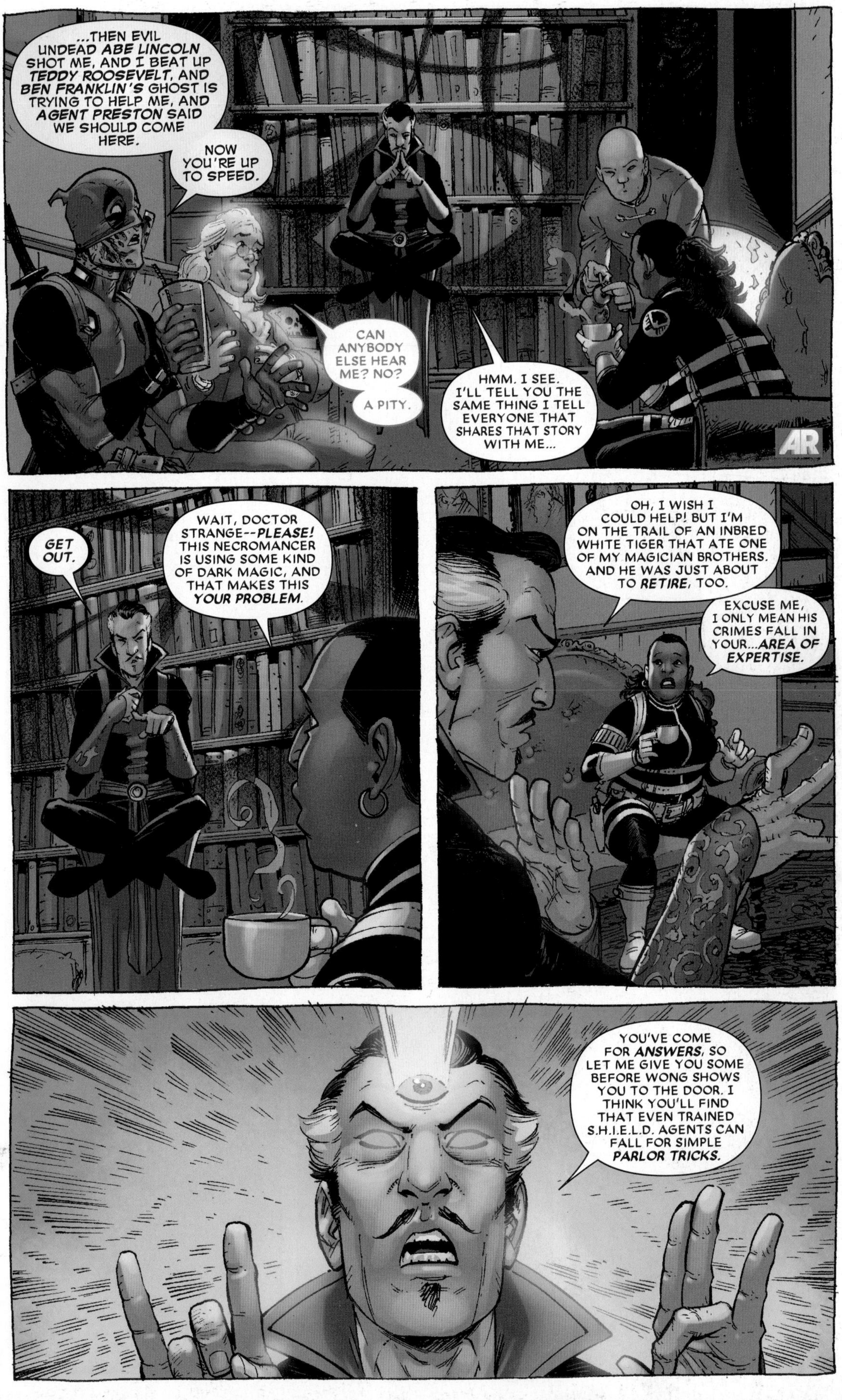
...THEN EVIL UNDEAD ABE LINCOLN SHOT ME, AND I BEAT UP TEDDY ROOSEVELT, AND BEN FRANKLIN'S GHOST IS TRYING TO HELP ME, AND AGENT PRESTON SAID WE SHOULD COME HERE.
NOW YOU'RE UP TO SPEED.
CAN ANYBODY ELSE HEAR ME? NO?
A PITY.
HMM. I SEE. I'LL TELL YOU THE SAME THING I TELL EVERYONE THAT SHARES THAT STORY WITH ME...
AR
GET OUT.
WAIT, DOCTOR STRANGE--PLEASE! THIS NECROMANCER IS USING SOME KIND OF DARK MAGIC, AND THAT MAKES THIS YOUR PROBLEM.
OH, I WISH I COULD HELP! BUT I'M ON THE TRAIL OF AN INBRED WHITE TIGER THAT ATE ONE OF MY MAGICIAN BROTHERS. AND HE WAS JUST ABOUT TO RETIRE, TOO.
EXCUSE ME, I ONLY MEAN HIS CRIMES FALL IN YOUR...AREA OF EXPERTISE.
YOU'VE COME FOR ANSWERS, SO LET ME GIVE YOU SOME BEFORE WONG SHOWS YOU TO THE DOOR. I THINK YOU'LL FIND THAT EVEN TRAINED S.H.I.E.L.D. AGENTS CAN FALL FOR SIMPLE PARLOR TRICKS.

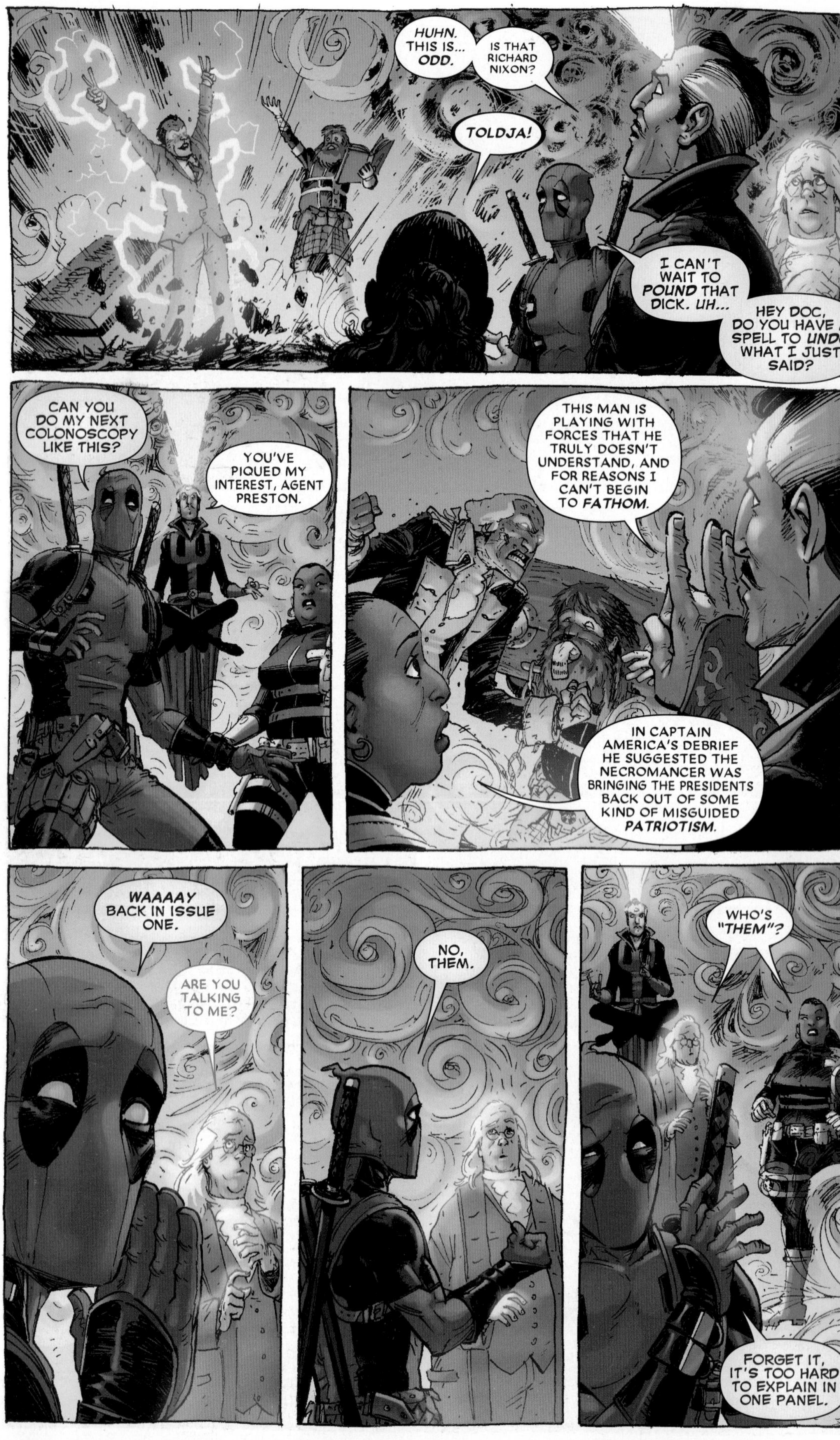
HUHN. THIS IS... ODD.
IS THAT RICHARD NIXON?
TOLDJA!
I CAN'T WAIT TO POUND THAT DICK. UH...
HEY DOC, DO YOU HAVE A SPELL TO UNDO WHAT I JUST SAID?
CAN YOU DO MY NEXT COLONOSCOPY LIKE THIS?
YOU'VE PIQUED MY INTEREST, AGENT PRESTON.
THIS MAN IS PLAYING WITH FORCES THAT HE TRULY DOESN'T UNDERSTAND, AND FOR REASONS I CAN'T BEGIN TO FATHOM.
IN CAPTAIN AMERICA'S DEBRIEF HE SUGGESTED THE NECROMANCER WAS BRINGING THE PRESIDENTS BACK OUT OF SOME KIND OF MISGUIDED PATRIOTISM.
WAAAAY BACK IN ISSUE ONE.
ARE YOU TALKING TO ME?
NO, THEM.
WHO'S "THEM"?
FORGET IT, IT'S TOO HARD TO EXPLAIN IN ONE PANEL.

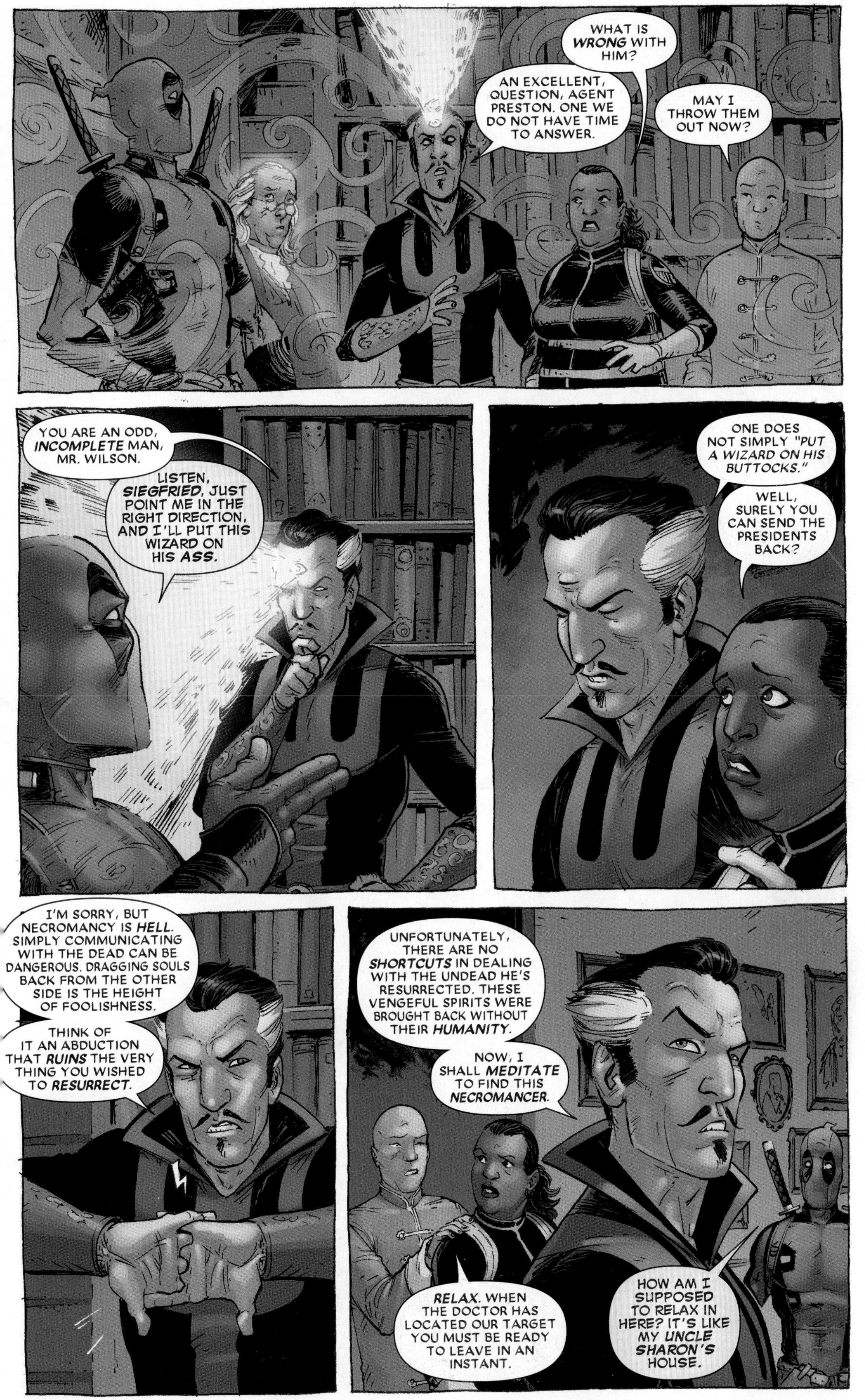
WHAT IS WRONG WITH HIM?
AN EXCELLENT, QUESTION, AGENT PRESTON. ONE WE DO NOT HAVE TIME TO ANSWER.
MAY I THROW THEM OUT NOW?
YOU ARE AN ODD, INCOMPLETE MAN, MR. WILSON.
LISTEN, SIEGFRIED, JUST POINT ME IN THE RIGHT DIRECTION, AND I'LL PUT THIS WIZARD ON HIS ASS.
ONE DOES NOT SIMPLY "PUT A WIZARD ON HIS BUTTOCKS."
WELL, SURELY YOU CAN SEND THE PRESIDENTS BACK?
I'M SORRY, BUT NECROMANCY IS HELL. SIMPLY COMMUNICATING WITH THE DEAD CAN BE DANGEROUS. DRAGGING SOULS BACK FROM THE OTHER SIDE IS THE HEIGHT OF FOOLISHNESS.
THINK OF IT AN ABDUCTION THAT RUINS THE VERY THING YOU WISHED TO RESURRECT.
UNFORTUNATELY, THERE ARE NO SHORTCUTS IN DEALING WITH THE UNDEAD HE'S RESURRECTED. THESE VENGEFUL SPIRITS WERE BROUGHT BACK WITHOUT THEIR HUMANITY.
NOW, I SHALL MEDITATE TO FIND THIS NECROMANCER.
RELAX. WHEN THE DOCTOR HAS LOCATED OUR TARGET YOU MUST BE READY TO LEAVE IN AN INSTANT.
HOW AM I SUPPOSED TO RELAX IN HERE? IT'S LIKE MY UNCLE SHARON'S HOUSE.

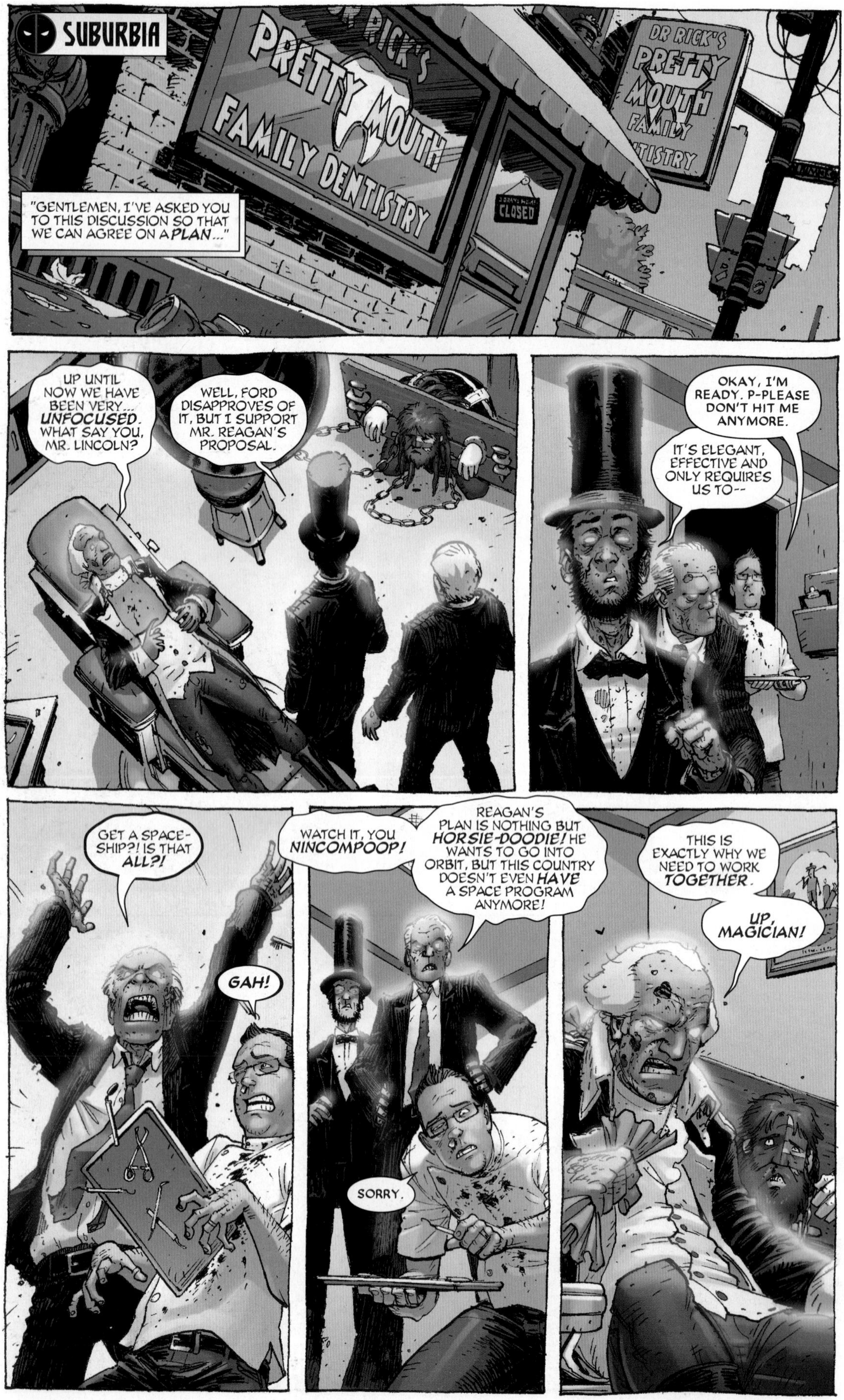

SUBURBIA
PRETTY MOUTH FAMILY DENTISTRY
DR RICK'S PRETTY MOUTH FAMILY
CLOSED
"GENTLEMEN, I'VE ASKED YOU TO THIS DISCUSSION SO THAT WE CAN AGREE ON A PLAN..."
UP UNTIL NOW WE HAVE BEEN VERY... UNFOCUSED. WHAT SAY YOU, MR. LINCOLN?
WELL, FORD DISAPPROVES OF IT, BUT I SUPPORT MR. REAGAN'S PROPOSAL.
OKAY, I'M READY. P-PLEASE DON'T HIT ME ANYMORE.
IT'S ELEGANT, EFFECTIVE AND ONLY REQUIRES US TO--
GET A SPACE-SHIP?! IS THAT ALL?!
GAH!
WATCH IT, YOU NINCOMPOOP!
REAGAN'S PLAN IS NOTHING BUT HORSIE-DOODIE! HE WANTS TO GO INTO ORBIT, BUT THIS COUNTRY DOESN'T EVEN HAVE A SPACE PROGRAM ANYMORE!
SORRY.
THIS IS EXACTLY WHY WE NEED TO WORK TOGETHER.
UP, MAGICIAN!

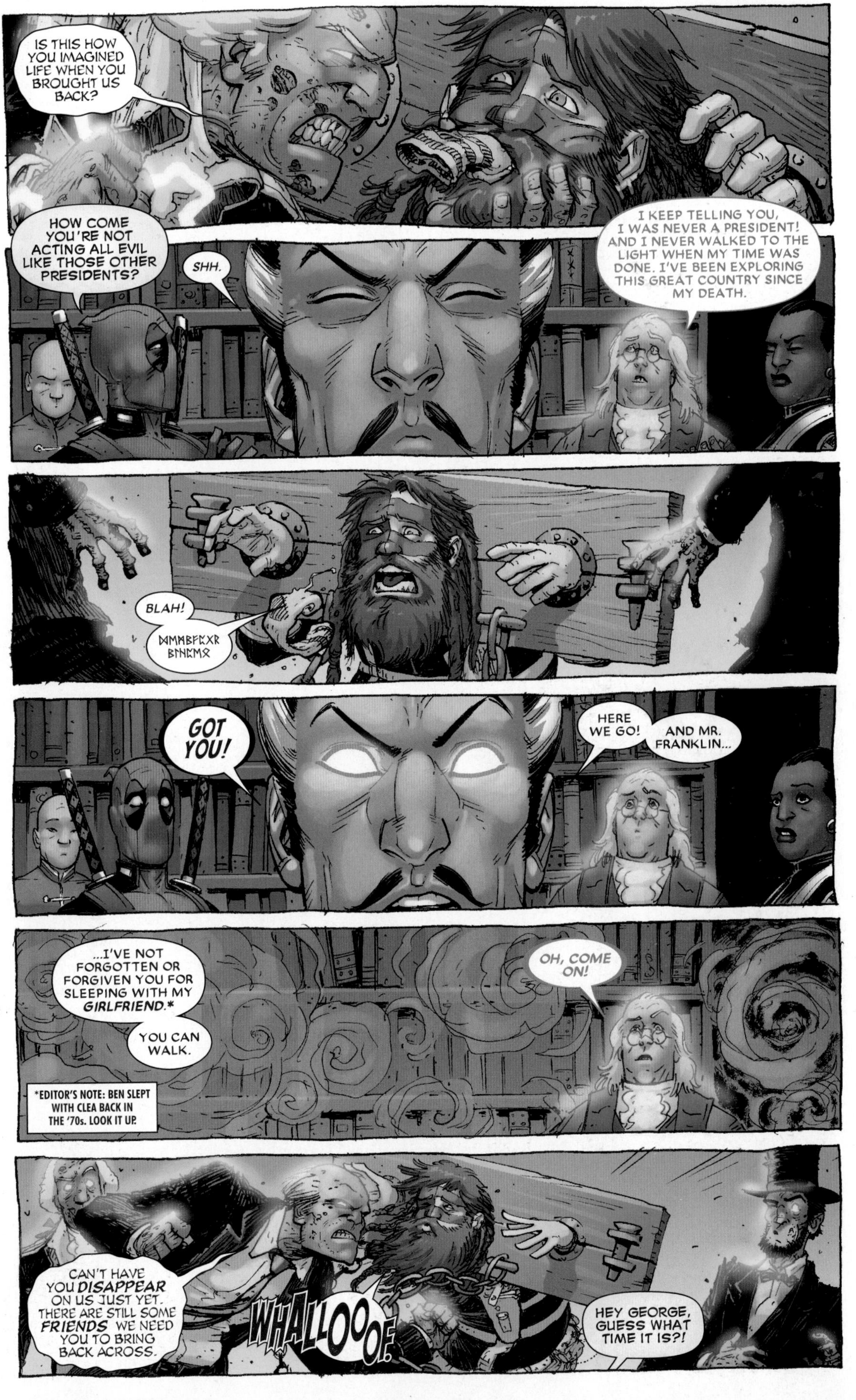
IS THIS HOW YOU IMAGINED LIFE WHEN YOU BROUGHT US BACK?
HOW COME YOU'RE NOT ACTING ALL EVIL LIKE THOSE OTHER PRESIDENTS?
SHH.
I KEEP TELLING YOU, I WAS NEVER A PRESIDENT! AND I NEVER WALKED TO THE LIGHT WHEN MY TIME WAS DONE. I'VE BEEN EXPLORING THIS GREAT COUNTRY SINCE MY DEATH.
BLAH!
GOT YOU!
HERE WE GO!
AND MR. FRANKLIN...
...I'VE NOT FORGOTTEN OR FORGIVEN YOU FOR SLEEPING WITH MY GIRLFRIEND.*
YOU CAN WALK.
OH, COME ON!
*EDITOR'S NOTE: BEN SLEPT WITH CLEA BACK IN THE '70s. LOOK IT UP.
CAN'T HAVE YOU DISAPPEAR ON US JUST YET. THERE ARE STILL SOME FRIENDS WE NEED YOU TO BRING BACK ACROSS.
WHALLOOOF.
HEY GEORGE, GUESS WHAT TIME IT IS?!

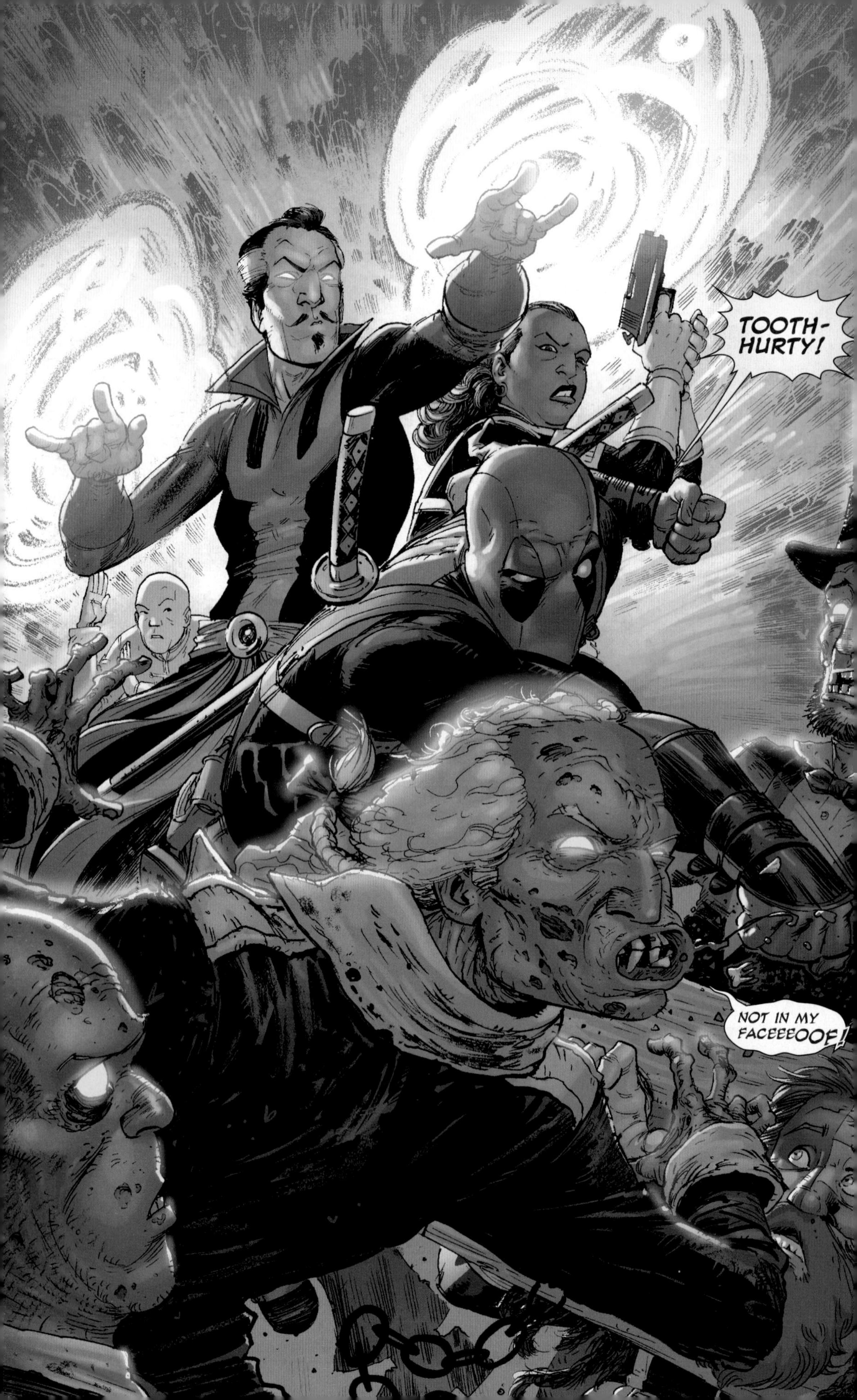
TOOTH-HURTY!
NOT IN MY FACEEEEOOF!

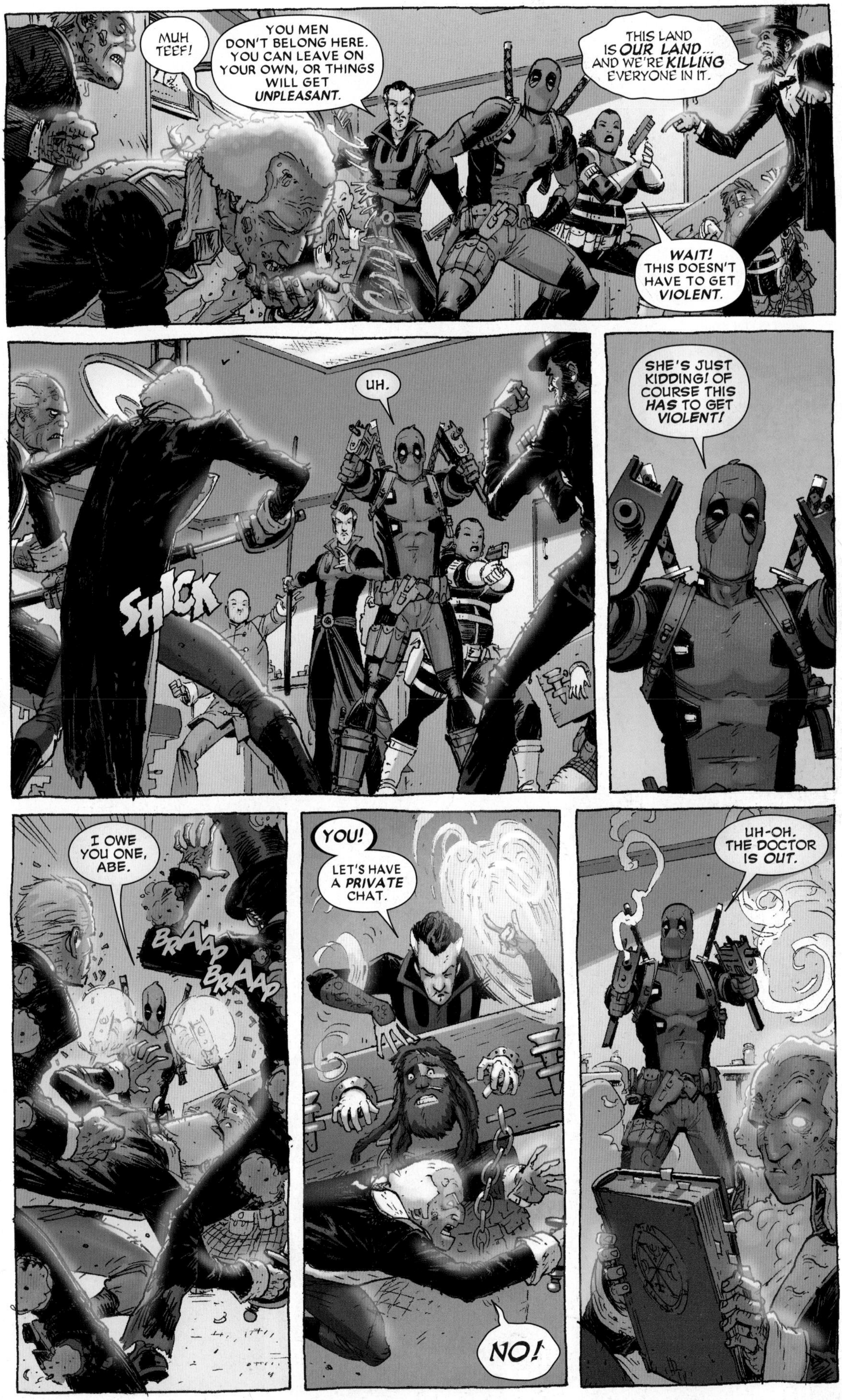
MUH TEEF!
YOU MEN DON'T BELONG HERE. YOU CAN LEAVE ON YOUR OWN, OR THINGS WILL GET UNPLEASANT.
THIS LAND IS OUR LAND... AND WE'RE KILLING EVERYONE IN IT.
WAIT! THIS DOESN'T HAVE TO GET VIOLENT.
UH.
SHICK
SHE'S JUST KIDDING! OF COURSE THIS HAS TO GET VIOLENT!
I OWE YOU ONE, ABE.
BRAAAP BRAAAP
YOU!
LET'S HAVE A PRIVATE CHAT.
NO!
UH-OH. THE DOCTOR IS OUT.

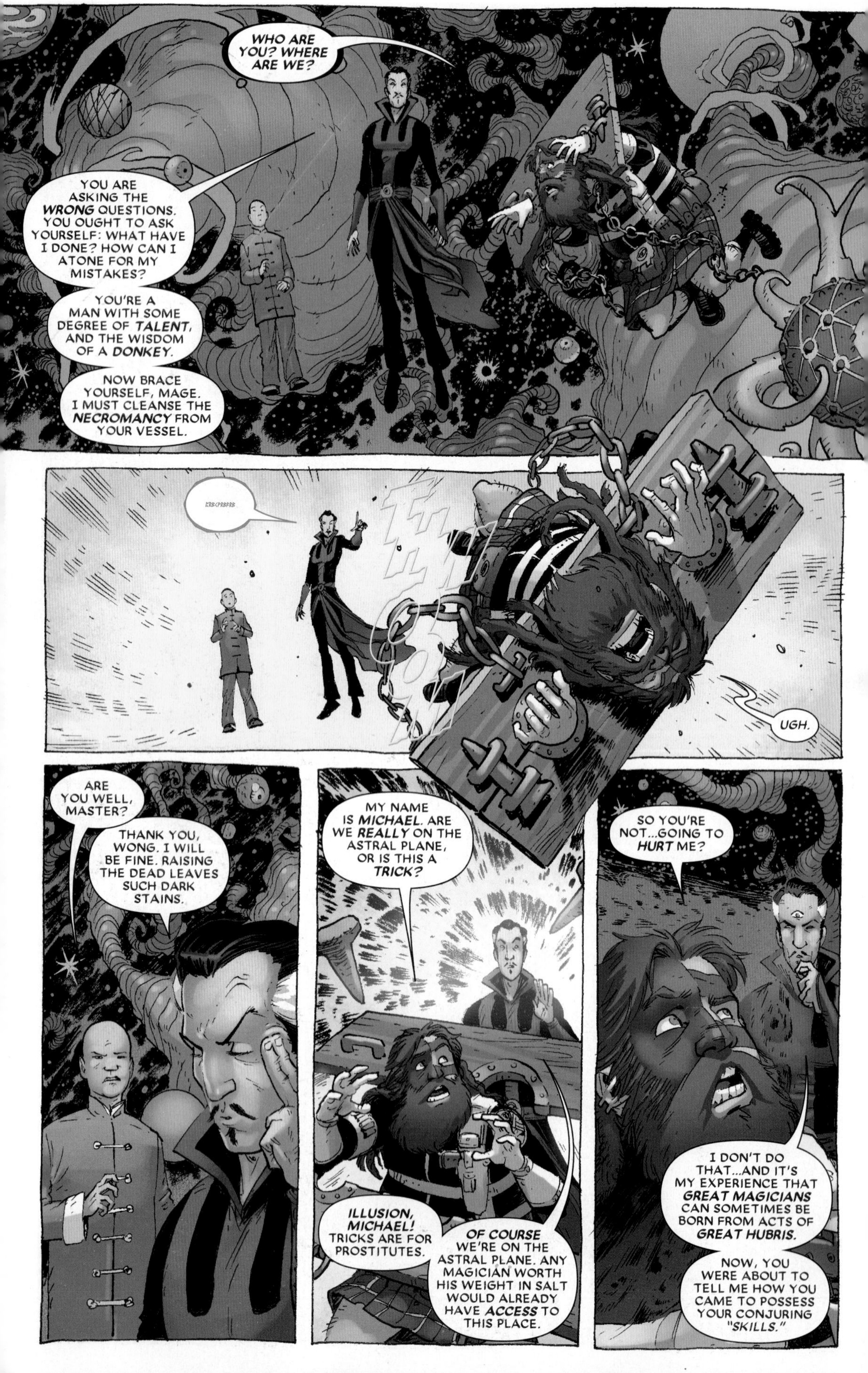

WHO ARE YOU? WHERE ARE WE?
YOU ARE ASKING THE WRONG QUESTIONS. YOU OUGHT TO ASK YOURSELF: WHAT HAVE I DONE? HOW CAN I ATONE FOR MY MISTAKES?
YOU'RE A MAN WITH SOME DEGREE OF TALENT, AND THE WISDOM OF A DONKEY.
NOW BRACE YOURSELF, MAGE. I MUST CLEANSE THE NECROMANCY FROM YOUR VESSEL.
UGH.
ARE YOU WELL, MASTER?
THANK YOU, WONG. I WILL BE FINE. RAISING THE DEAD LEAVES SUCH DARK STAINS.
MY NAME IS MICHAEL. ARE WE REALLY ON THE ASTRAL PLANE, OR IS THIS A TRICK?
ILLUSION, MICHAEL! TRICKS ARE FOR PROSTITUTES.
OF COURSE WE'RE ON THE ASTRAL PLANE. ANY MAGICIAN WORTH HIS WEIGHT IN SALT WOULD ALREADY HAVE ACCESS TO THIS PLACE.
SO YOU'RE NOT...GOING TO HURT ME?
I DON'T DO THAT...AND IT'S MY EXPERIENCE THAT GREAT MAGICIANS CAN SOMETIMES BE BORN FROM ACTS OF GREAT HUBRIS.
NOW, YOU WERE ABOUT TO TELL ME HOW YOU CAME TO POSSESS YOUR CONJURING "SKILLS."

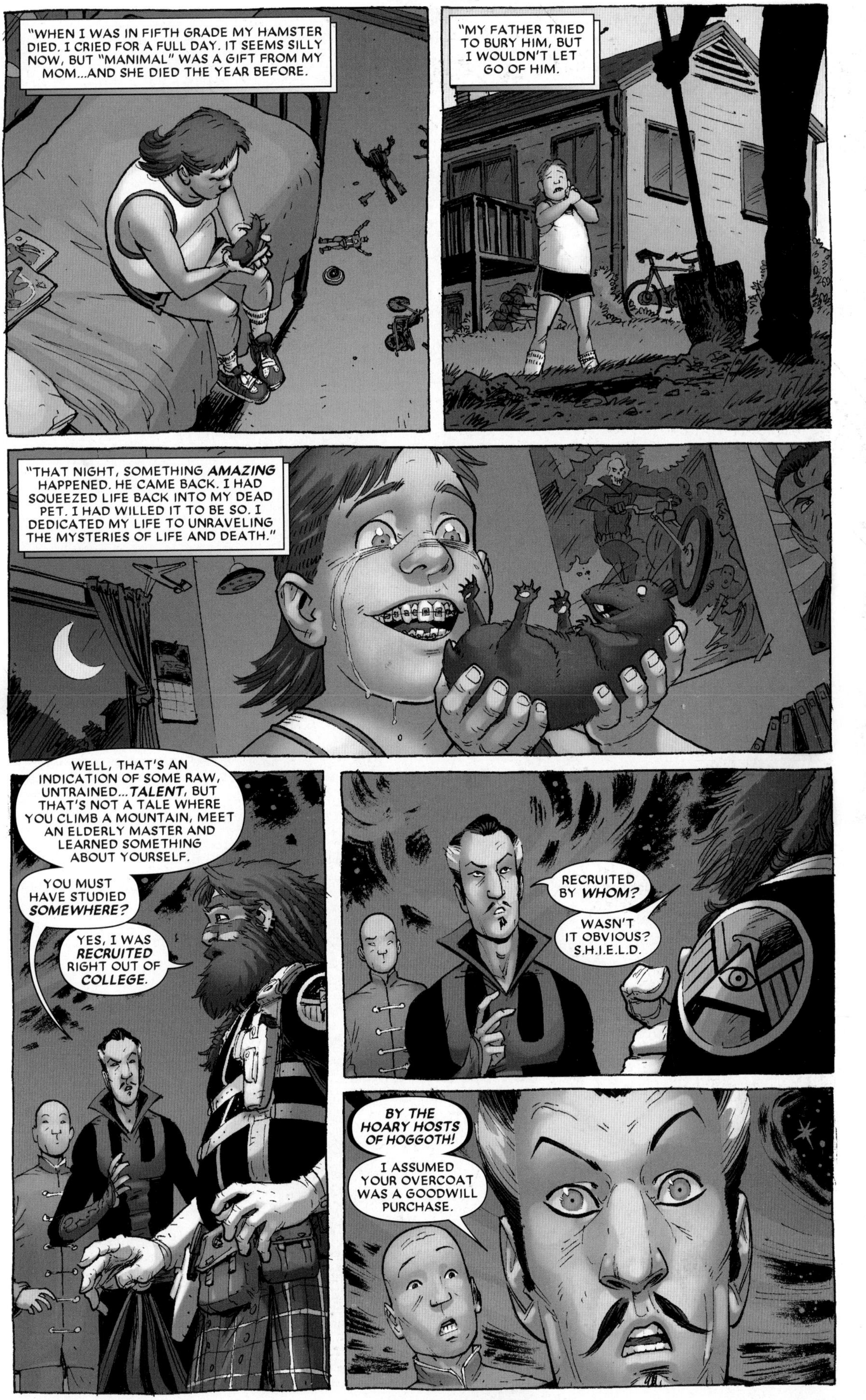
"WHEN I WAS IN FIFTH GRADE MY HAMSTER DIED. I CRIED FOR A FULL DAY. IT SEEMS SILLY NOW, BUT "MANIMAL" WAS A GIFT FROM MY MOM...AND SHE DIED THE YEAR BEFORE.
"MY FATHER TRIED TO BURY HIM, BUT I WOULDN'T LET GO OF HIM.
"THAT NIGHT, SOMETHING AMAZING HAPPENED. HE CAME BACK. I HAD SQUEEZED LIFE BACK INTO MY DEAD PET. I HAD WILLED IT TO BE SO. I DEDICATED MY LIFE TO UNRAVELING THE MYSTERIES OF LIFE AND DEATH."
WELL, THAT'S AN INDICATION OF SOME RAW, UNTRAINED...TALENT, BUT THAT'S NOT A TALE WHERE YOU CLIMB A MOUNTAIN, MEET AN ELDERLY MASTER AND LEARNED SOMETHING ABOUT YOURSELF.
YOU MUST HAVE STUDIED SOMEWHERE?
YES, I WAS RECRUITED RIGHT OUT OF COLLEGE.
RECRUITED BY WHOM?
WASN'T IT OBVIOUS? S.H.I.E.L.D.
BY THE HOARY HOSTS OF HOGGOTH!
I ASSUMED YOUR OVERCOAT WAS A GOODWILL PURCHASE.

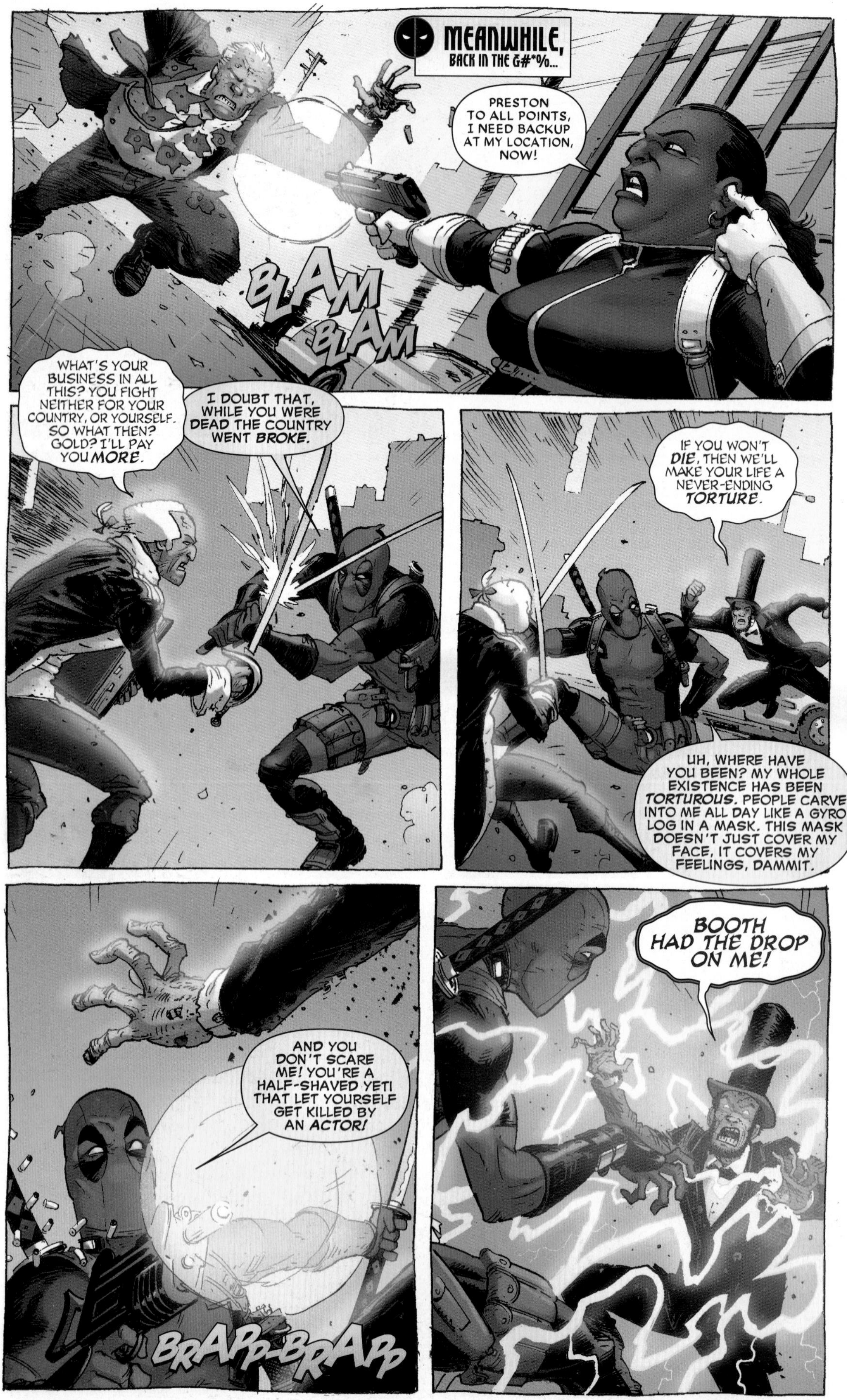
MEANWHILE, BACK IN THE G#*%...
PRESTON TO ALL POINTS, I NEED BACKUP AT MY LOCATION, NOW!
BLAM BLAM
WHAT'S YOUR BUSINESS IN ALL THIS? YOU FIGHT NEITHER FOR YOUR COUNTRY, OR YOURSELF. SO WHAT THEN? GOLD? I'LL PAY YOU MORE.
I DOUBT THAT, WHILE YOU WERE DEAD THE COUNTRY WENT BROKE.
IF YOU WON'T DIE, THEN WE'LL MAKE YOUR LIFE A NEVER-ENDING TORTURE.
UH, WHERE HAVE YOU BEEN? MY WHOLE EXISTENCE HAS BEEN TORTUROUS. PEOPLE CARVE INTO ME ALL DAY LIKE A GYRO LOG IN A MASK. THIS MASK DOESN'T JUST COVER MY FACE, IT COVERS MY FEELINGS, DAMMIT.
AND YOU DON'T SCARE ME! YOU'RE A HALF-SHAVED YETI THAT LET YOURSELF GET KILLED BY AN ACTOR!
BRAPP-BRAPP
BOOTH HAD THE DROP ON ME!

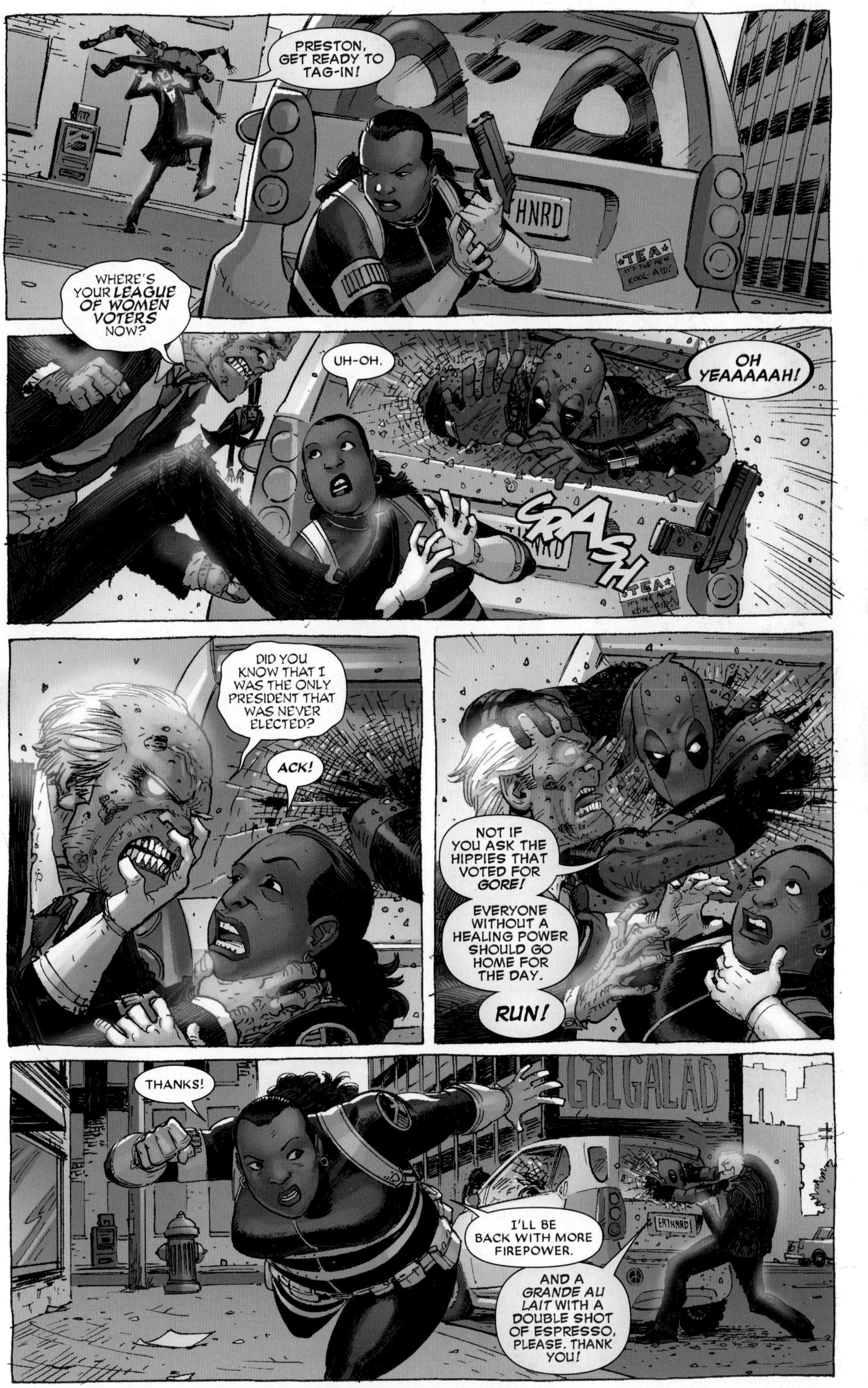
PRESTON, GET READY TO TAG-IN!
HNRD
TEA IT'S THE NEW KOOL-AID!
WHERE'S YOUR LEAGUE OF WOMEN VOTERS NOW?
UH-OH.
OH YEAAAAAH!
CRASH
DID YOU KNOW THAT I WAS THE ONLY PRESIDENT THAT WAS NEVER ELECTED?
ACK!
NOT IF YOU ASK THE HIPPIES THAT VOTED FOR GORE!
EVERYONE WITHOUT A HEALING POWER SHOULD GO HOME FOR THE DAY.
RUN!
GILGALAD
THANKS!
I'LL BE BACK WITH MORE FIREPOWER.
AND A GRANDE AU LAIT WITH A DOUBLE SHOT OF ESPRESSO, PLEASE. THANK YOU!

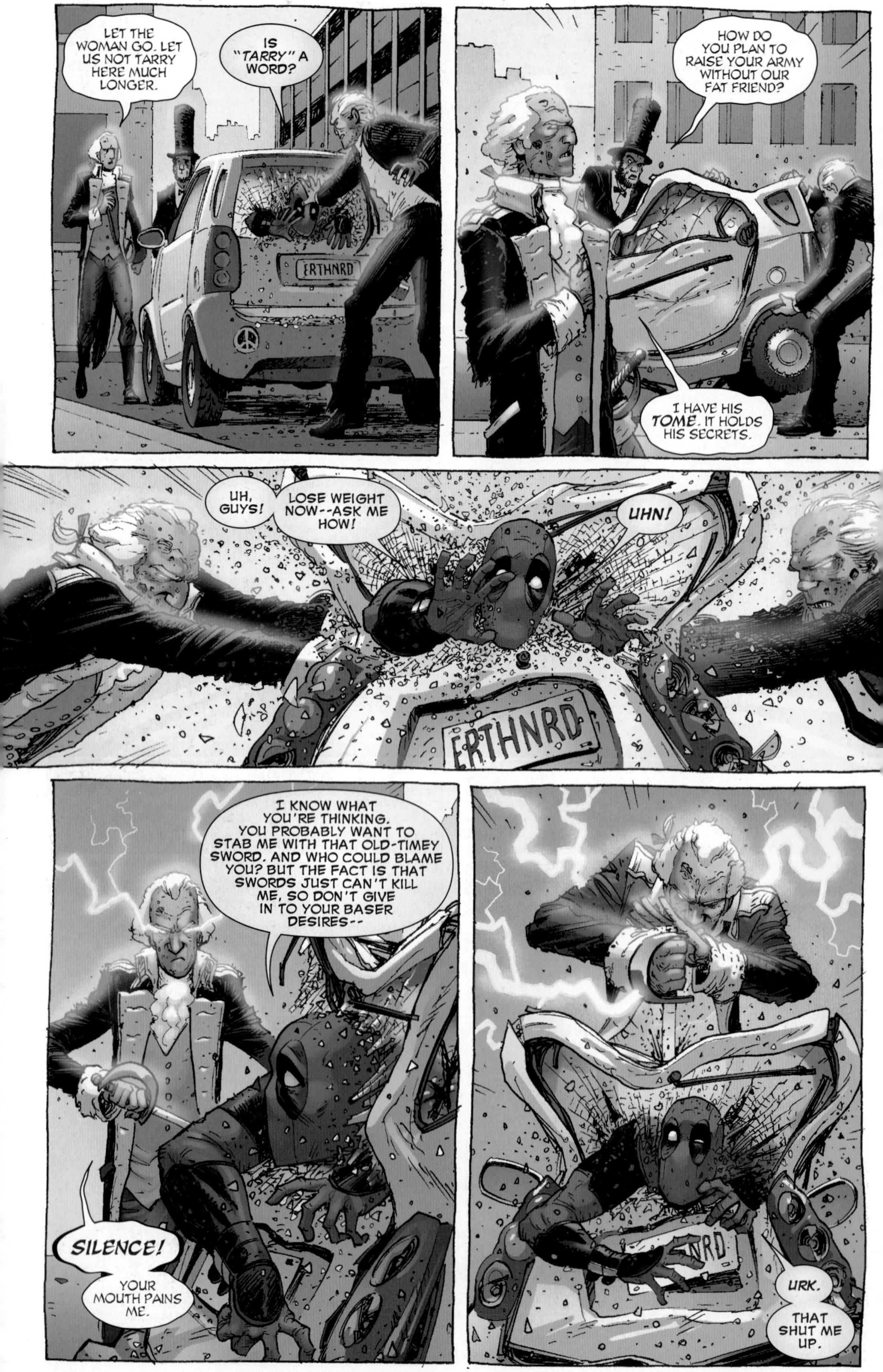

LET THE WOMAN GO. LET US NOT TARRY HERE MUCH LONGER.
IS "TARRY" A WORD?
ERTHNRD
HOW DO YOU PLAN TO RAISE YOUR ARMY WITHOUT OUR FAT FRIEND?
I HAVE HIS TOME. IT HOLDS HIS SECRETS.
UH, GUYS!
LOSE WEIGHT NOW--ASK ME HOW!
UHN!
ERTHNRD
I KNOW WHAT YOU'RE THINKING. YOU PROBABLY WANT TO STAB ME WITH THAT OLD-TIMEY SWORD. AND WHO COULD BLAME YOU? BUT THE FACT IS THAT SWORDS JUST CAN'T KILL ME, SO DON'T GIVE IN TO YOUR BASER DESIRES--
SILENCE!
YOUR MOUTH PAINS ME.
URK.
THAT SHUT ME UP.

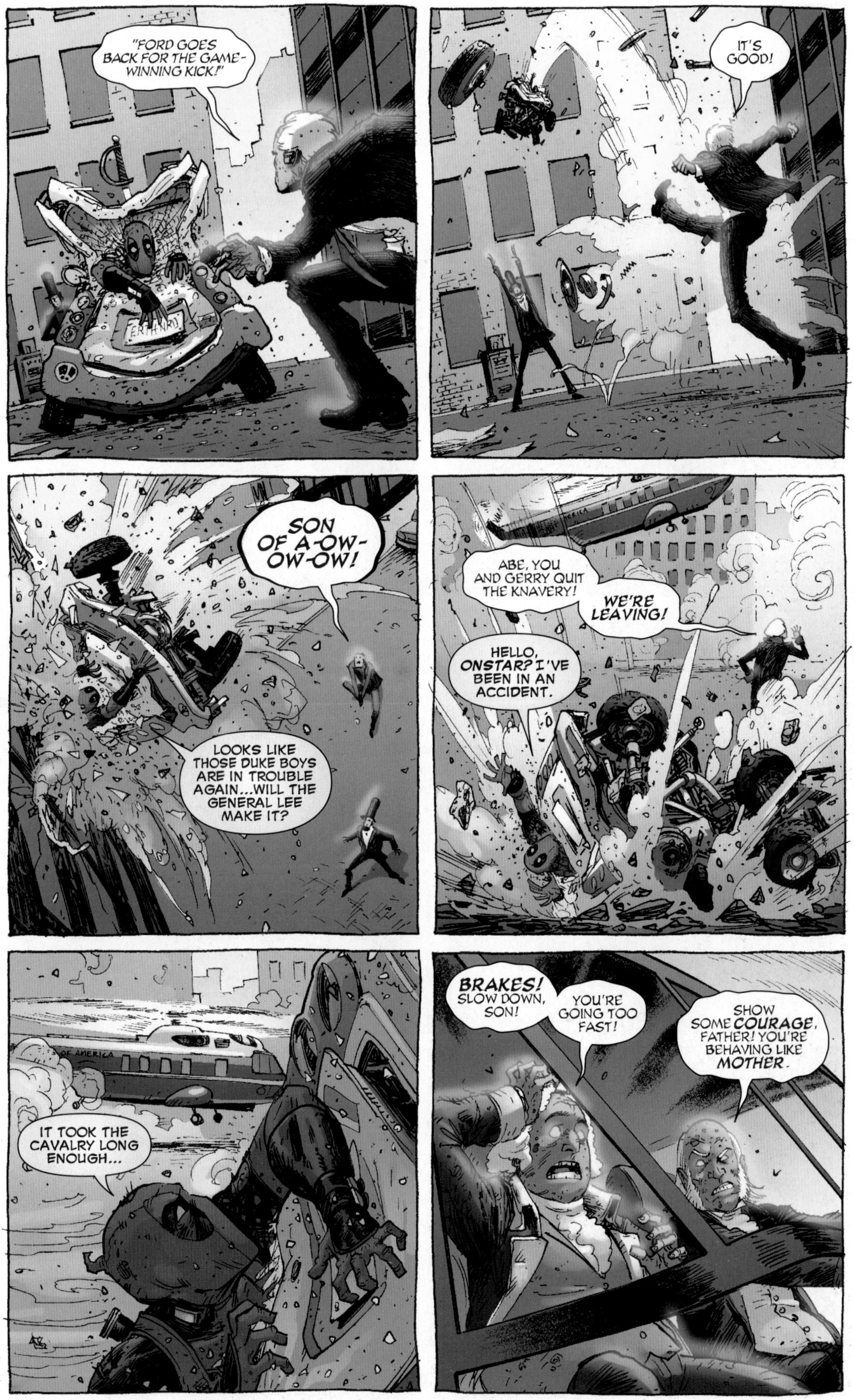
"FORD GOES BACK FOR THE GAME-WINNING KICK!"
IT'S GOOD!
SON OF A-OW-OW-OW!
LOOKS LIKE THOSE DUKE BOYS ARE IN TROUBLE AGAIN...WILL THE GENERAL LEE MAKE IT?
ABE, YOU AND GERRY QUIT THE KNAVERY!
WE'RE LEAVING!
HELLO, ONSTAR? I'VE BEEN IN AN ACCIDENT.
IT TOOK THE CAVALRY LONG ENOUGH...
BRAKES! SLOW DOWN, SON!
YOU'RE GOING TOO FAST!
SHOW SOME COURAGE, FATHER! YOU'RE BEHAVING LIKE MOTHER.

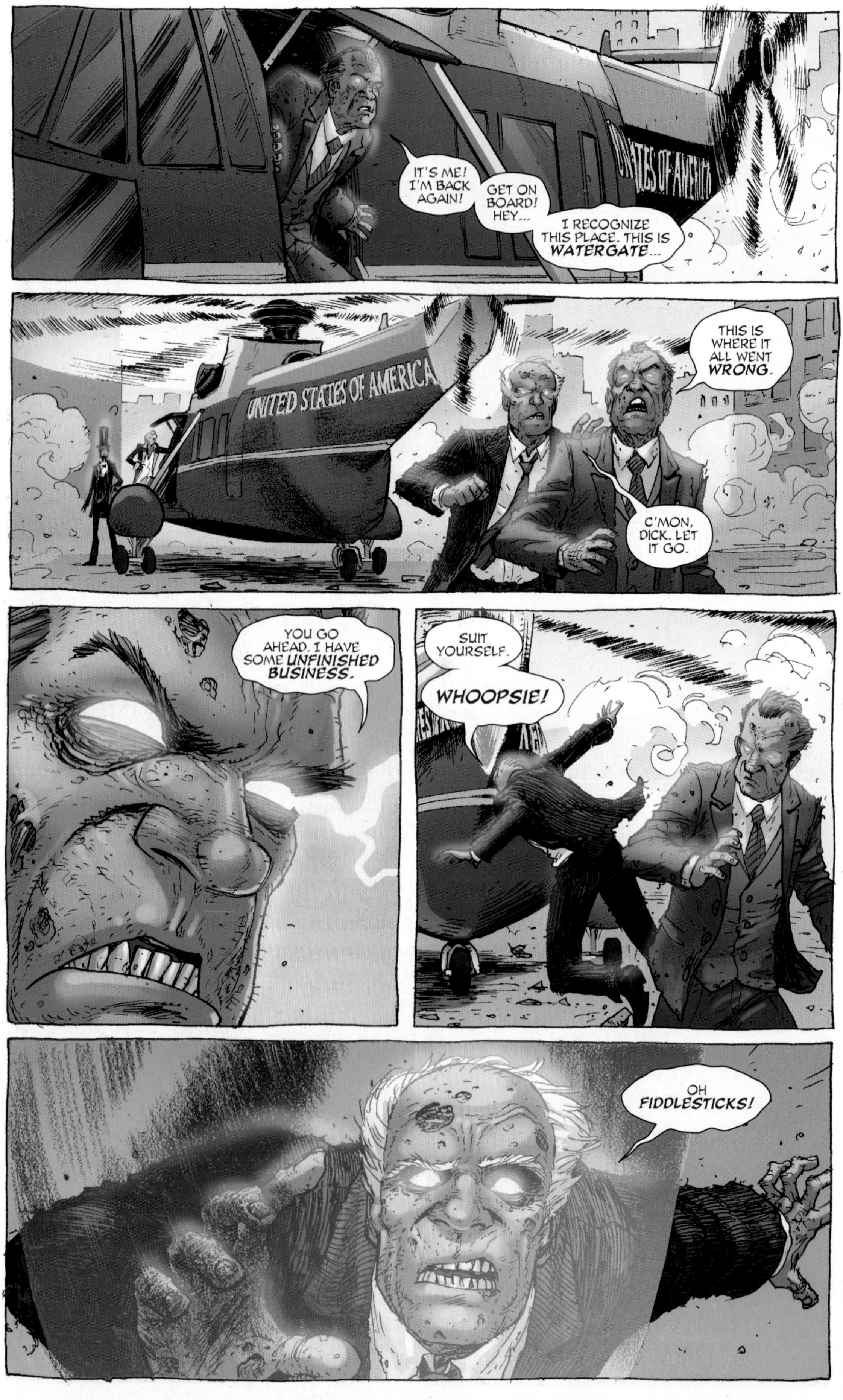
IT'S ME! I'M BACK AGAIN!
GET ON BOARD! HEY...
I RECOGNIZE THIS PLACE. THIS IS WATERGATE...
UNITED STATES OF AMERICA
THIS IS WHERE IT ALL WENT WRONG.
C'MON, DICK. LET IT GO.
YOU GO AHEAD. I HAVE SOME UNFINISHED BUSINESS.
SUIT YOURSELF.
WHOOPSIE!
OH FIDDLESTICKS!

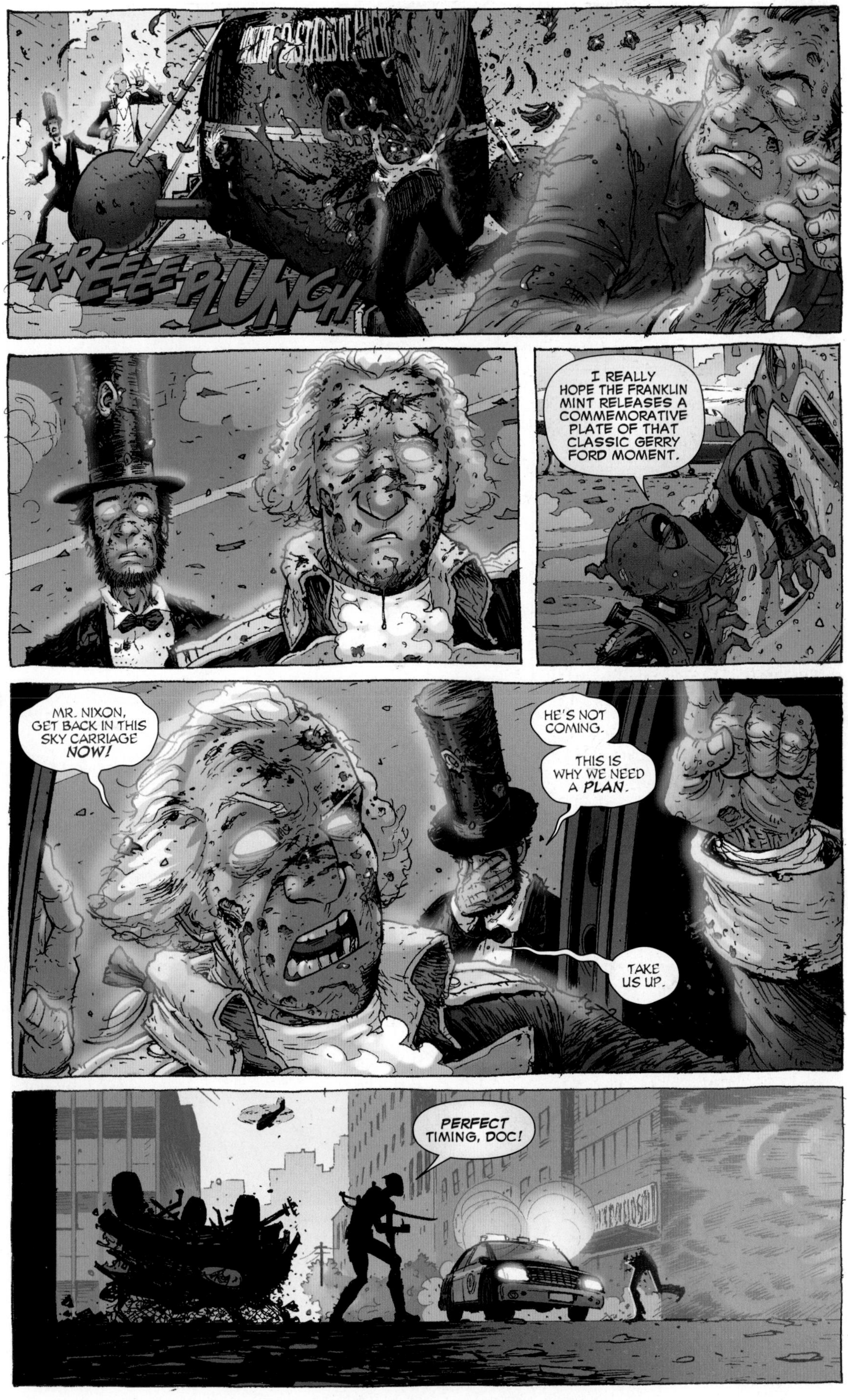
SKREEEEPLUNCH
I REALLY HOPE THE FRANKLIN MINT RELEASES A COMMEMORATIVE PLATE OF THAT CLASSIC GERRY FORD MOMENT.
MR. NIXON, GET BACK IN THIS SKY CARRIAGE NOW!
HE'S NOT COMING.
THIS IS WHY WE NEED A PLAN.
TAKE US UP.
PERFECT TIMING, DOC!

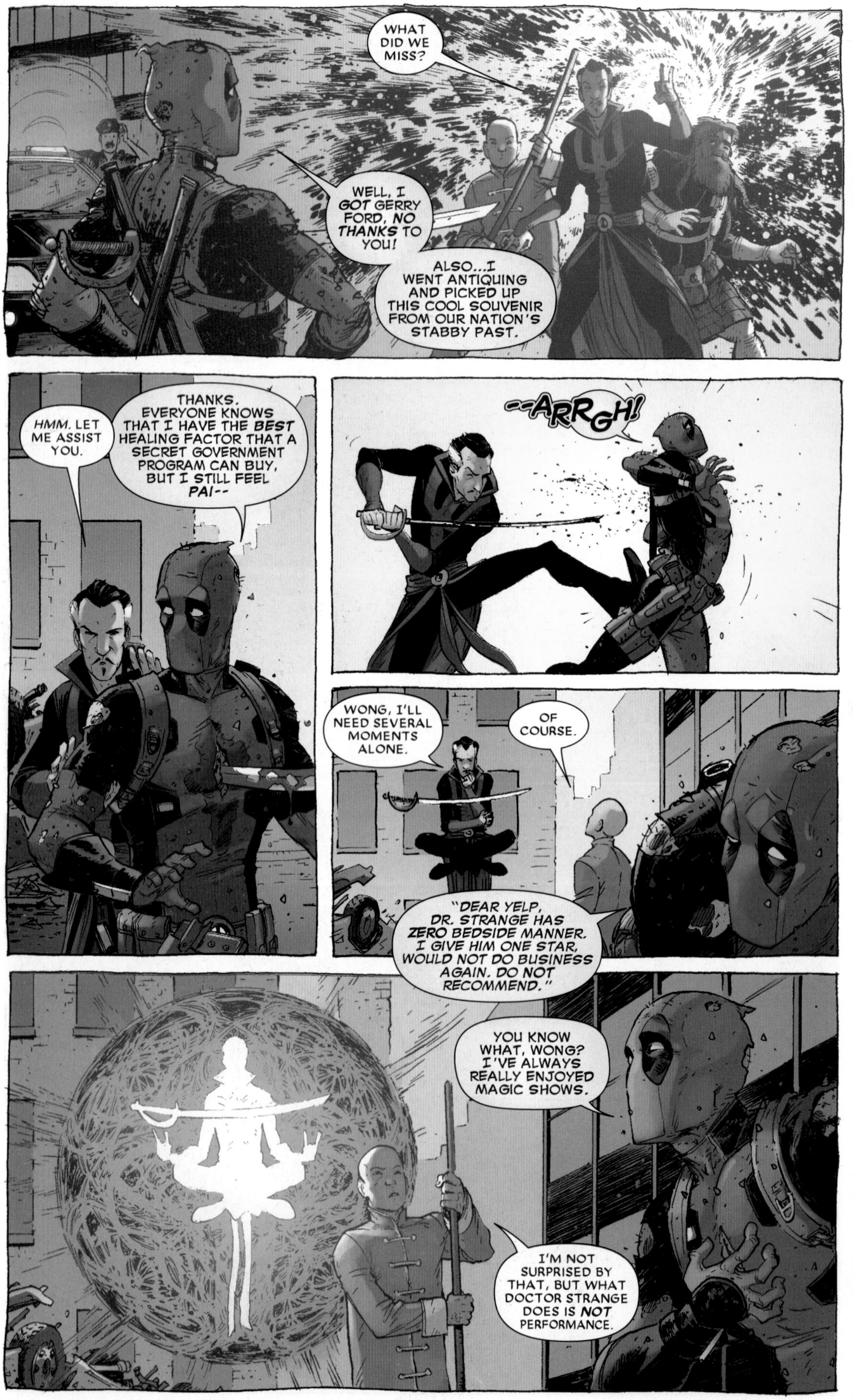

WHAT DID WE MISS?
WELL, I GOT GERRY FORD, NO THANKS TO YOU!
ALSO...I WENT ANTIQUING AND PICKED UP THIS COOL SOUVENIR FROM OUR NATION'S STABBY PAST.
THANKS. EVERYONE KNOWS THAT I HAVE THE BEST HEALING FACTOR THAT A SECRET GOVERNMENT PROGRAM CAN BUY, BUT I STILL FEEL PAI--
HMM. LET ME ASSIST YOU.
--ARRGH!
WONG, I'LL NEED SEVERAL MOMENTS ALONE.
OF COURSE.
"DEAR YELP, DR. STRANGE HAS ZERO BEDSIDE MANNER. I GIVE HIM ONE STAR, WOULD NOT DO BUSINESS AGAIN. DO NOT RECOMMEND."
YOU KNOW WHAT, WONG? I'VE ALWAYS REALLY ENJOYED MAGIC SHOWS.
I'M NOT SURPRISED BY THAT, BUT WHAT DOCTOR STRANGE DOES IS NOT PERFORMANCE.

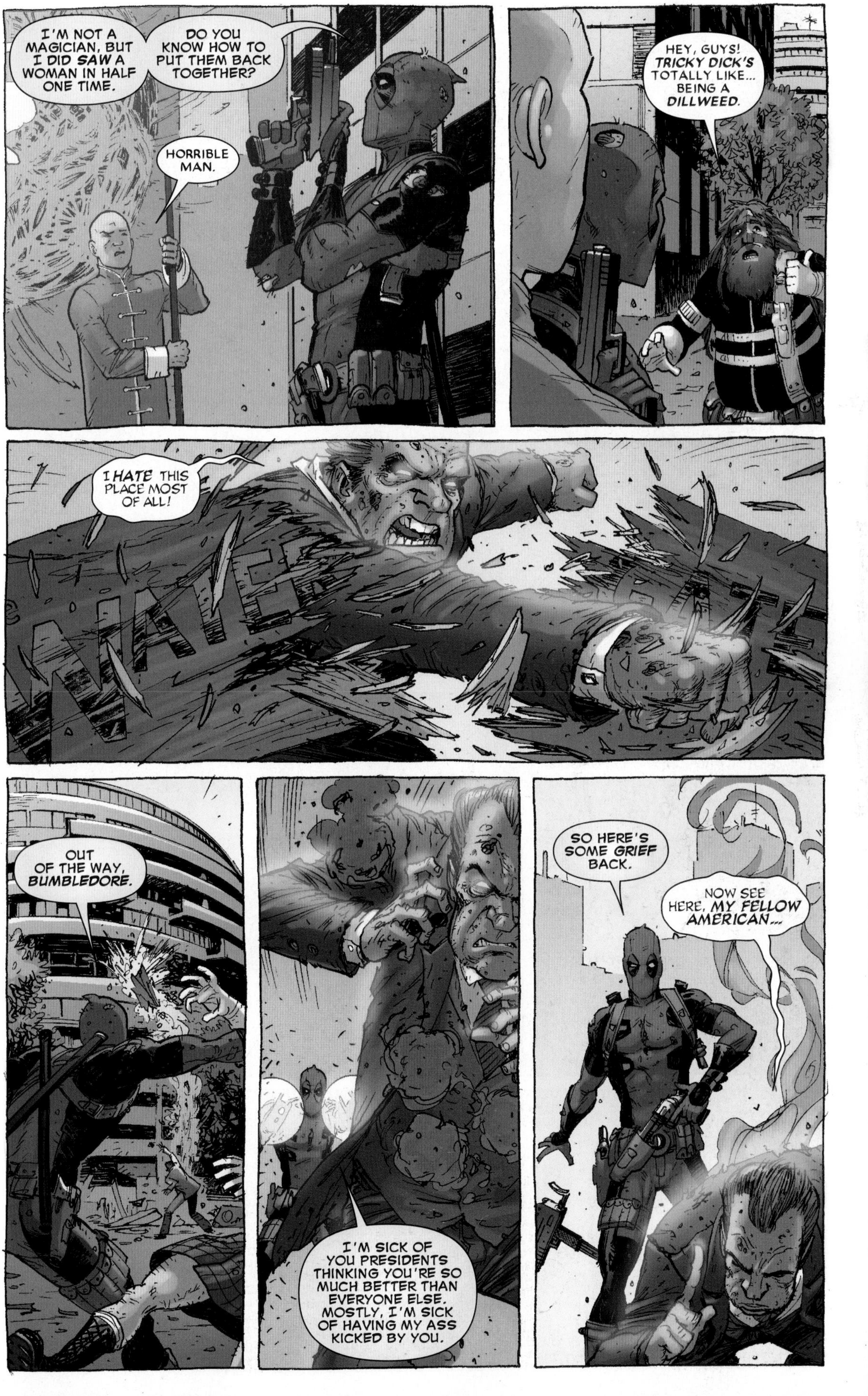
I'M NOT A MAGICIAN, BUT I DID SAW A WOMAN IN HALF ONE TIME.
DO YOU KNOW HOW TO PUT THEM BACK TOGETHER?
HORRIBLE MAN.
HEY, GUYS! TRICKY DICK'S TOTALLY LIKE... BEING A DILLWEED.
I HATE THIS PLACE MOST OF ALL!
OUT OF THE WAY, BUMBLEDORE.
I'M SICK OF YOU PRESIDENTS THINKING YOU'RE SO MUCH BETTER THAN EVERYONE ELSE. MOSTLY, I'M SICK OF HAVING MY ASS KICKED BY YOU.
SO HERE'S SOME GRIEF BACK.
NOW SEE HERE, MY FELLOW AMERICAN...

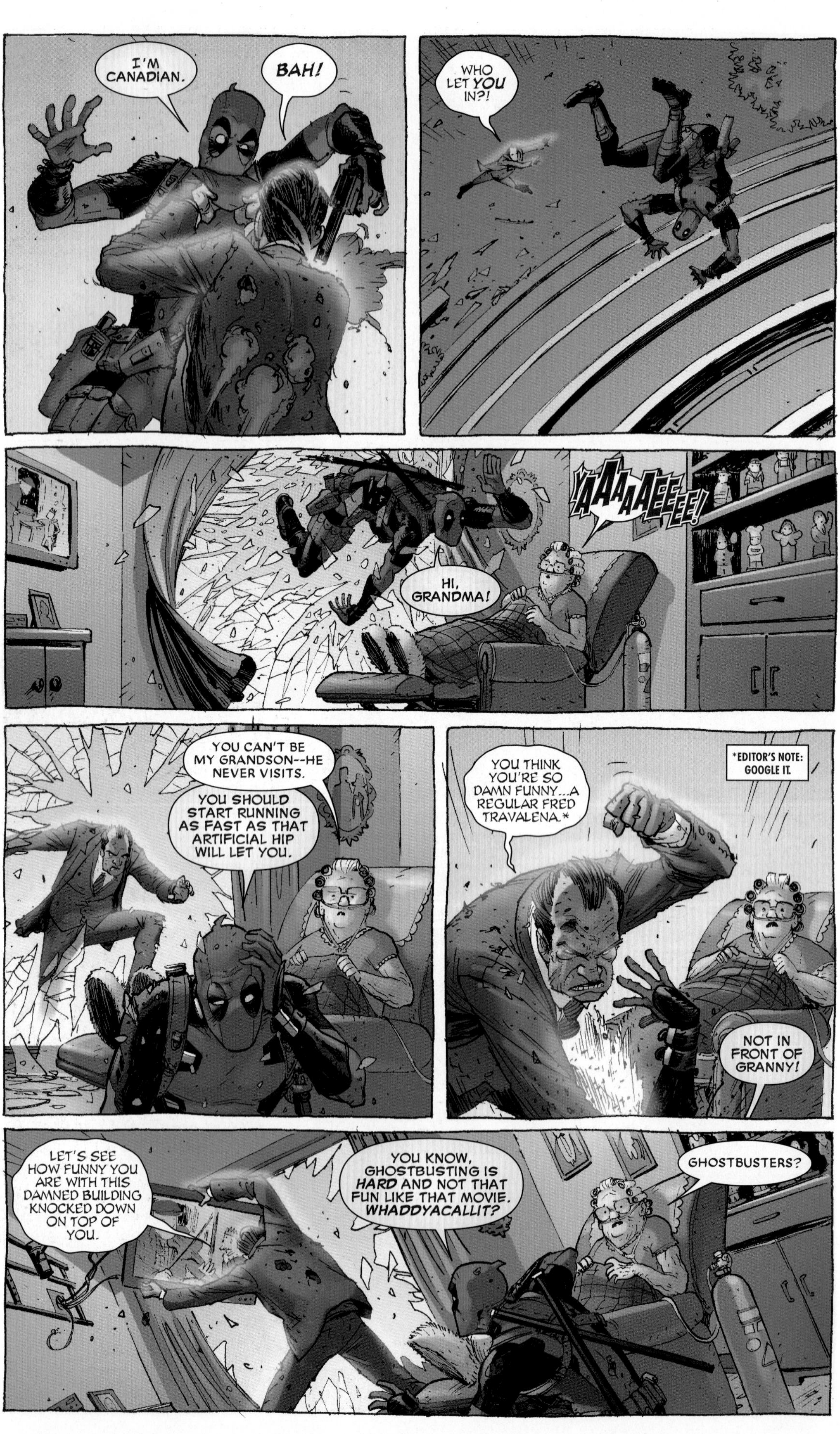
I'M CANADIAN.
BAH!
WHO LET YOU IN?!
YAAAAAEEEEE!
HI, GRANDMA!
YOU CAN'T BE MY GRANDSON--HE NEVER VISITS.
YOU SHOULD START RUNNING AS FAST AS THAT ARTIFICIAL HIP WILL LET YOU.
YOU THINK YOU'RE SO DAMN FUNNY...A REGULAR FRED TRAVALENA.*
*EDITOR'S NOTE: GOOGLE IT.
NOT IN FRONT OF GRANNY!
LET'S SEE HOW FUNNY YOU ARE WITH THIS DAMNED BUILDING KNOCKED DOWN ON TOP OF YOU.
YOU KNOW, GHOSTBUSTING IS HARD AND NOT THAT FUN LIKE THAT MOVIE. WHADDYACALLIT?
GHOSTBUSTERS?

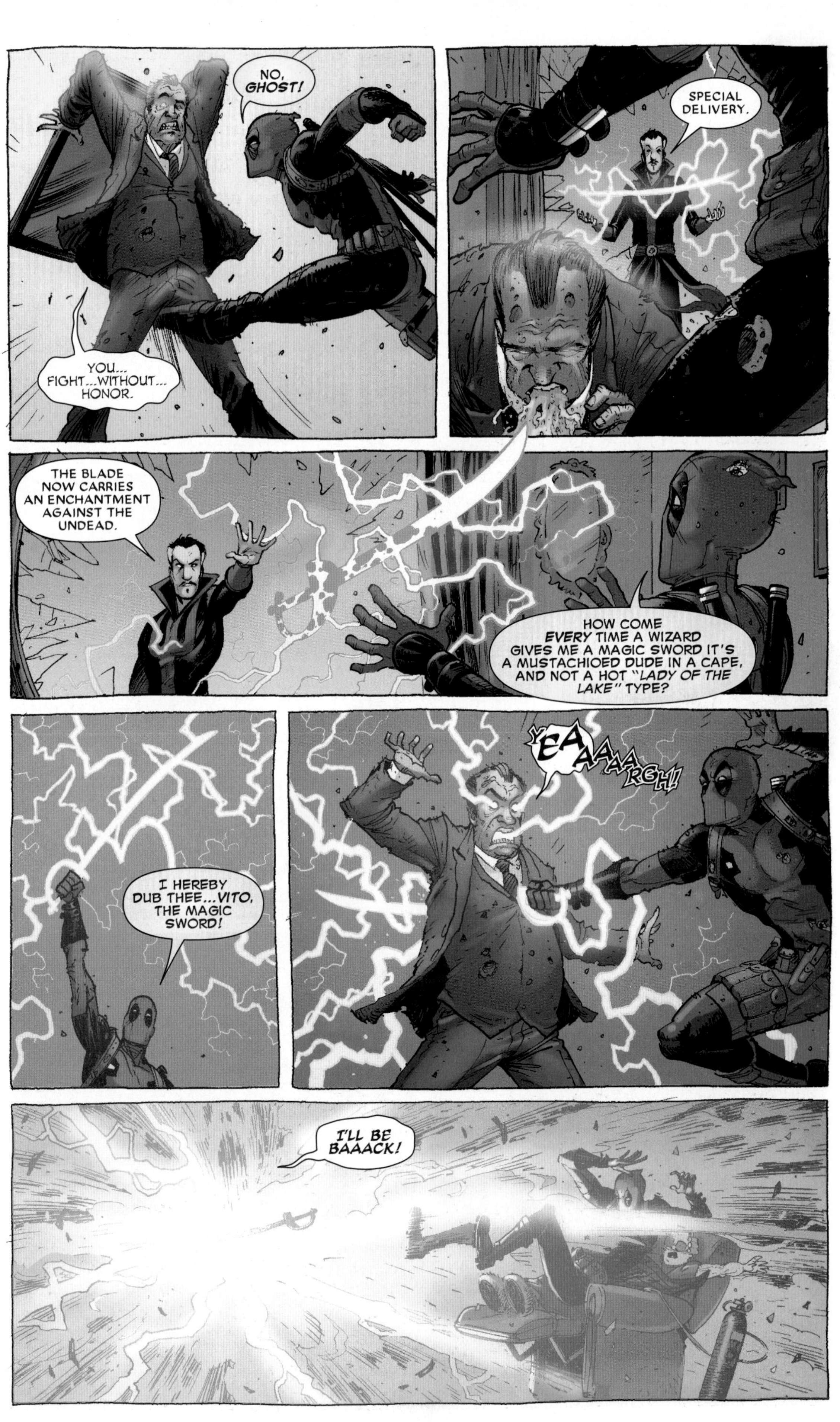
NO, GHOST!
YOU... FIGHT...WITHOUT... HONOR.
SPECIAL DELIVERY.
THE BLADE NOW CARRIES AN ENCHANTMENT AGAINST THE UNDEAD.
HOW COME EVERY TIME A WIZARD GIVES ME A MAGIC SWORD IT'S A MUSTACHIOED DUDE IN A CAPE, AND NOT A HOT "LADY OF THE LAKE" TYPE?
I HEREBY DUB THEE...VITO, THE MAGIC SWORD!
YEAAAAARGH!
I'LL BE BAAACK!

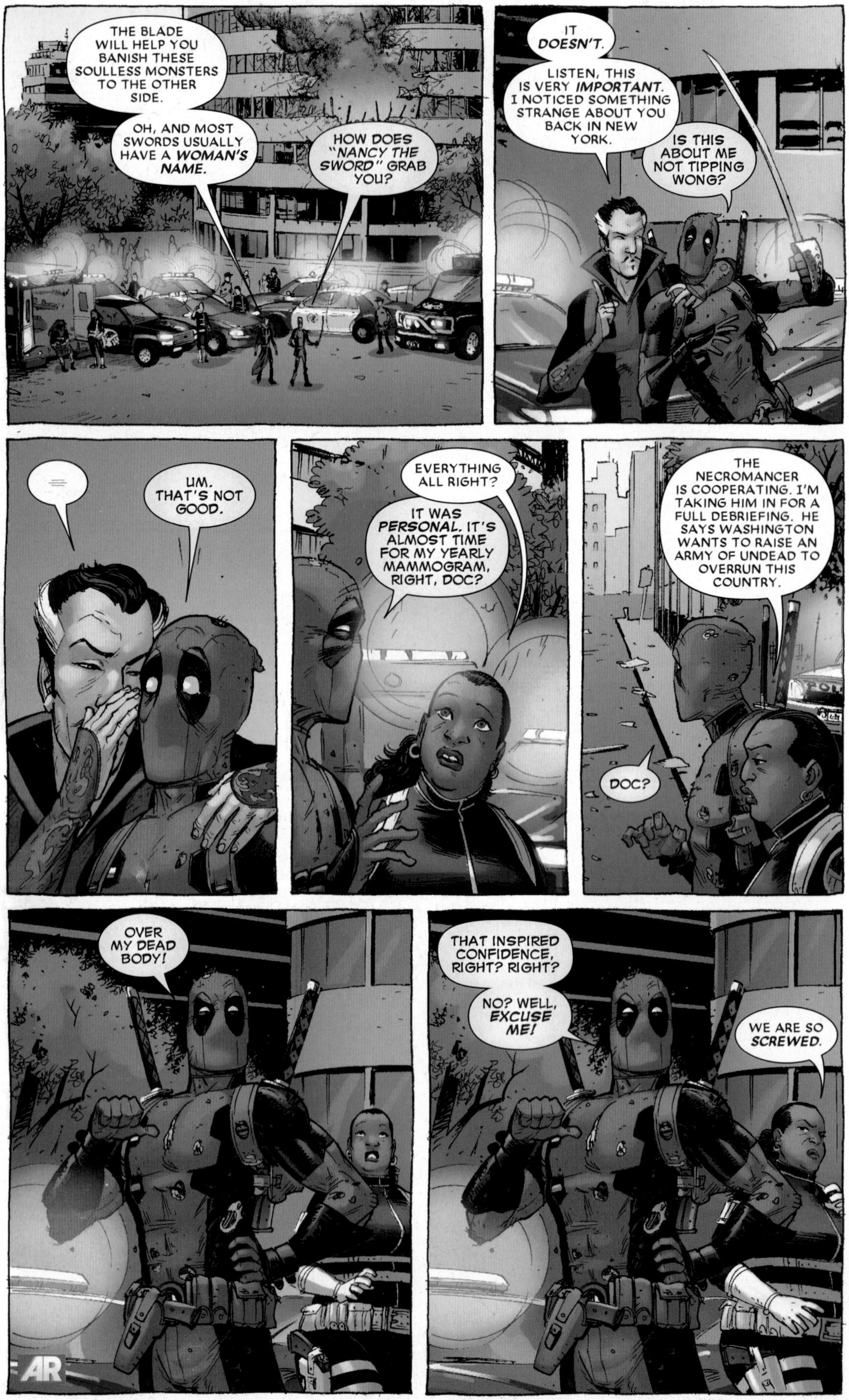
THE BLADE WILL HELP YOU BANISH THESE SOULLESS MONSTERS TO THE OTHER SIDE.
OH, AND MOST SWORDS USUALLY HAVE A WOMAN'S NAME.
HOW DOES "NANCY THE SWORD" GRAB YOU?
IT DOESN'T.
LISTEN, THIS IS VERY IMPORTANT. I NOTICED SOMETHING STRANGE ABOUT YOU BACK IN NEW YORK.
IS THIS ABOUT ME NOT TIPPING WONG?
UM. THAT'S NOT GOOD.
EVERYTHING ALL RIGHT?
IT WAS PERSONAL. IT'S ALMOST TIME FOR MY YEARLY MAMMOGRAM, RIGHT, DOC?
THE NECROMANCER IS COOPERATING. I'M TAKING HIM IN FOR A FULL DEBRIEFING. HE SAYS WASHINGTON WANTS TO RAISE AN ARMY OF UNDEAD TO OVERRUN THIS COUNTRY.
DOC?
OVER MY DEAD BODY!
THAT INSPIRED CONFIDENCE, RIGHT? RIGHT?
NO? WELL, EXCUSE ME!
WE ARE SO SCREWED.

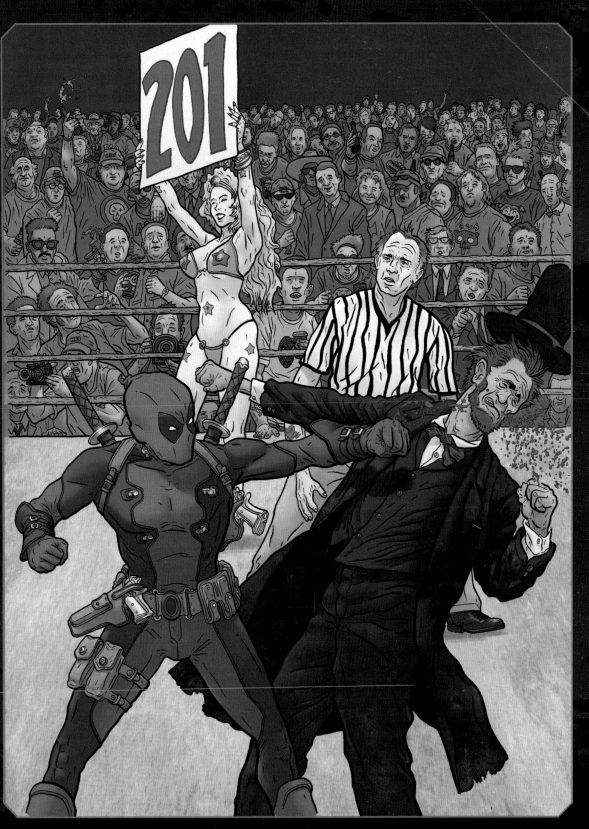

THE QUICK AND THE DEAD AND THE REALLY DEAD

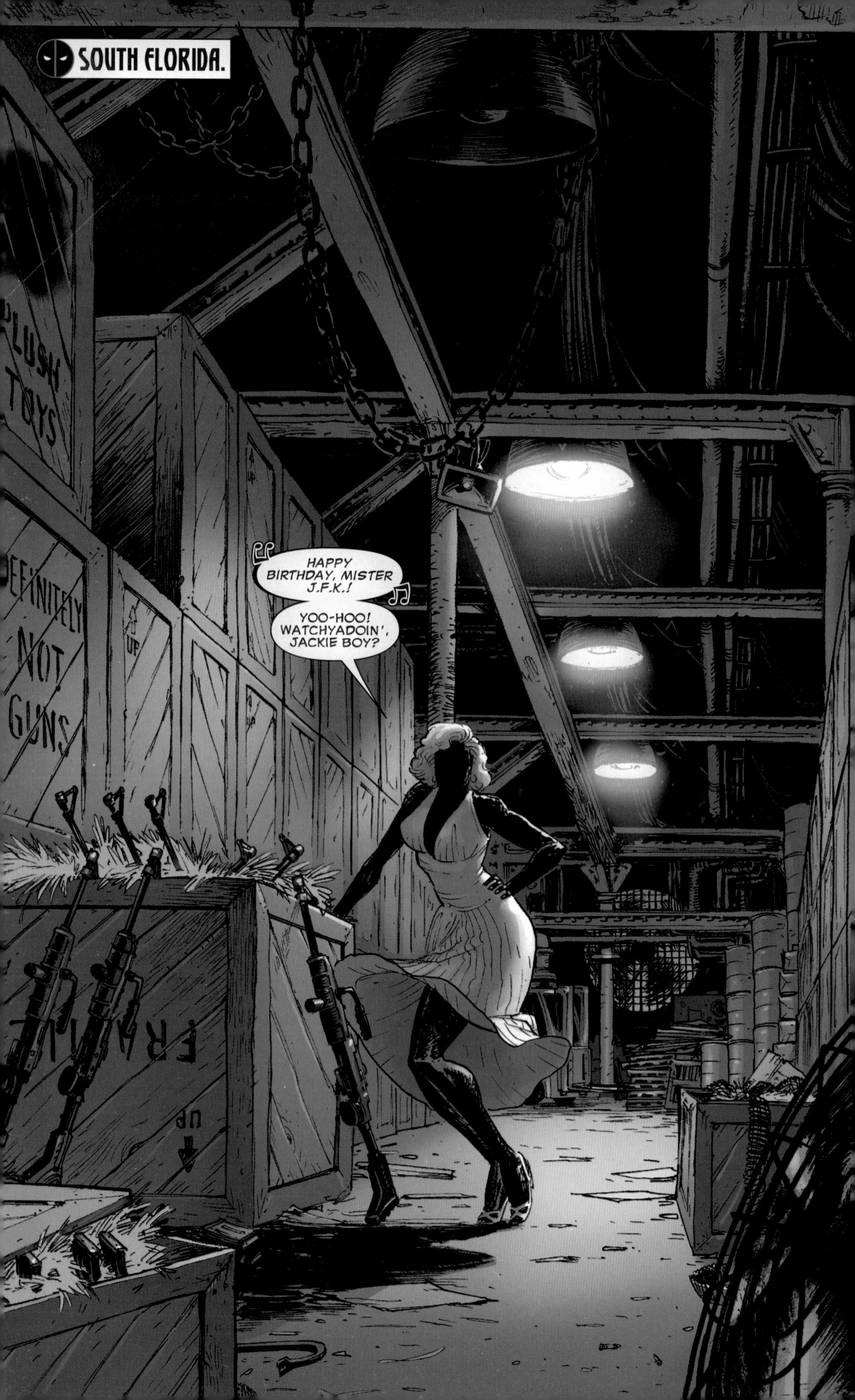
SOUTH FLORIDA.
PLUSH TOYS
DEFINITELY NOT GUNS
HAPPY BIRTHDAY, MISTER J.F.K.!
YOO-HOO! WATCHYADOIN', JACKIE BOY?

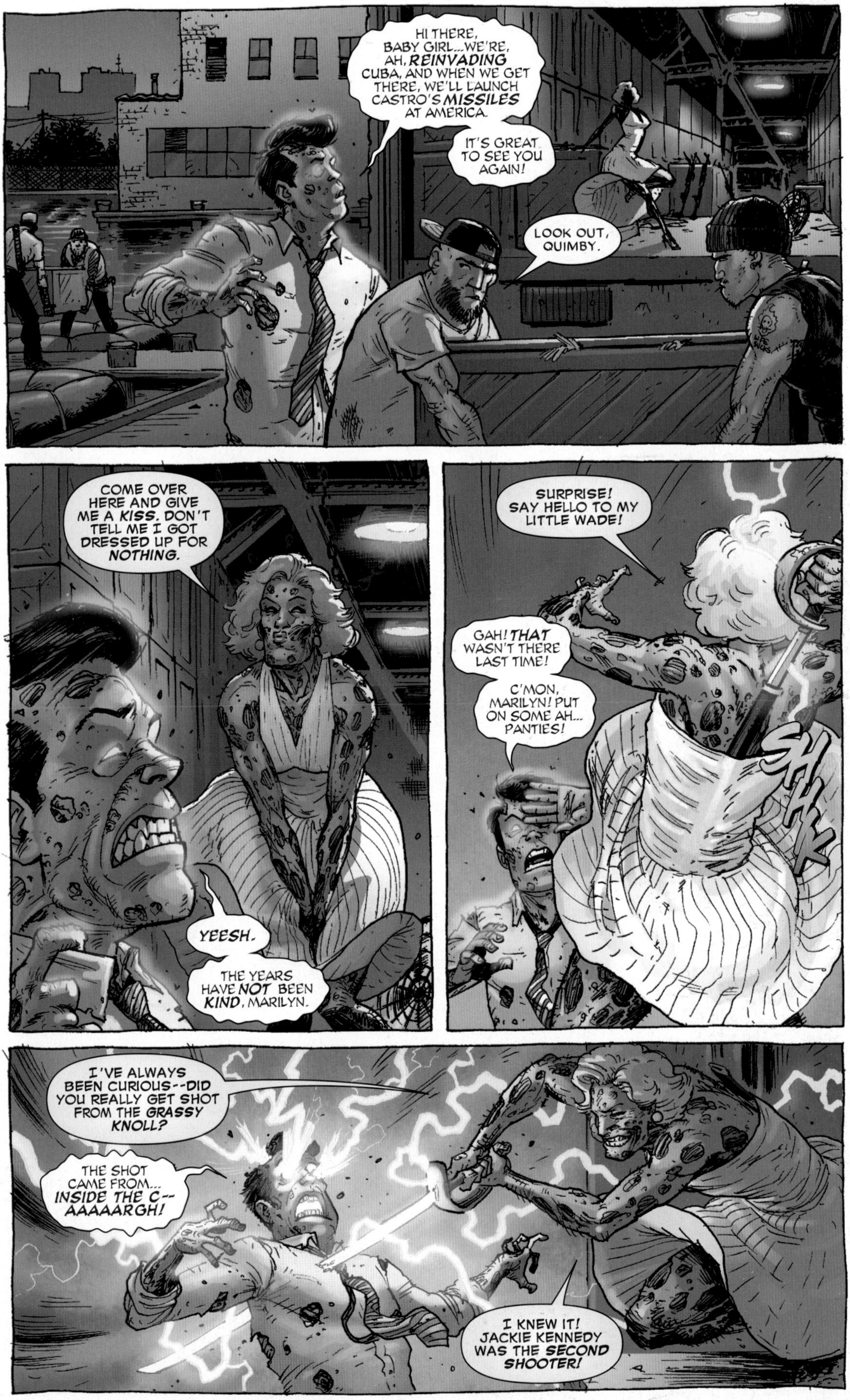
HI THERE, BABY GIRL... WE'RE, AH, REINVADING CUBA, AND WHEN WE GET THERE, WE'LL LAUNCH CASTRO'S MISSILES AT AMERICA.
IT'S GREAT TO SEE YOU AGAIN!
LOOK OUT, QUIMBY.
COME OVER HERE AND GIVE ME A KISS. DON'T TELL ME I GOT DRESSED UP FOR NOTHING.
YEESH.
THE YEARS HAVE NOT BEEN KIND, MARILYN.
SURPRISE! SAY HELLO TO MY LITTLE WADE!
GAH! THAT WASN'T THERE LAST TIME!
C'MON, MARILYN! PUT ON SOME AH... PANTIES!
SHNK
I'VE ALWAYS BEEN CURIOUS--DID YOU REALLY GET SHOT FROM THE GRASSY KNOLL?
THE SHOT CAME FROM... INSIDE THE C-- AAAAARGH!
I KNEW IT! JACKIE KENNEDY WAS THE SECOND SHOOTER!

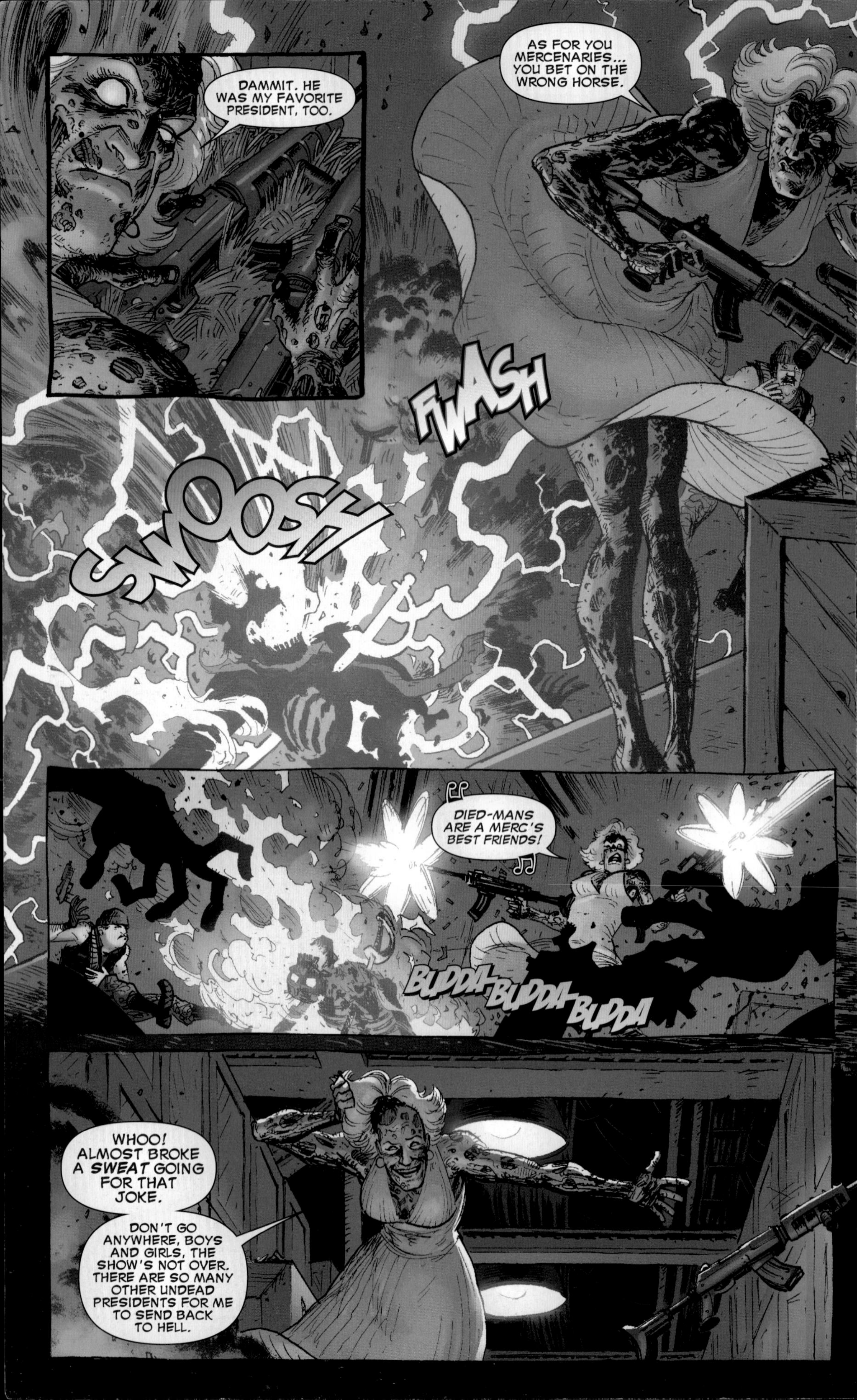
DAMMIT. HE WAS MY FAVORITE PRESIDENT, TOO.
AS FOR YOU MERCENARIES... YOU BET ON THE WRONG HORSE.
FWASH
SWOOSH
DIED-MANS ARE A MERC'S BEST FRIENDS!
BUDDA-BUDDA-BUDDA
WHOO! ALMOST BROKE A SWEAT GOING FOR THAT JOKE.
DON'T GO ANYWHERE, BOYS AND GIRLS, THE SHOW'S NOT OVER. THERE ARE SO MANY OTHER UNDEAD PRESIDENTS FOR ME TO SEND BACK TO HELL.

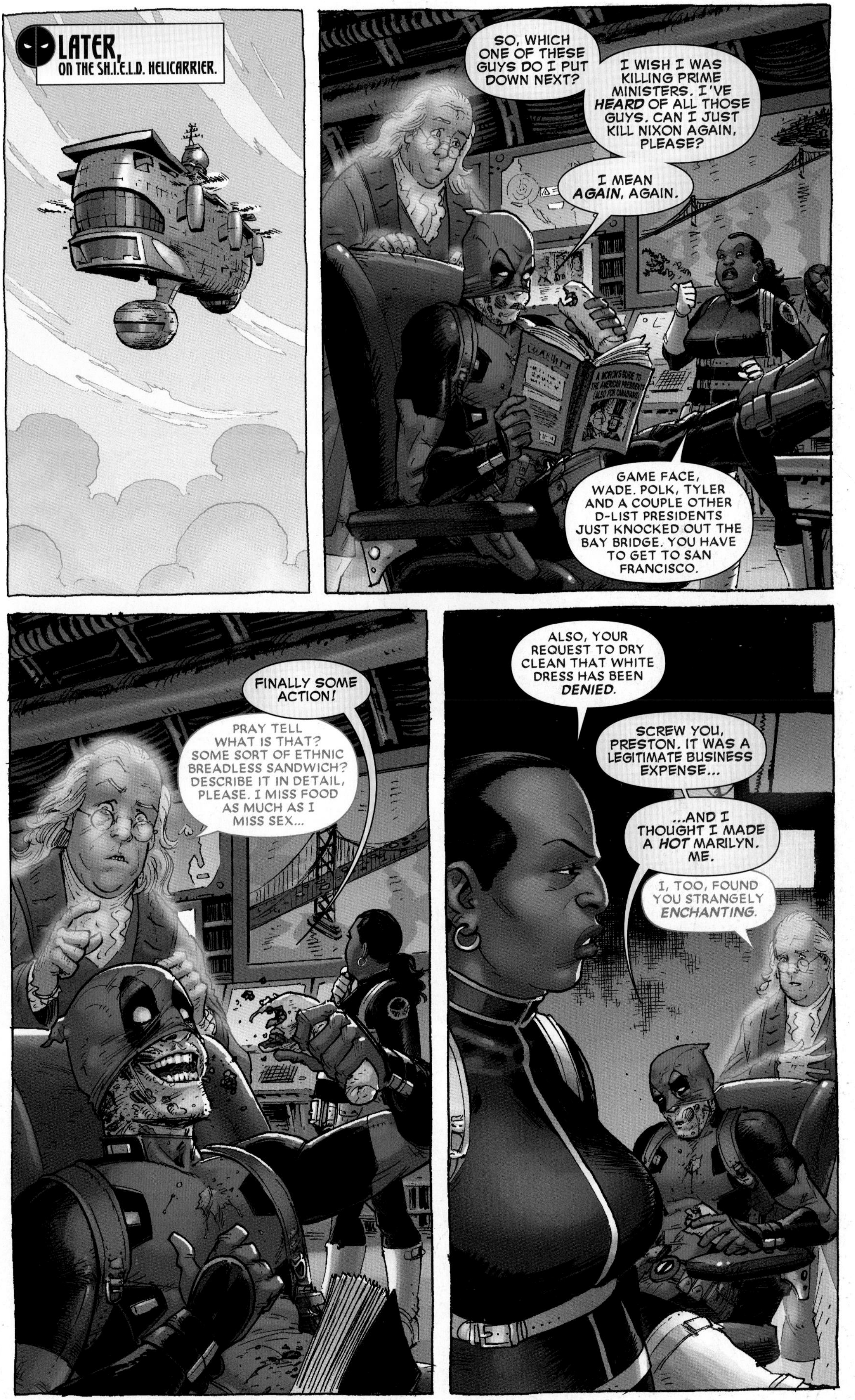
LATER,
ON THE SH.I.E.L.D. HELICARRIER.
SO, WHICH ONE OF THESE GUYS DO I PUT DOWN NEXT?
I WISH I WAS KILLING PRIME MINISTERS. I'VE HEARD OF ALL THOSE GUYS. CAN I JUST KILL NIXON AGAIN, PLEASE?
I MEAN AGAIN, AGAIN.
A MORON'S GUIDE TO THE AMERICAN PRESIDENTS (ALSO FOR CANADIANS!)
GAME FACE, WADE. POLK, TYLER AND A COUPLE OTHER D-LIST PRESIDENTS JUST KNOCKED OUT THE BAY BRIDGE. YOU HAVE TO GET TO SAN FRANCISCO.
FINALLY SOME ACTION!
PRAY TELL WHAT IS THAT? SOME SORT OF ETHNIC BREADLESS SANDWICH? DESCRIBE IT IN DETAIL, PLEASE. I MISS FOOD AS MUCH AS I MISS SEX...
ALSO, YOUR REQUEST TO DRY CLEAN THAT WHITE DRESS HAS BEEN DENIED.
SCREW YOU, PRESTON. IT WAS A LEGITIMATE BUSINESS EXPENSE...
...AND I THOUGHT I MADE A HOT MARILYN. ME.
I, TOO, FOUND YOU STRANGELY ENCHANTING.

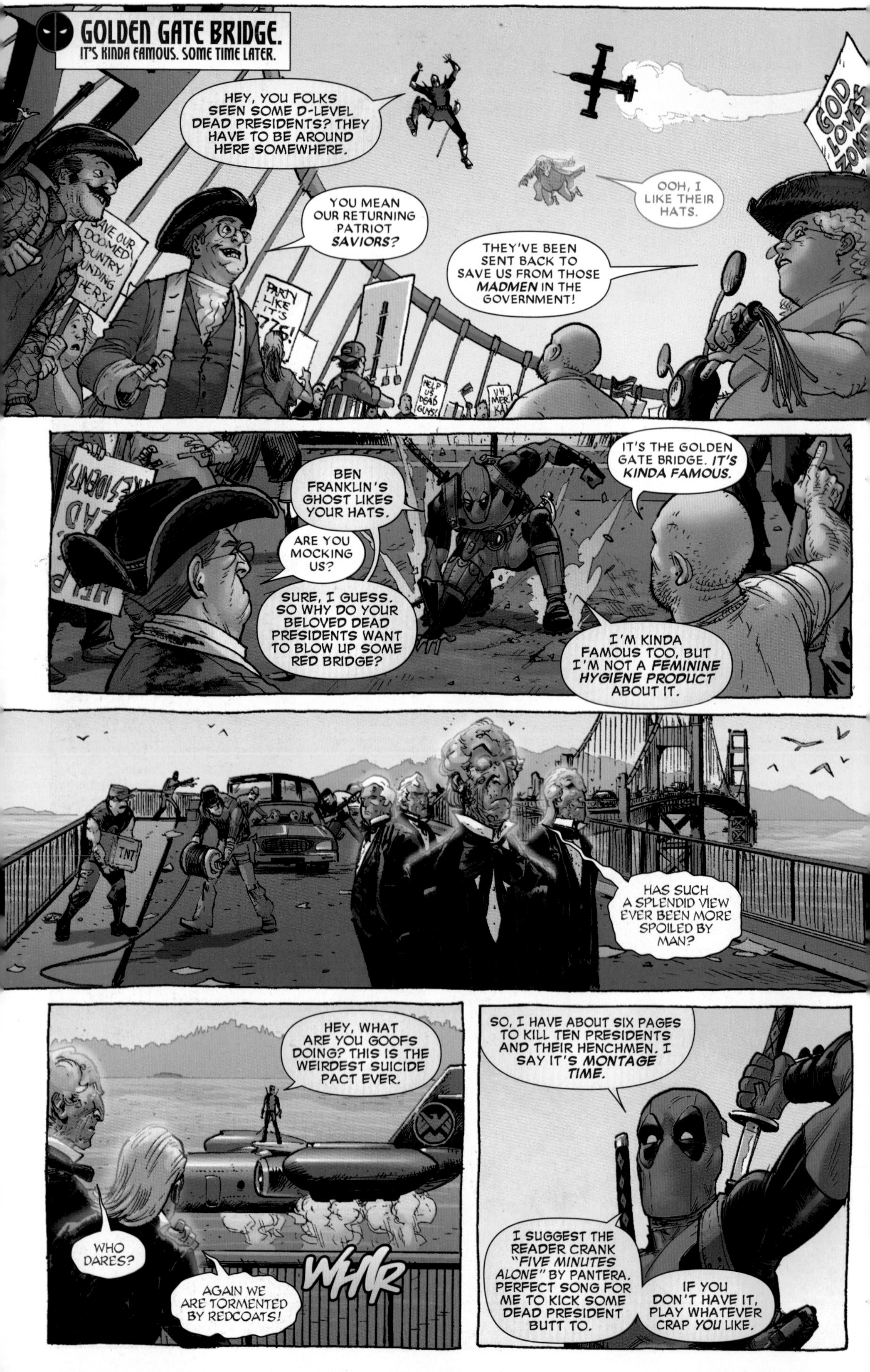
GOLDEN GATE BRIDGE.
IT'S KINDA FAMOUS. SOME TIME LATER.
HEY, YOU FOLKS SEEN SOME D-LEVEL DEAD PRESIDENTS? THEY HAVE TO BE AROUND HERE SOMEWHERE.
YOU MEAN OUR RETURNING PATRIOT *SAVIORS?*
THEY'VE BEEN SENT BACK TO SAVE US FROM THOSE *MADMEN* IN THE GOVERNMENT!
OOH, I LIKE THEIR HATS.
BEN FRANKLIN'S GHOST LIKES YOUR HATS.
ARE YOU MOCKING US?
SURE, I GUESS. SO WHY DO YOUR BELOVED DEAD PRESIDENTS WANT TO BLOW UP SOME RED BRIDGE?
IT'S THE GOLDEN GATE BRIDGE. *IT'S KINDA FAMOUS.*
I'M KINDA FAMOUS TOO, BUT I'M NOT A *FEMININE HYGIENE PRODUCT* ABOUT IT.
TNT
HAS SUCH A SPLENDID VIEW EVER BEEN MORE SPOILED BY MAN?
HEY, WHAT ARE YOU GOOFS DOING? THIS IS THE WEIRDEST SUICIDE PACT EVER.
WHO DARES?
AGAIN WE ARE TORMENTED BY REDCOATS!
WHIR
SO, I HAVE ABOUT SIX PAGES TO KILL TEN PRESIDENTS AND THEIR HENCHMEN. I SAY IT'S *MONTAGE TIME.*
I SUGGEST THE READER CRANK "*FIVE MINUTES ALONE*" BY PANTERA. PERFECT SONG FOR ME TO KICK SOME DEAD PRESIDENT BUTT TO.
IF YOU DON'T HAVE IT, PLAY WHATEVER CRAP *YOU* LIKE.

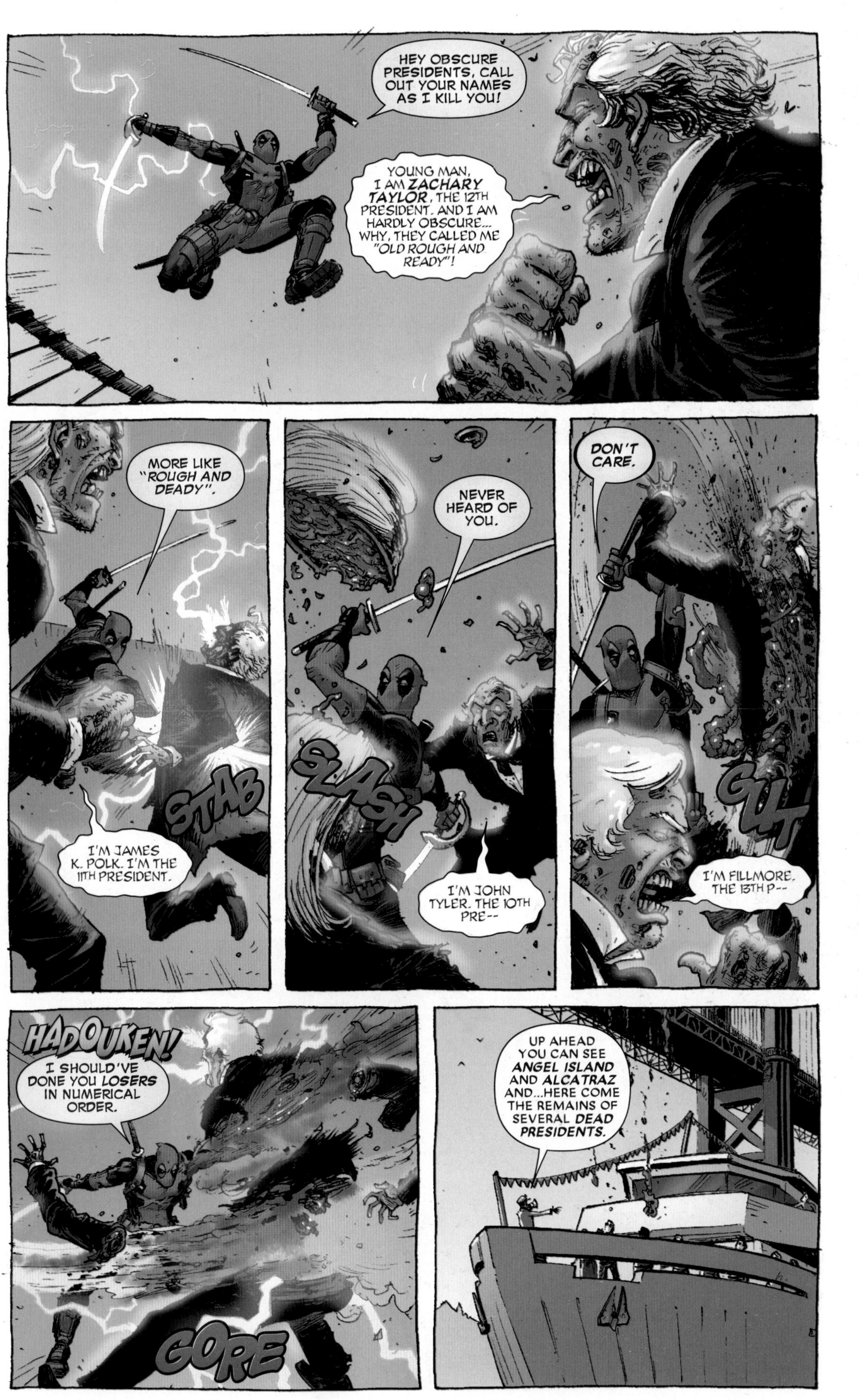
HEY OBSCURE PRESIDENTS, CALL OUT YOUR NAMES AS I KILL YOU!
YOUNG MAN, I AM ZACHARY TAYLOR, THE 12TH PRESIDENT. AND I AM HARDLY OBSCURE... WHY, THEY CALLED ME "OLD ROUGH AND READY"!
MORE LIKE "ROUGH AND DEADY".
STAB
I'M JAMES K. POLK. I'M THE 11TH PRESIDENT.
NEVER HEARD OF YOU.
SLASH
I'M JOHN TYLER. THE 10TH PRE--
DON'T CARE.
GUT
I'M FILLMORE. THE 13TH P--
HADOUKEN!
I SHOULD'VE DONE YOU LOSERS IN NUMERICAL ORDER.
GORE
UP AHEAD YOU CAN SEE ANGEL ISLAND AND ALCATRAZ AND...HERE COME THE REMAINS OF SEVERAL DEAD PRESIDENTS.

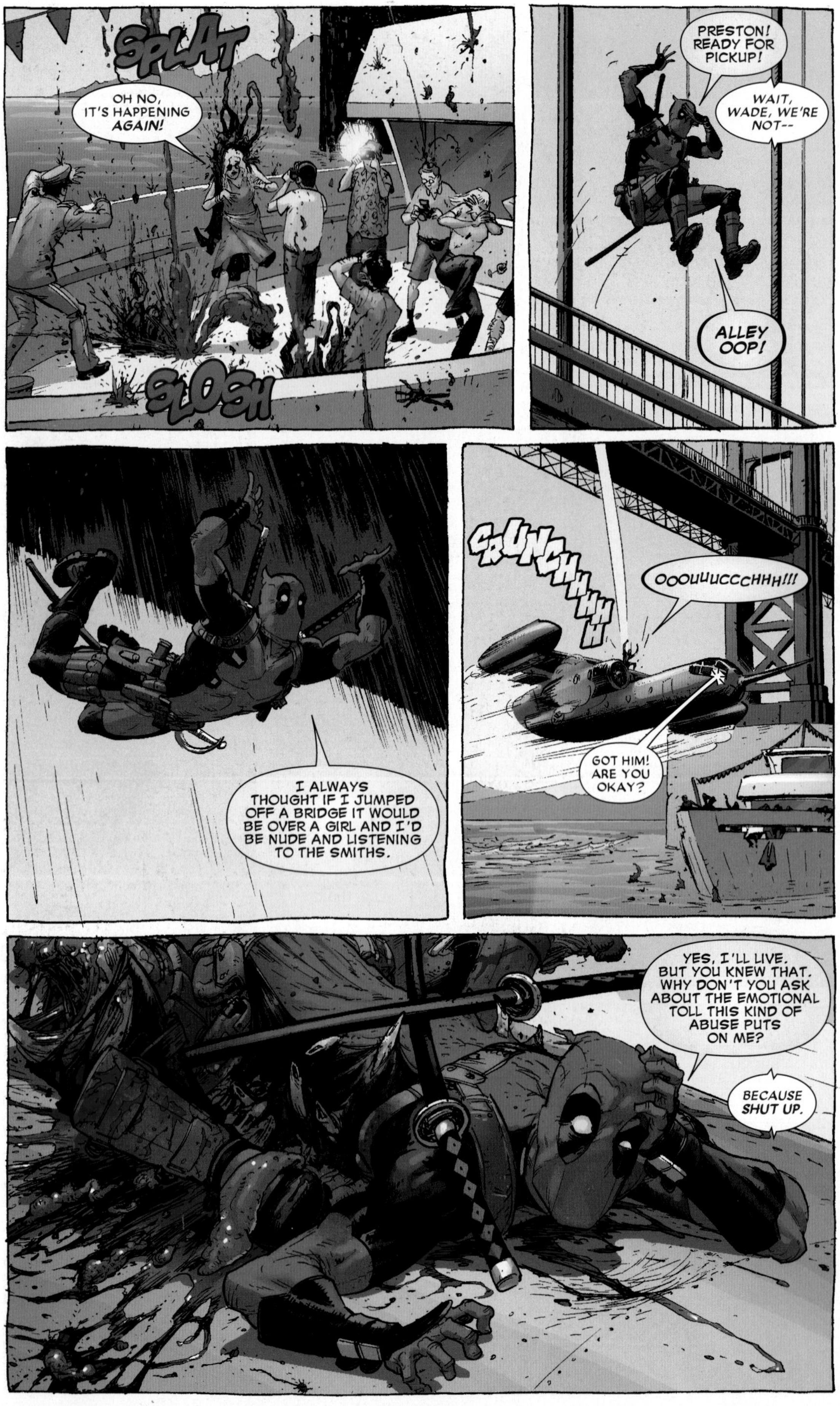
SPLAT
OH NO, IT'S HAPPENING AGAIN!
SLOSH
PRESTON! READY FOR PICKUP!
WAIT, WADE, WE'RE NOT--
ALLEY OOP!
I ALWAYS THOUGHT IF I JUMPED OFF A BRIDGE IT WOULD BE OVER A GIRL AND I'D BE NUDE AND LISTENING TO THE SMITHS.
CRUNCHHHHH
OOOUUUCCCHHH!!!
GOT HIM! ARE YOU OKAY?
YES, I'LL LIVE. BUT YOU KNEW THAT. WHY DON'T YOU ASK ABOUT THE EMOTIONAL TOLL THIS KIND OF ABUSE PUTS ON ME?
BECAUSE SHUT UP.

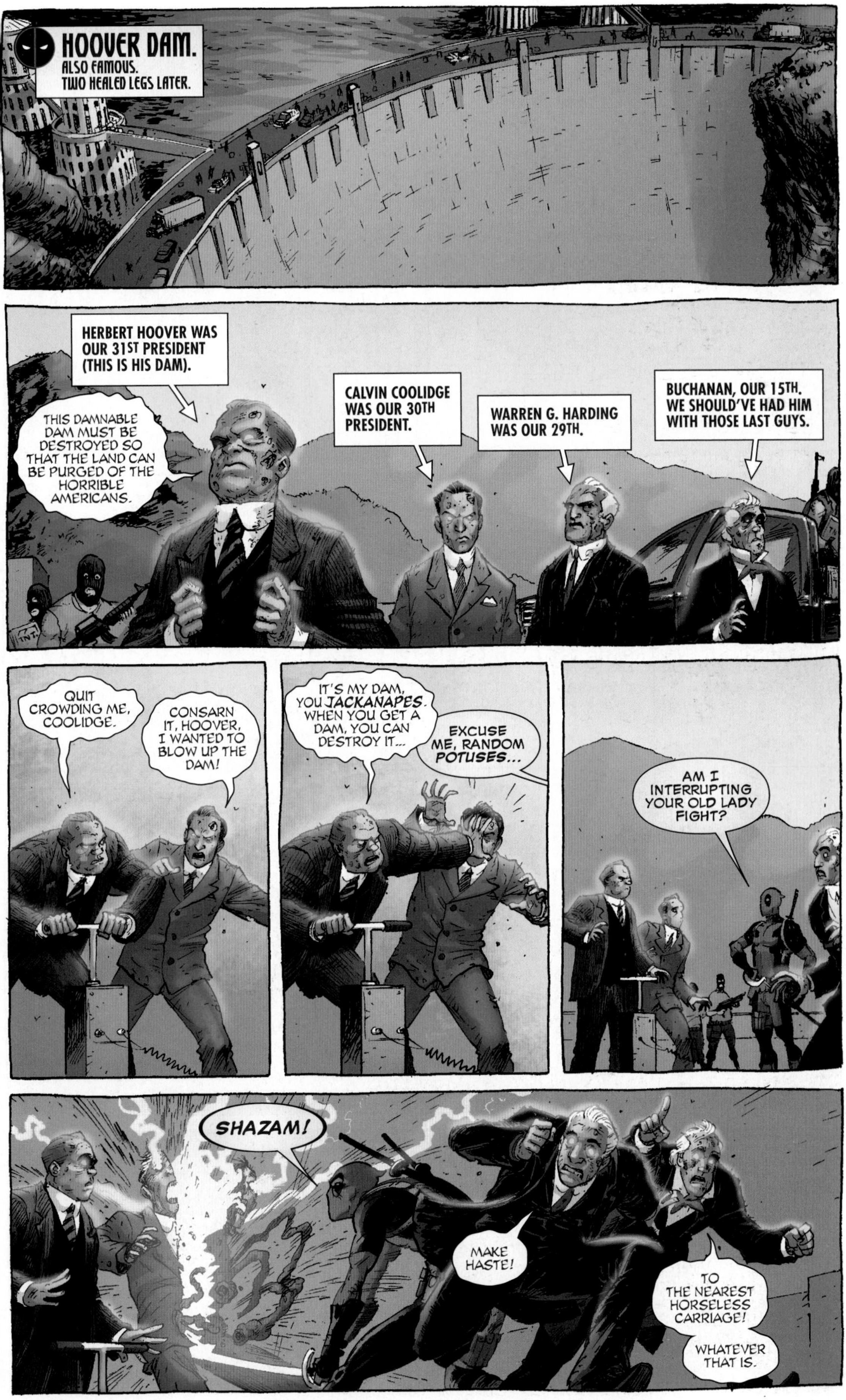
HOOVER DAM.
ALSO FAMOUS.
TWO HEALED LEGS LATER.
HERBERT HOOVER WAS OUR 31ST PRESIDENT (THIS IS HIS DAM).
THIS DAMNABLE DAM MUST BE DESTROYED SO THAT THE LAND CAN BE PURGED OF THE HORRIBLE AMERICANS.
CALVIN COOLIDGE WAS OUR 30TH PRESIDENT.
WARREN G. HARDING WAS OUR 29TH.
BUCHANAN, OUR 15TH. WE SHOULD'VE HAD HIM WITH THOSE LAST GUYS.
QUIT CROWDING ME, COOLIDGE.
CONSARN IT, HOOVER, I WANTED TO BLOW UP THE DAM!
IT'S MY DAM, YOU JACKANAPES. WHEN YOU GET A DAM, YOU CAN DESTROY IT...
EXCUSE ME, RANDOM POTUSES...
AM I INTERRUPTING YOUR OLD LADY FIGHT?
SHAZAM!
MAKE HASTE!
TO THE NEAREST HORSELESS CARRIAGE!
WHATEVER THAT IS.

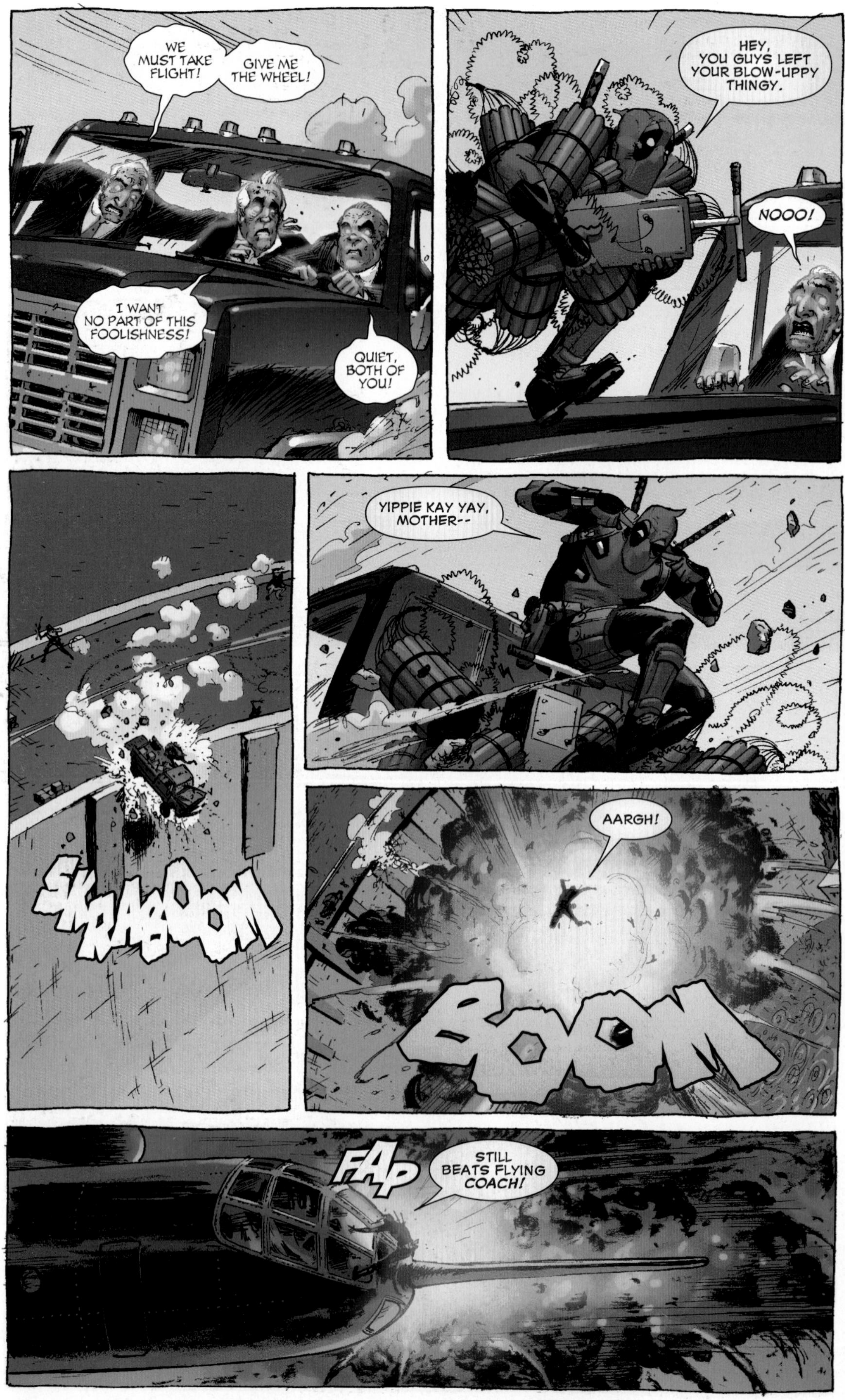
WE MUST TAKE FLIGHT!
GIVE ME THE WHEEL!
I WANT NO PART OF THIS FOOLISHNESS!
QUIET, BOTH OF YOU!
HEY, YOU GUYS LEFT YOUR BLOW-UPPY THINGY.
NOOO!
SKRABOOM
YIPPIE KAY YAY, MOTHER--
AARGH!
BOOM
FAP
STILL BEATS FLYING COACH!

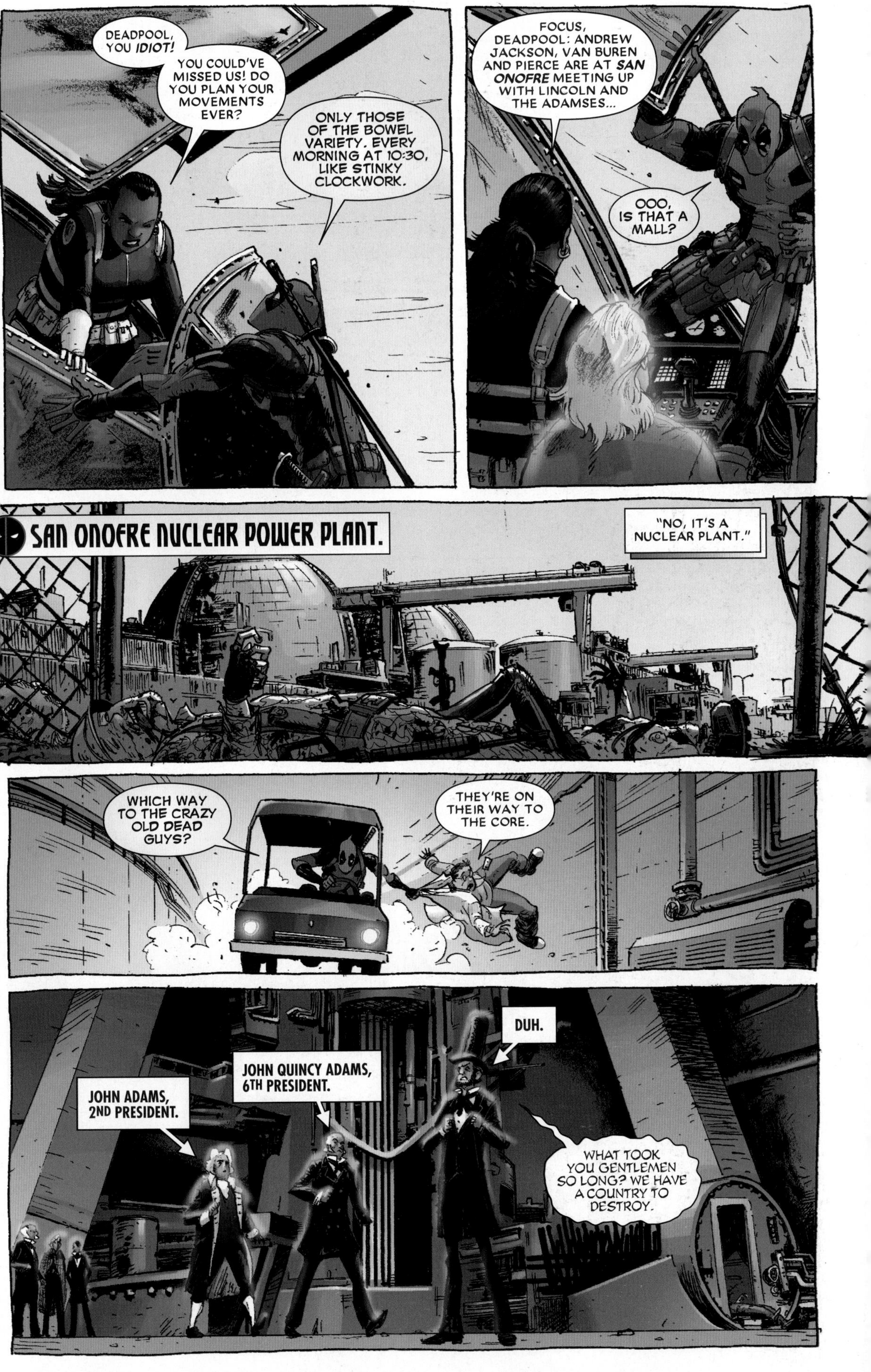
DEADPOOL, YOU IDIOT!
YOU COULD'VE MISSED US! DO YOU PLAN YOUR MOVEMENTS EVER?
ONLY THOSE OF THE BOWEL VARIETY. EVERY MORNING AT 10:30, LIKE STINKY CLOCKWORK.
FOCUS, DEADPOOL: ANDREW JACKSON, VAN BUREN AND PIERCE ARE AT SAN ONOFRE MEETING UP WITH LINCOLN AND THE ADAMSES...
OOO, IS THAT A MALL?
SAN ONOFRE NUCLEAR POWER PLANT.
"NO, IT'S A NUCLEAR PLANT."
WHICH WAY TO THE CRAZY OLD DEAD GUYS?
THEY'RE ON THEIR WAY TO THE CORE.
DUH.
JOHN QUINCY ADAMS, 6TH PRESIDENT.
JOHN ADAMS, 2ND PRESIDENT.
WHAT TOOK YOU GENTLEMEN SO LONG? WE HAVE A COUNTRY TO DESTROY.

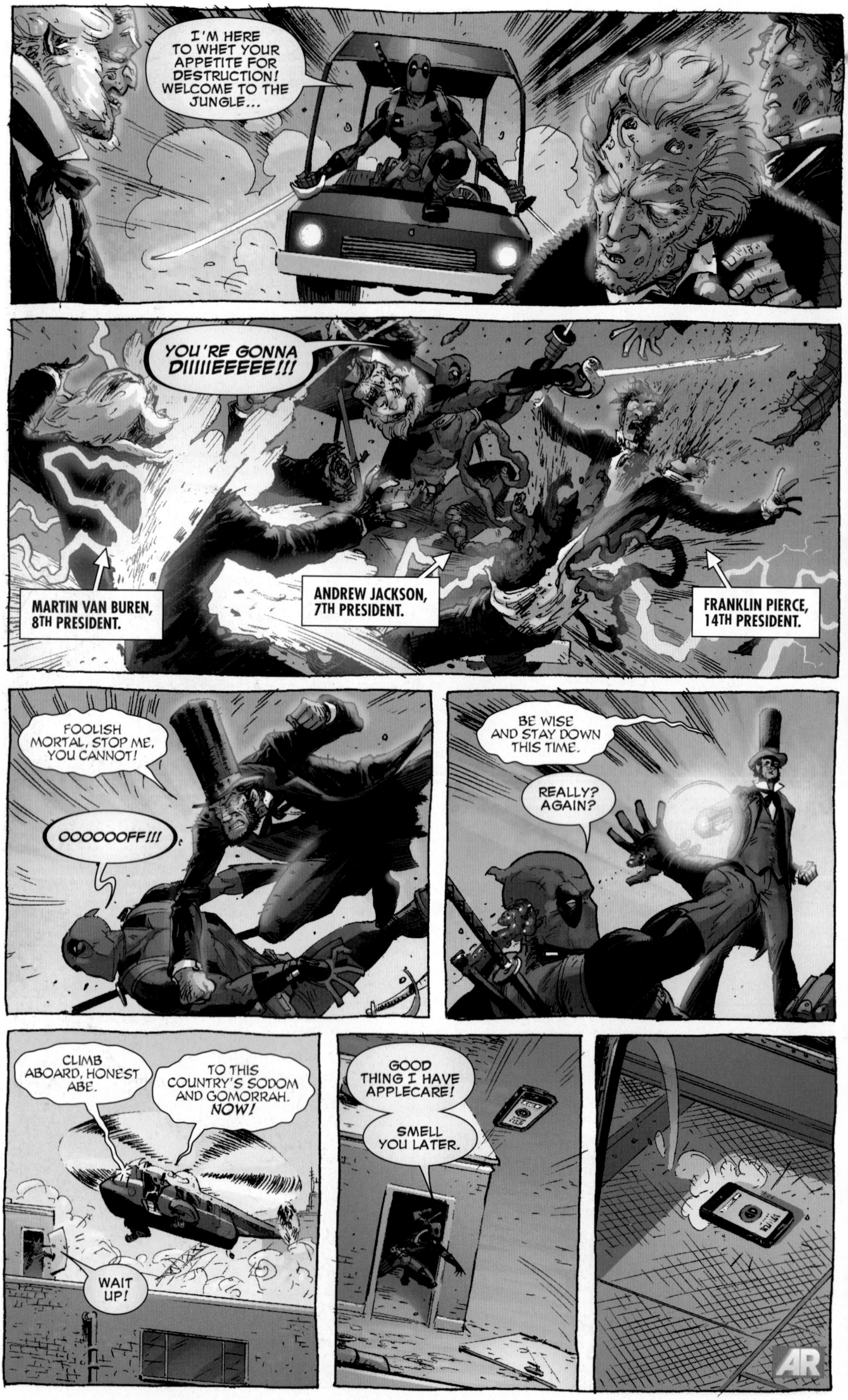
I'M HERE TO WHET YOUR APPETITE FOR DESTRUCTION! WELCOME TO THE JUNGLE...
YOU'RE GONNA DIIIIEEEEE!!!
MARTIN VAN BUREN, 8TH PRESIDENT.
ANDREW JACKSON, 7TH PRESIDENT.
FRANKLIN PIERCE, 14TH PRESIDENT.
FOOLISH MORTAL, STOP ME, YOU CANNOT!
OOOOOOFF!!!
BE WISE AND STAY DOWN THIS TIME.
REALLY? AGAIN?
CLIMB ABOARD, HONEST ABE.
TO THIS COUNTRY'S SODOM AND GOMORRAH. NOW!
WAIT UP!
GOOD THING I HAVE APPLECARE!
SMELL YOU LATER.

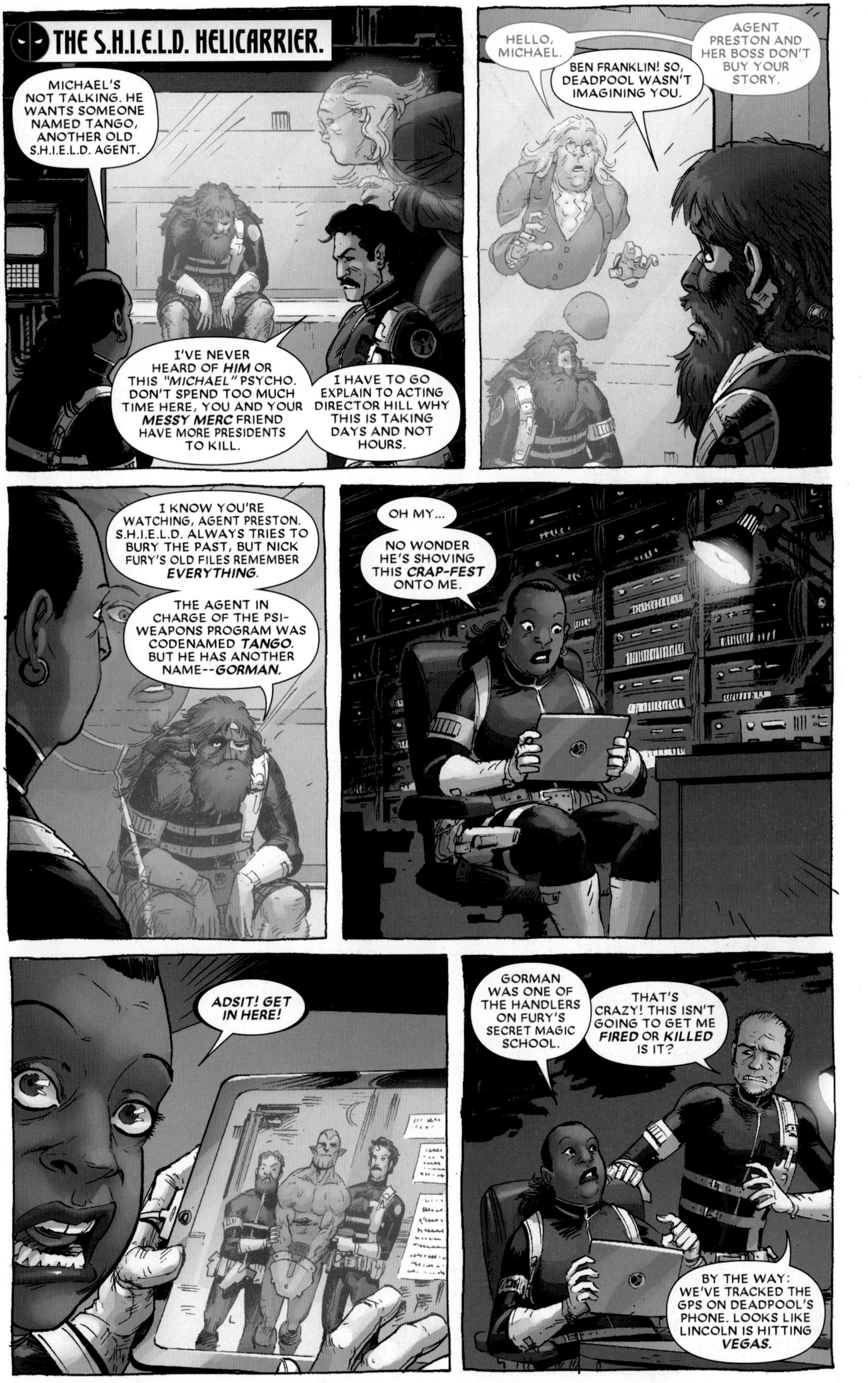
THE S.H.I.E.L.D. HELICARRIER.
MICHAEL'S NOT TALKING. HE WANTS SOMEONE NAMED TANGO, ANOTHER OLD S.H.I.E.L.D. AGENT.
I'VE NEVER HEARD OF HIM OR THIS "MICHAEL" PSYCHO. DON'T SPEND TOO MUCH TIME HERE, YOU AND YOUR MESSY MERC FRIEND HAVE MORE PRESIDENTS TO KILL.
I HAVE TO GO EXPLAIN TO ACTING DIRECTOR HILL WHY THIS IS TAKING DAYS AND NOT HOURS.
HELLO, MICHAEL.
BEN FRANKLIN! SO, DEADPOOL WASN'T IMAGINING YOU.
AGENT PRESTON AND HER BOSS DON'T BUY YOUR STORY.
I KNOW YOU'RE WATCHING, AGENT PRESTON. S.H.I.E.L.D. ALWAYS TRIES TO BURY THE PAST, BUT NICK FURY'S OLD FILES REMEMBER EVERYTHING.
THE AGENT IN CHARGE OF THE PSI-WEAPONS PROGRAM WAS CODENAMED TANGO. BUT HE HAS ANOTHER NAME--GORMAN.
OH MY...
NO WONDER HE'S SHOVING THIS CRAP-FEST ONTO ME.
ADSIT! GET IN HERE!
GORMAN WAS ONE OF THE HANDLERS ON FURY'S SECRET MAGIC SCHOOL.
THAT'S CRAZY! THIS ISN'T GOING TO GET ME FIRED OR KILLED IS IT?
BY THE WAY: WE'VE TRACKED THE GPS ON DEADPOOL'S PHONE. LOOKS LIKE LINCOLN IS HITTING VEGAS.

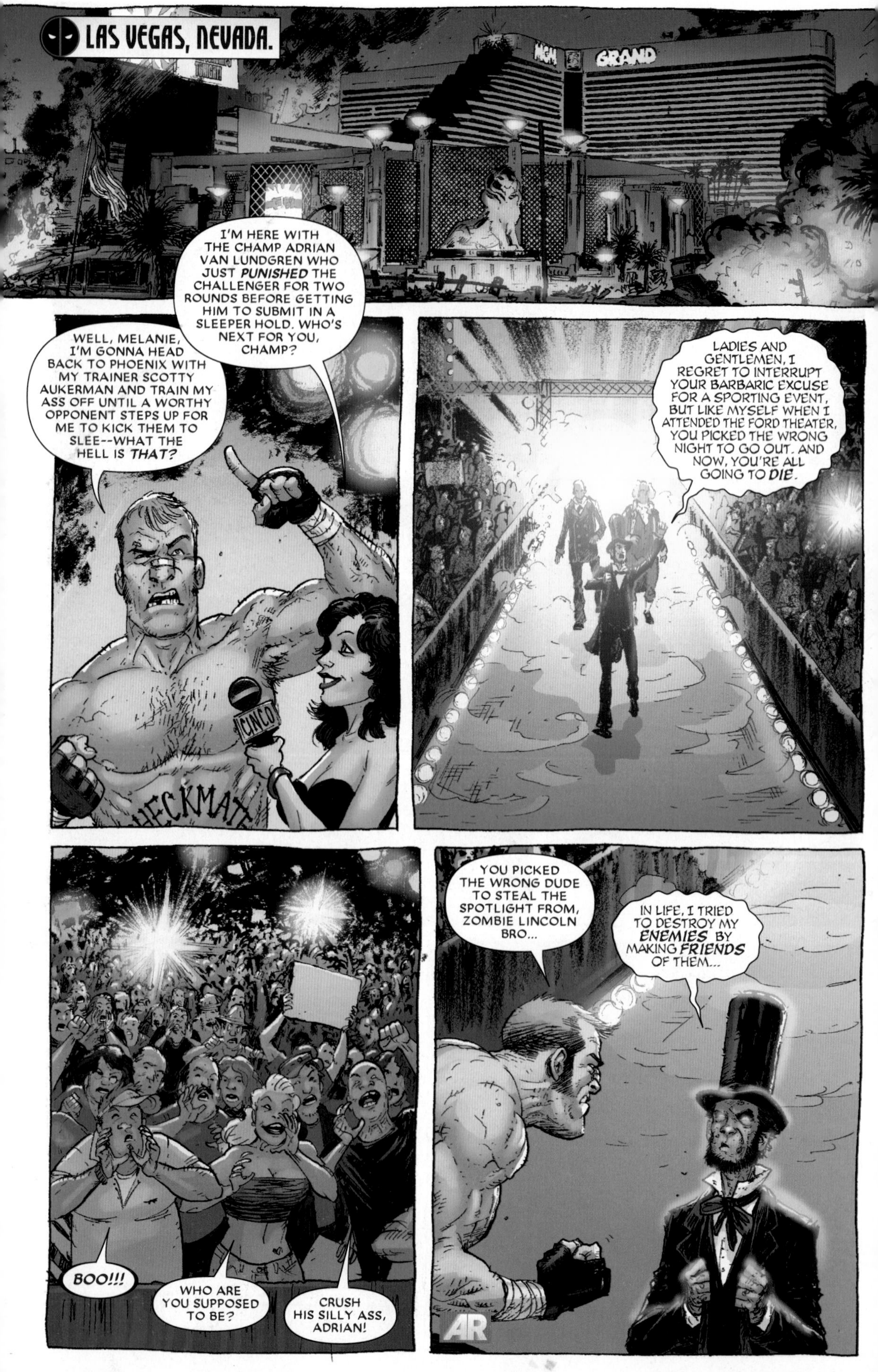
LAS VEGAS, NEVADA.
MGM GRAND
I'M HERE WITH THE CHAMP ADRIAN VAN LUNDGREN WHO JUST PUNISHED THE CHALLENGER FOR TWO ROUNDS BEFORE GETTING HIM TO SUBMIT IN A SLEEPER HOLD. WHO'S NEXT FOR YOU, CHAMP?
WELL, MELANIE, I'M GONNA HEAD BACK TO PHOENIX WITH MY TRAINER SCOTTY AUKERMAN AND TRAIN MY ASS OFF UNTIL A WORTHY OPPONENT STEPS UP FOR ME TO KICK THEM TO SLEE--WHAT THE HELL IS THAT?
CINCO
LADIES AND GENTLEMEN, I REGRET TO INTERRUPT YOUR BARBARIC EXCUSE FOR A SPORTING EVENT, BUT LIKE MYSELF WHEN I ATTENDED THE FORD THEATER, YOU PICKED THE WRONG NIGHT TO GO OUT. AND NOW, YOU'RE ALL GOING TO DIE.
BOO!!!
WHO ARE YOU SUPPOSED TO BE?
CRUSH HIS SILLY ASS, ADRIAN!
YOU PICKED THE WRONG DUDE TO STEAL THE SPOTLIGHT FROM, ZOMBIE LINCOLN BRO...
IN LIFE, I TRIED TO DESTROY MY ENEMIES BY MAKING FRIENDS OF THEM...

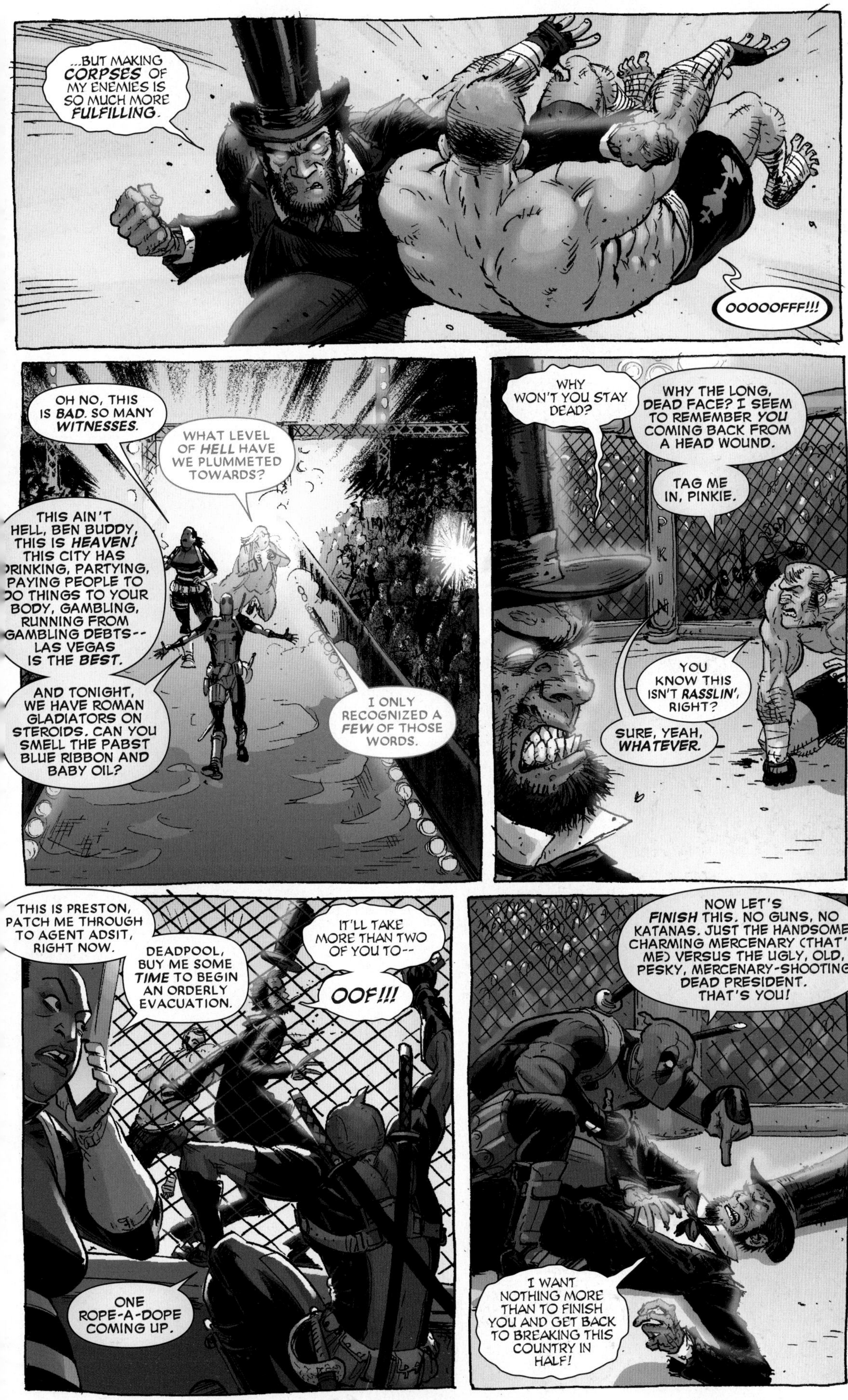
...BUT MAKING CORPSES OF MY ENEMIES IS SO MUCH MORE FULFILLING.
OOOOOFFF!!!
OH NO, THIS IS BAD. SO MANY WITNESSES.
WHAT LEVEL OF HELL HAVE WE PLUMMETED TOWARDS?
THIS AIN'T HELL, BEN BUDDY, THIS IS HEAVEN! THIS CITY HAS DRINKING, PARTYING, PAYING PEOPLE TO DO THINGS TO YOUR BODY, GAMBLING, RUNNING FROM GAMBLING DEBTS-- LAS VEGAS IS THE BEST.
AND TONIGHT, WE HAVE ROMAN GLADIATORS ON STEROIDS. CAN YOU SMELL THE PABST BLUE RIBBON AND BABY OIL?
I ONLY RECOGNIZED A FEW OF THOSE WORDS.
WHY WON'T YOU STAY DEAD?
WHY THE LONG, DEAD FACE? I SEEM TO REMEMBER YOU COMING BACK FROM A HEAD WOUND.
TAG ME IN, PINKIE.
YOU KNOW THIS ISN'T RASSLIN', RIGHT?
SURE, YEAH, WHATEVER.
THIS IS PRESTON, PATCH ME THROUGH TO AGENT ADSIT, RIGHT NOW.
DEADPOOL, BUY ME SOME TIME TO BEGIN AN ORDERLY EVACUATION.
IT'LL TAKE MORE THAN TWO OF YOU TO--
OOF!!!
ONE ROPE-A-DOPE COMING UP.
NOW LET'S FINISH THIS. NO GUNS, NO KATANAS. JUST THE HANDSOME, CHARMING MERCENARY (THAT'S ME) VERSUS THE UGLY, OLD, PESKY, MERCENARY-SHOOTING DEAD PRESIDENT. THAT'S YOU!
I WANT NOTHING MORE THAN TO FINISH YOU AND GET BACK TO BREAKING THIS COUNTRY IN HALF!

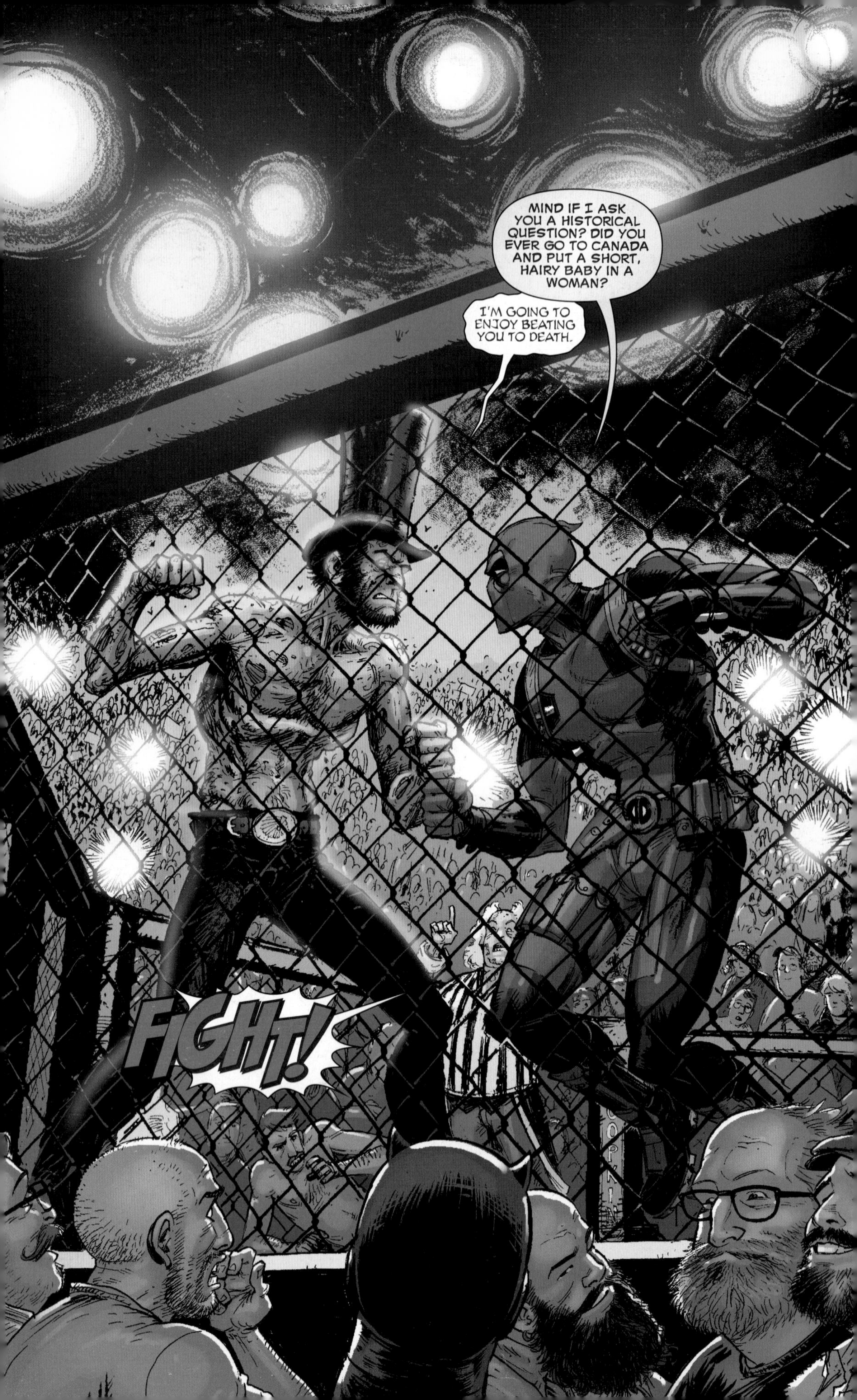
MIND IF I ASK YOU A HISTORICAL QUESTION? DID YOU EVER GO TO CANADA AND PUT A SHORT, HAIRY BABY IN A WOMAN?
I'M GOING TO ENJOY BEATING YOU TO DEATH.
FIGHT!

YOU GUYS WATCH THESE.

I HAVEN'T GOT ALL DAY!

ANY ADVICE?

YOU LACK THE PHYSICAL PROWESS FOR A STRAIGHTFORWARD CONFRONTATION, SO STAY MOBILE.

AND GIVE 'EM HELL!

THE UPPER LEVELS ARE CLEARING OUT, AND S.H.I.E.L.D. SWAT TEAMS ARE INBOUND.

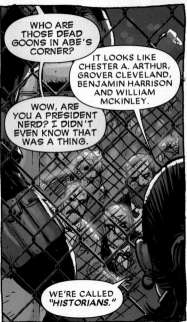

WHO ARE THOSE DEAD GOONS IN ABE'S CORNER?

IT LOOKS LIKE CHESTER A. ARTHUR, GROVER CLEVELAND, BENJAMIN HARRISON AND WILLIAM MCKINLEY.

WOW, ARE YOU A PRESIDENT NERD? I DIDN'T EVEN KNOW THAT WAS A THING.

WE'RE CALLED "HISTORIANS."

MY STARS, WHO ARE THOSE STRUMPETS?

DING DING DING

OH, THEY'RE REALITY TV STARS FAMOUS FOR SHOPPING AND HAVING SEX WITH EVERY-- OOOLPH!

KRAK

LUCKY SHOT, DEAD-TIMER. AGAIN. YOU DON'T GET A FOURTH.

DO YOU EVER SHUT YOUR FOUL MOUTH?

ACTUALLY, NO, NOT REALL--

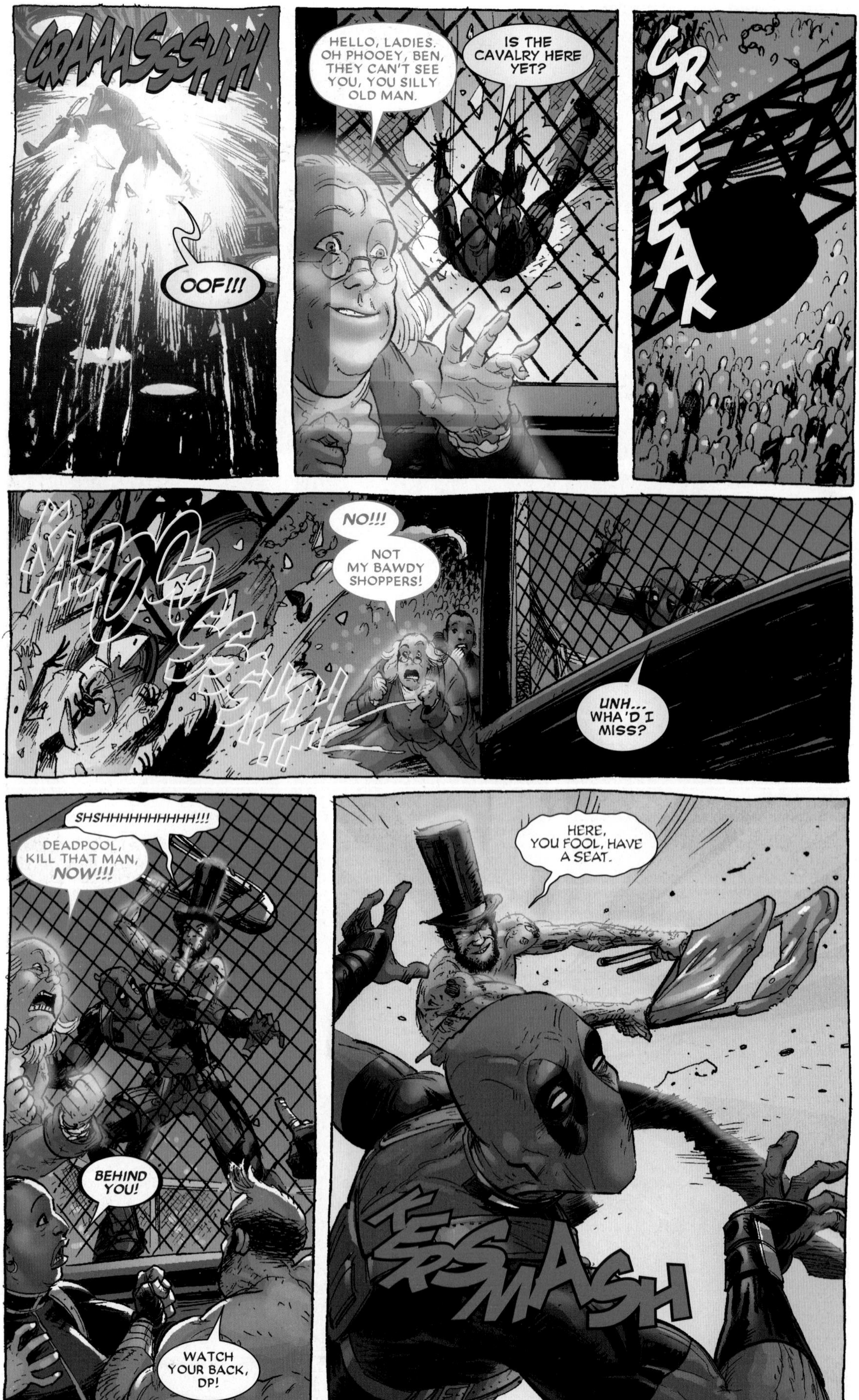
CRAAASSSHHH
OOF!!!
HELLO, LADIES. OH PHOOEY, BEN, THEY CAN'T SEE YOU, YOU SILLY OLD MAN.
IS THE CAVALRY HERE YET?
CREEEAK
KA-BOOOSSHHH
NO!!!
NOT MY BAWDY SHOPPERS!
UNH... WHA'D I MISS?
SHSHHHHHHHHHHH!!!
DEADPOOL, KILL THAT MAN, NOW!!!
BEHIND YOU!
WATCH YOUR BACK, DP!
HERE, YOU FOOL, HAVE A SEAT.
KERSMASH

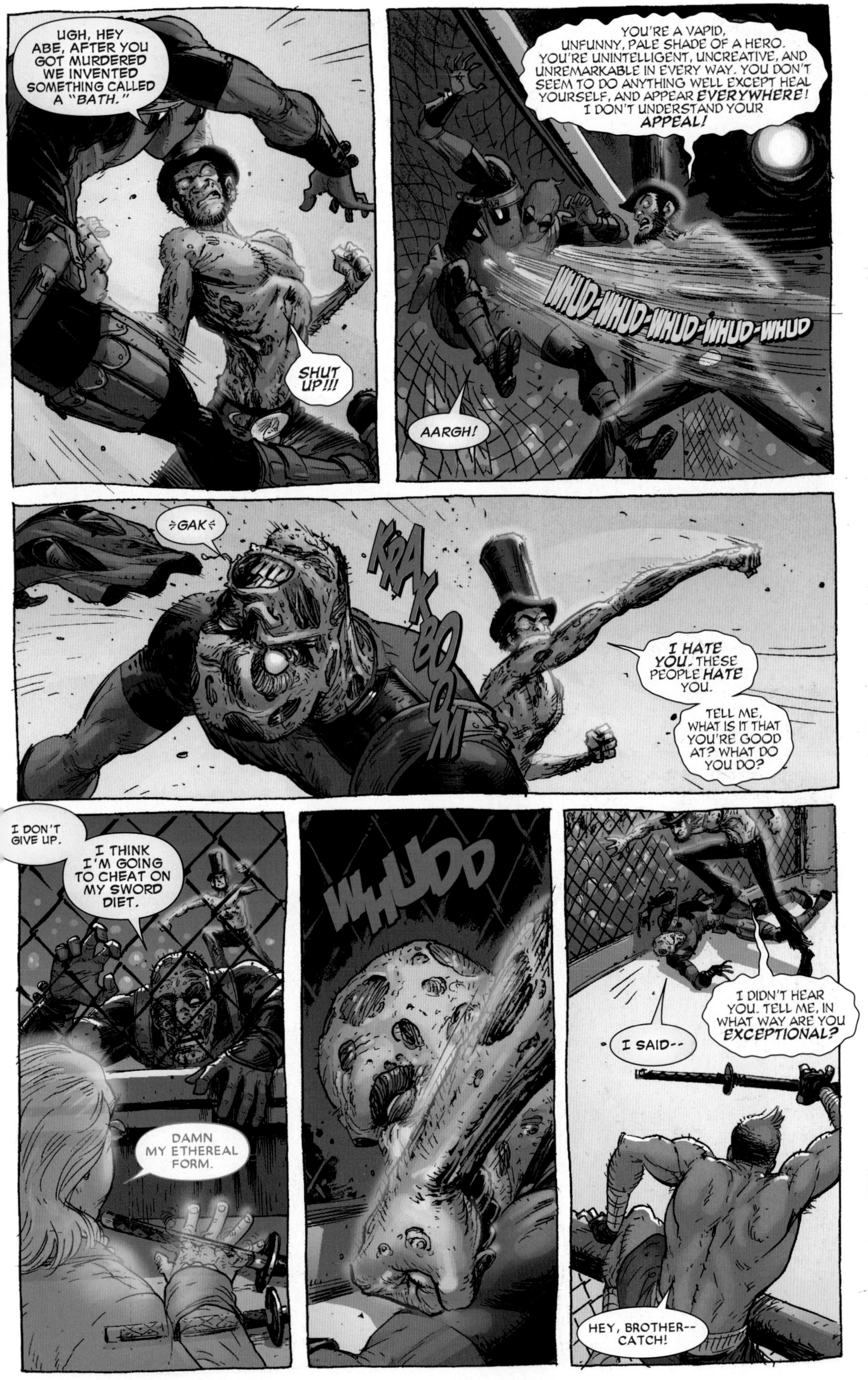
UGH, HEY ABE, AFTER YOU GOT MURDERED WE INVENTED SOMETHING CALLED A "BATH."
SHUT UP!!!
YOU'RE A VAPID, UNFUNNY, PALE SHADE OF A HERO. YOU'RE UNINTELLIGENT, UNCREATIVE, AND UNREMARKABLE IN EVERY WAY. YOU DON'T SEEM TO DO ANYTHING WELL EXCEPT HEAL YOURSELF, AND APPEAR EVERYWHERE! I DON'T UNDERSTAND YOUR APPEAL!
WHUD-WHUD-WHUD-WHUD-WHUD
AARGH!
GAK
KRAKBOOM
I HATE YOU. THESE PEOPLE HATE YOU.
TELL ME, WHAT IS IT THAT YOU'RE GOOD AT? WHAT DO YOU DO?
I DON'T GIVE UP.
I THINK I'M GOING TO CHEAT ON MY SWORD DIET.
DAMN MY ETHEREAL FORM.
WHUDD
I DIDN'T HEAR YOU. TELL ME, IN WHAT WAY ARE YOU EXCEPTIONAL?
I SAID--
HEY, BROTHER-- CATCH!

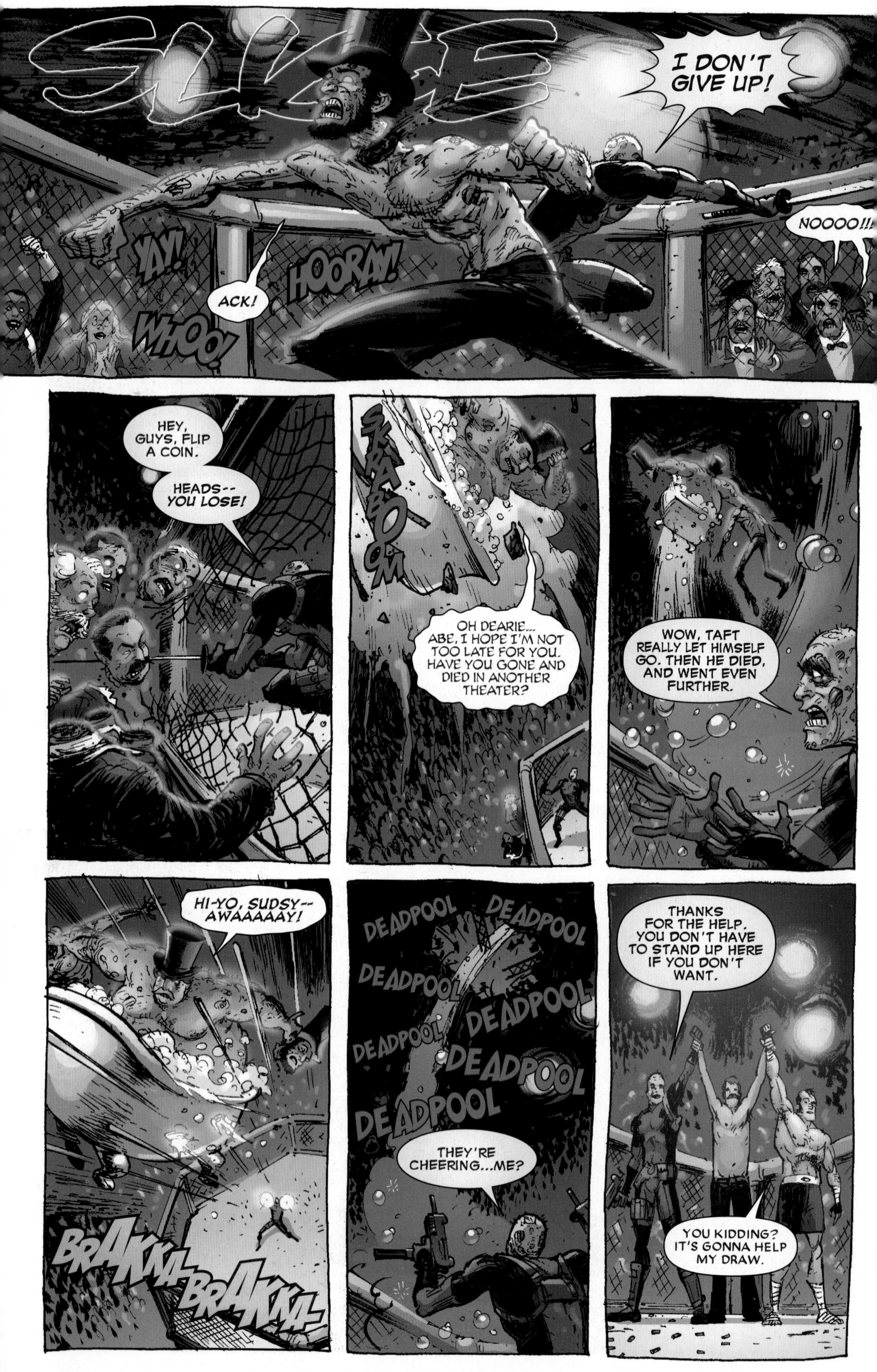

SLICE
I DON'T GIVE UP!
YAY!
ACK!
HOORAY!
WHOO!
NOOOO!!!
HEY, GUYS, FLIP A COIN.
HEADS-- YOU LOSE!
SKRABOOM
OH DEARIE... ABE, I HOPE I'M NOT TOO LATE FOR YOU. HAVE YOU GONE AND DIED IN ANOTHER THEATER?
WOW, TAFT REALLY LET HIMSELF GO. THEN HE DIED, AND WENT EVEN FURTHER.
HI-YO, SUDSY-- AWAAAAAY!
BRAKKA BRAKKA
DEADPOOL DEADPOOL DEADPOOL DEADPOOL DEADPOOL DEADPOOL DEADPOOL DEADPOOL
THEY'RE CHEERING...ME?
THANKS FOR THE HELP. YOU DON'T HAVE TO STAND UP HERE IF YOU DON'T WANT.
YOU KIDDING? IT'S GONNA HELP MY DRAW.

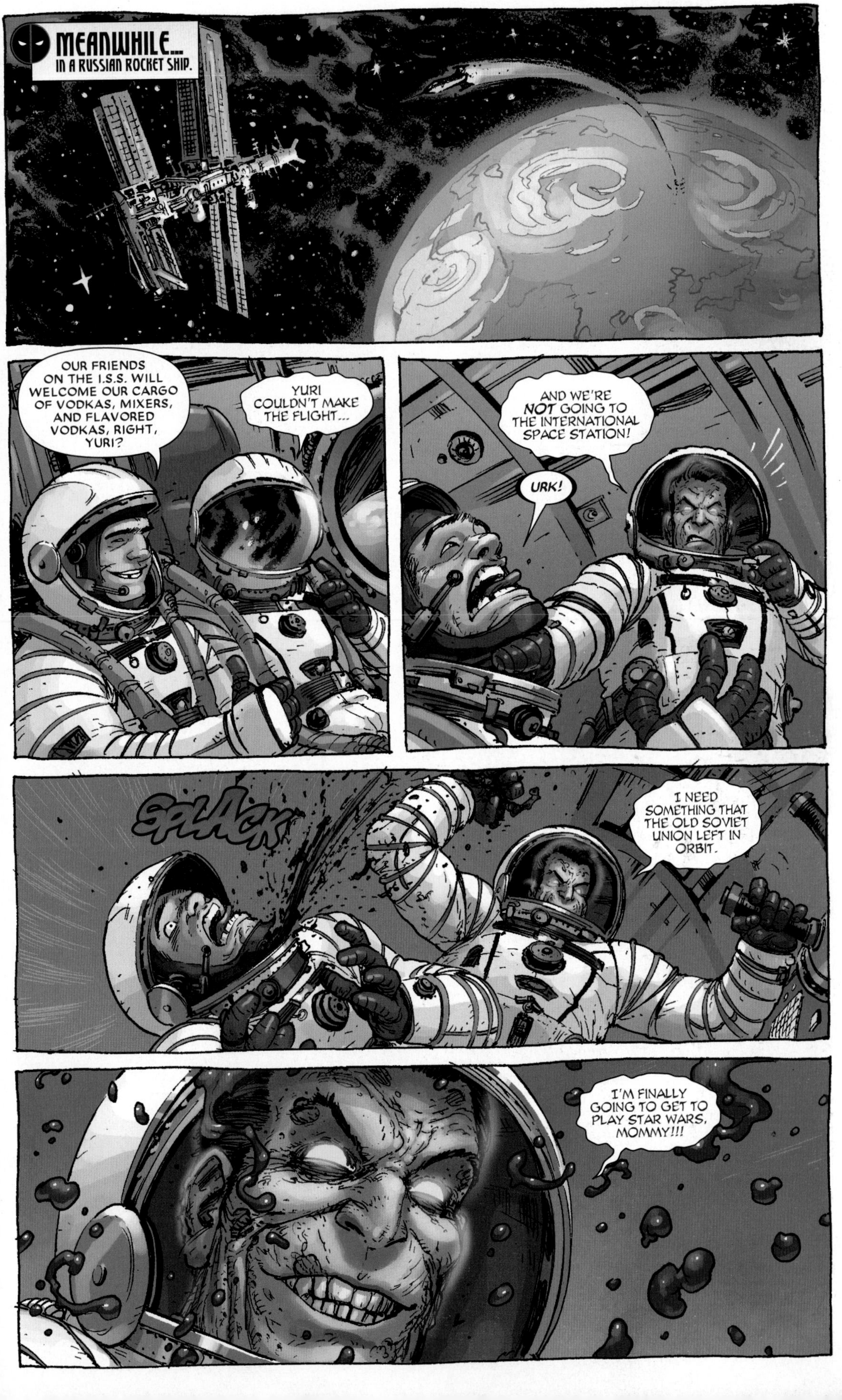
MEANWHILE... IN A RUSSIAN ROCKET SHIP.
OUR FRIENDS ON THE I.S.S. WILL WELCOME OUR CARGO OF VODKAS, MIXERS, AND FLAVORED VODKAS, RIGHT, YURI?
YURI COULDN'T MAKE THE FLIGHT...
AND WE'RE NOT GOING TO THE INTERNATIONAL SPACE STATION!
URK!
SPLACK
I NEED SOMETHING THAT THE OLD SOVIET UNION LEFT IN ORBIT.
I'M FINALLY GOING TO GET TO PLAY STAR WARS, MOMMY!!!

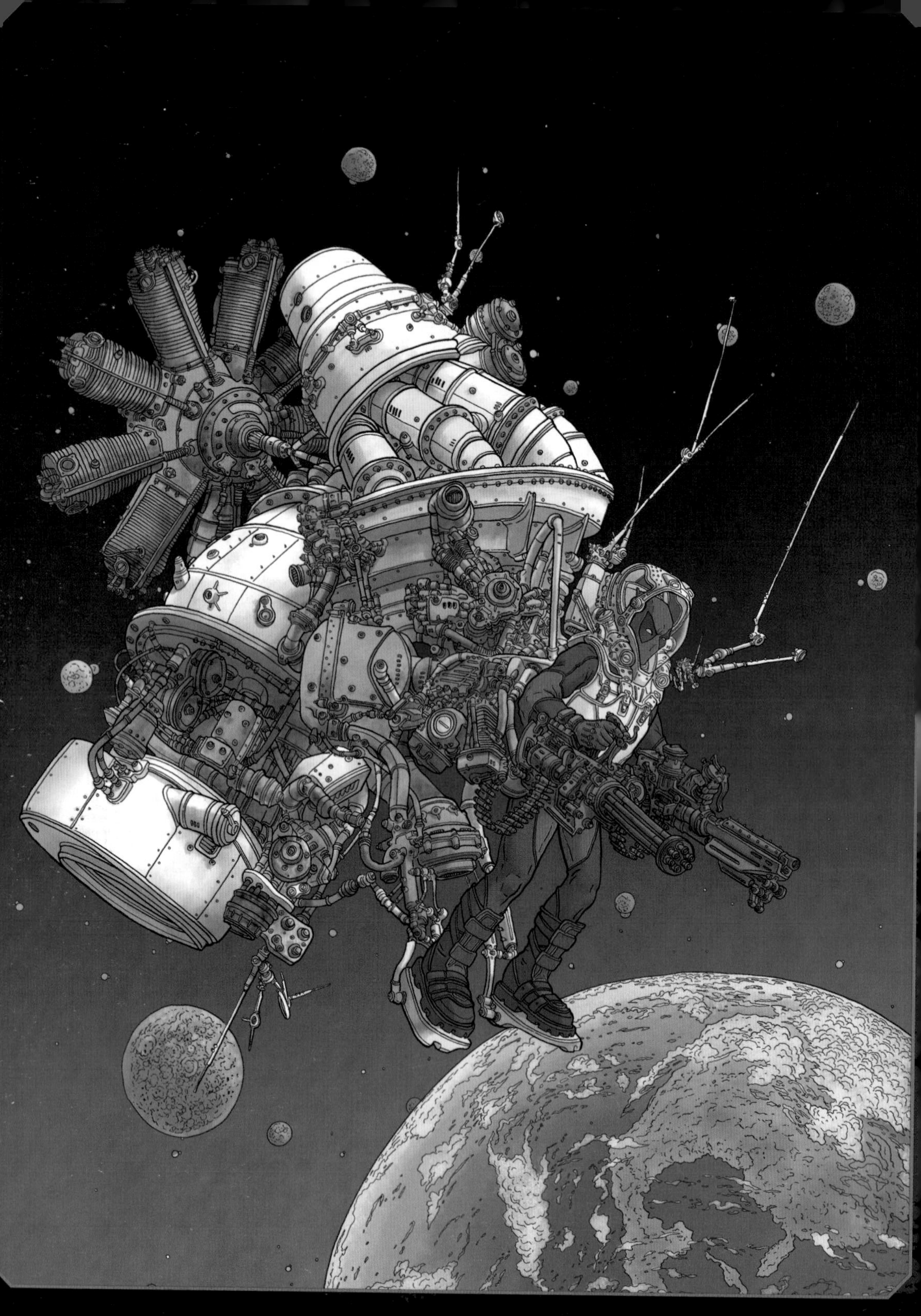

STAR WARS: REVENGE OF THE GIPPER

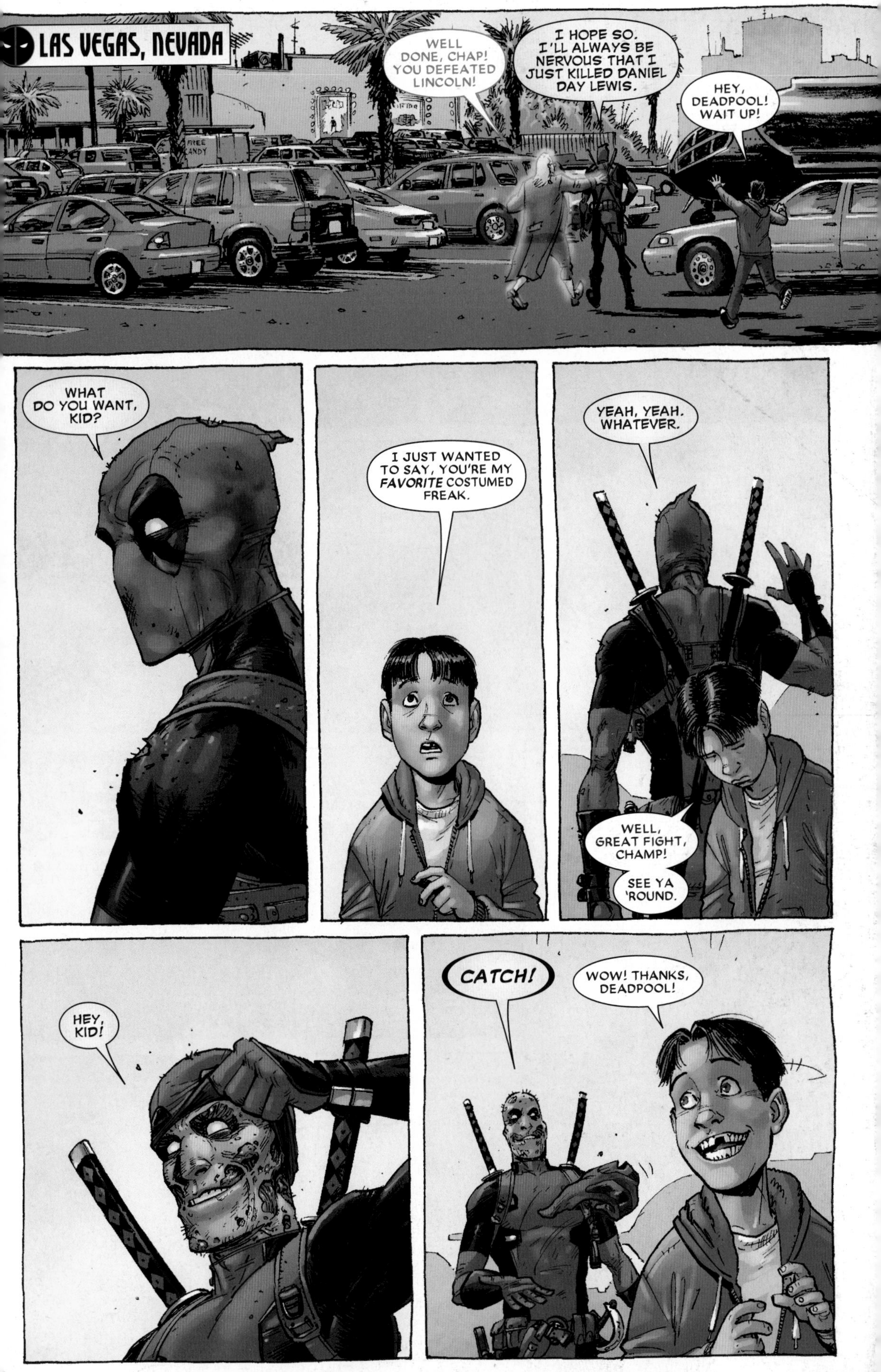

LAS VEGAS, NEVADA
WELL DONE, CHAP! YOU DEFEATED LINCOLN!
I HOPE SO. I'LL ALWAYS BE NERVOUS THAT I JUST KILLED DANIEL DAY LEWIS.
HEY, DEADPOOL! WAIT UP!
WHAT DO YOU WANT, KID?
I JUST WANTED TO SAY, YOU'RE MY FAVORITE COSTUMED FREAK.
YEAH, YEAH. WHATEVER.
WELL, GREAT FIGHT, CHAMP!
SEE YA 'ROUND.
HEY, KID!
CATCH!
WOW! THANKS, DEADPOOL!

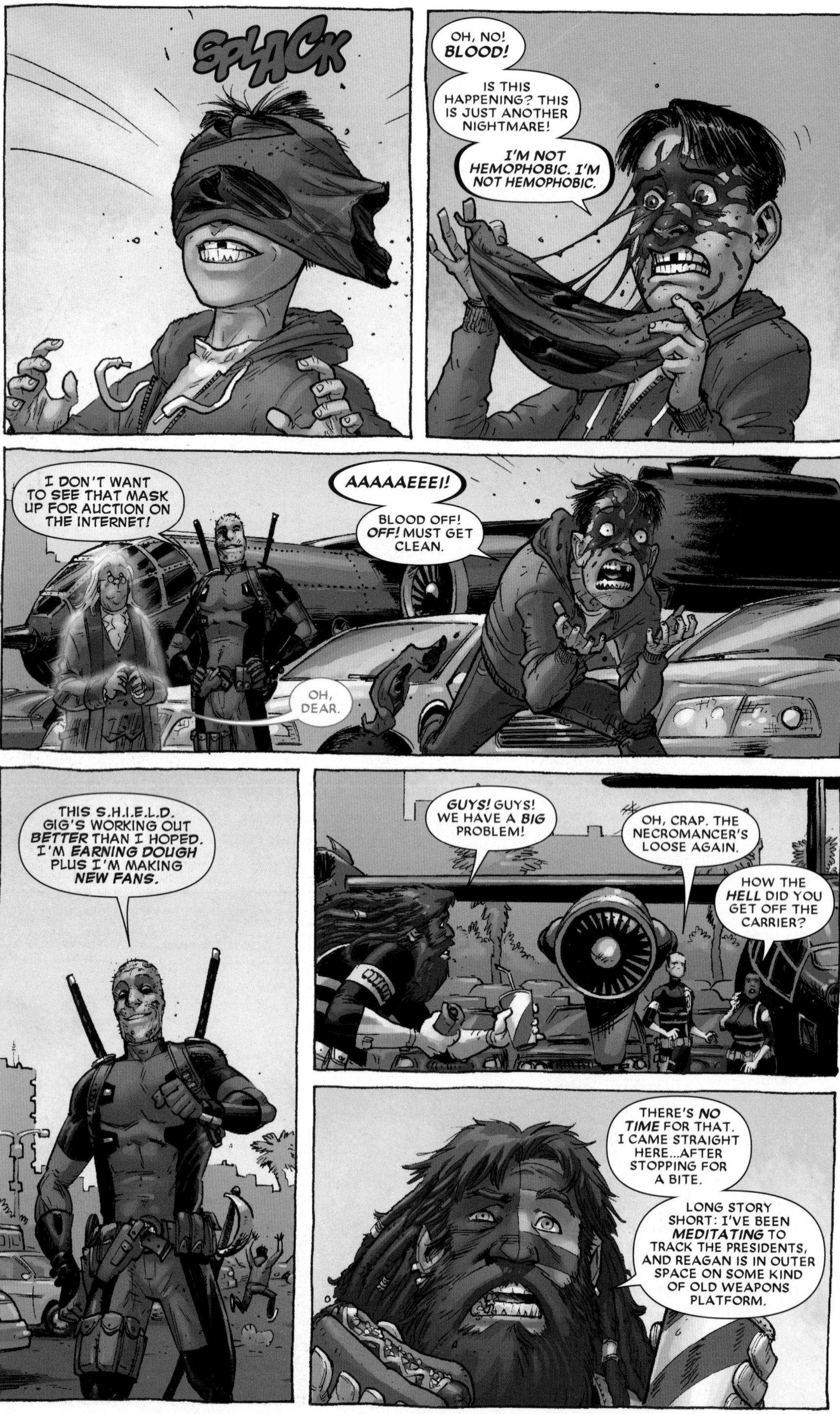
SPLACK
OH, NO! BLOOD!
IS THIS HAPPENING? THIS IS JUST ANOTHER NIGHTMARE!
I'M NOT HEMOPHOBIC. I'M NOT HEMOPHOBIC.
I DON'T WANT TO SEE THAT MASK UP FOR AUCTION ON THE INTERNET!
AAAAAEEEI!
BLOOD OFF! OFF! MUST GET CLEAN.
OH, DEAR.
THIS S.H.I.E.L.D. GIG'S WORKING OUT BETTER THAN I HOPED. I'M EARNING DOUGH PLUS I'M MAKING NEW FANS.
GUYS! GUYS! WE HAVE A BIG PROBLEM!
OH, CRAP. THE NECROMANCER'S LOOSE AGAIN.
HOW THE HELL DID YOU GET OFF THE CARRIER?
THERE'S NO TIME FOR THAT. I CAME STRAIGHT HERE...AFTER STOPPING FOR A BITE.
LONG STORY SHORT: I'VE BEEN MEDITATING TO TRACK THE PRESIDENTS, AND REAGAN IS IN OUTER SPACE ON SOME KIND OF OLD WEAPONS PLATFORM.

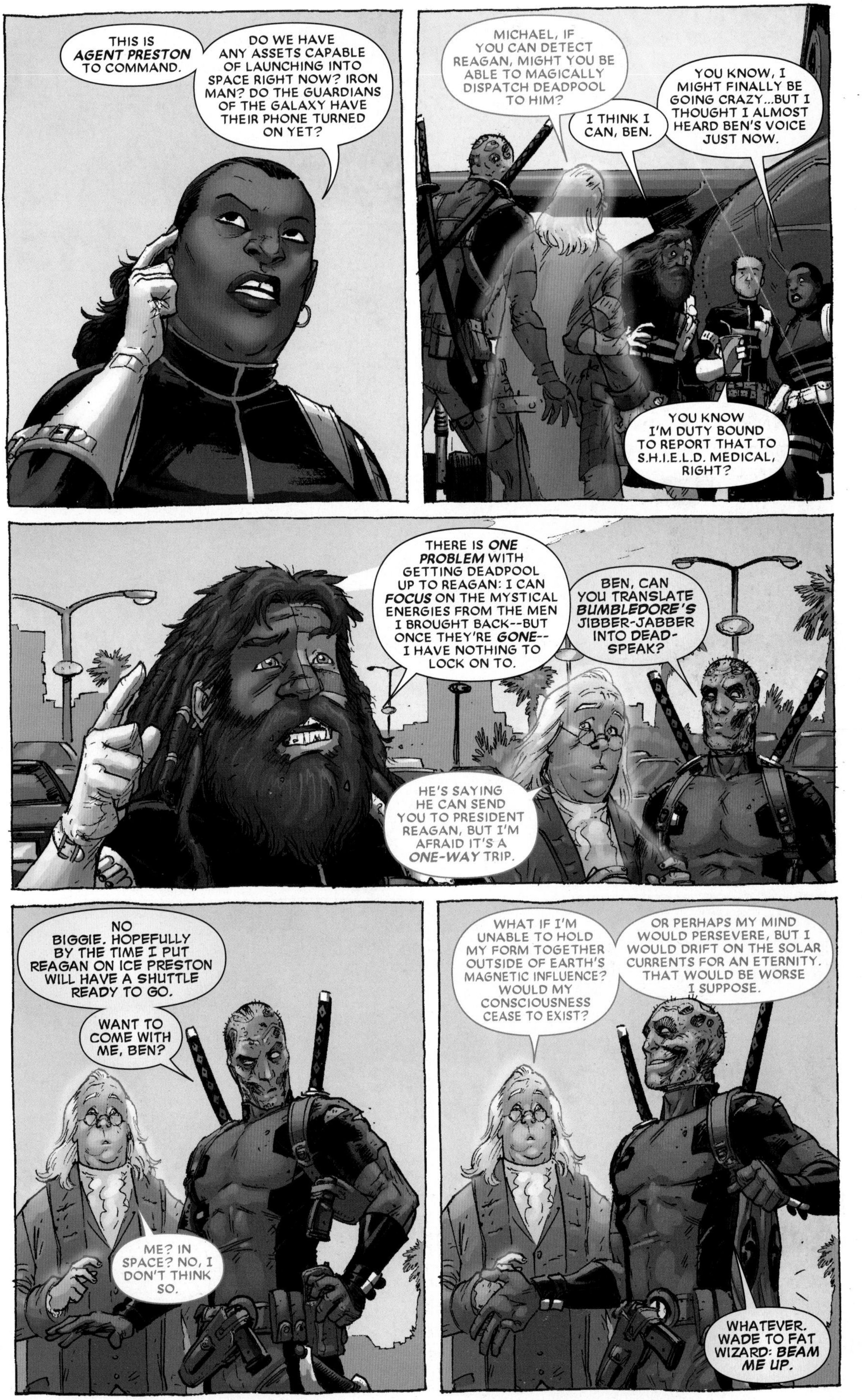
THIS IS AGENT PRESTON TO COMMAND.
DO WE HAVE ANY ASSETS CAPABLE OF LAUNCHING INTO SPACE RIGHT NOW? IRON MAN? DO THE GUARDIANS OF THE GALAXY HAVE THEIR PHONE TURNED ON YET?
MICHAEL, IF YOU CAN DETECT REAGAN, MIGHT YOU BE ABLE TO MAGICALLY DISPATCH DEADPOOL TO HIM?
I THINK I CAN, BEN.
YOU KNOW, I MIGHT FINALLY BE GOING CRAZY...BUT I THOUGHT I ALMOST HEARD BEN'S VOICE JUST NOW.
YOU KNOW I'M DUTY BOUND TO REPORT THAT TO S.H.I.E.L.D. MEDICAL, RIGHT?
THERE IS ONE PROBLEM WITH GETTING DEADPOOL UP TO REAGAN: I CAN FOCUS ON THE MYSTICAL ENERGIES FROM THE MEN I BROUGHT BACK--BUT ONCE THEY'RE GONE--I HAVE NOTHING TO LOCK ON TO.
BEN, CAN YOU TRANSLATE BUMBLEDORE'S JIBBER-JABBER INTO DEAD-SPEAK?
HE'S SAYING HE CAN SEND YOU TO PRESIDENT REAGAN, BUT I'M AFRAID IT'S A ONE-WAY TRIP.
NO BIGGIE. HOPEFULLY BY THE TIME I PUT REAGAN ON ICE PRESTON WILL HAVE A SHUTTLE READY TO GO.
WANT TO COME WITH ME, BEN?
ME? IN SPACE? NO, I DON'T THINK SO.
WHAT IF I'M UNABLE TO HOLD MY FORM TOGETHER OUTSIDE OF EARTH'S MAGNETIC INFLUENCE? WOULD MY CONSCIOUSNESS CEASE TO EXIST?
OR PERHAPS MY MIND WOULD PERSEVERE, BUT I WOULD DRIFT ON THE SOLAR CURRENTS FOR AN ETERNITY. THAT WOULD BE WORSE I SUPPOSE.
WHATEVER. WADE TO FAT WIZARD: BEAM ME UP.

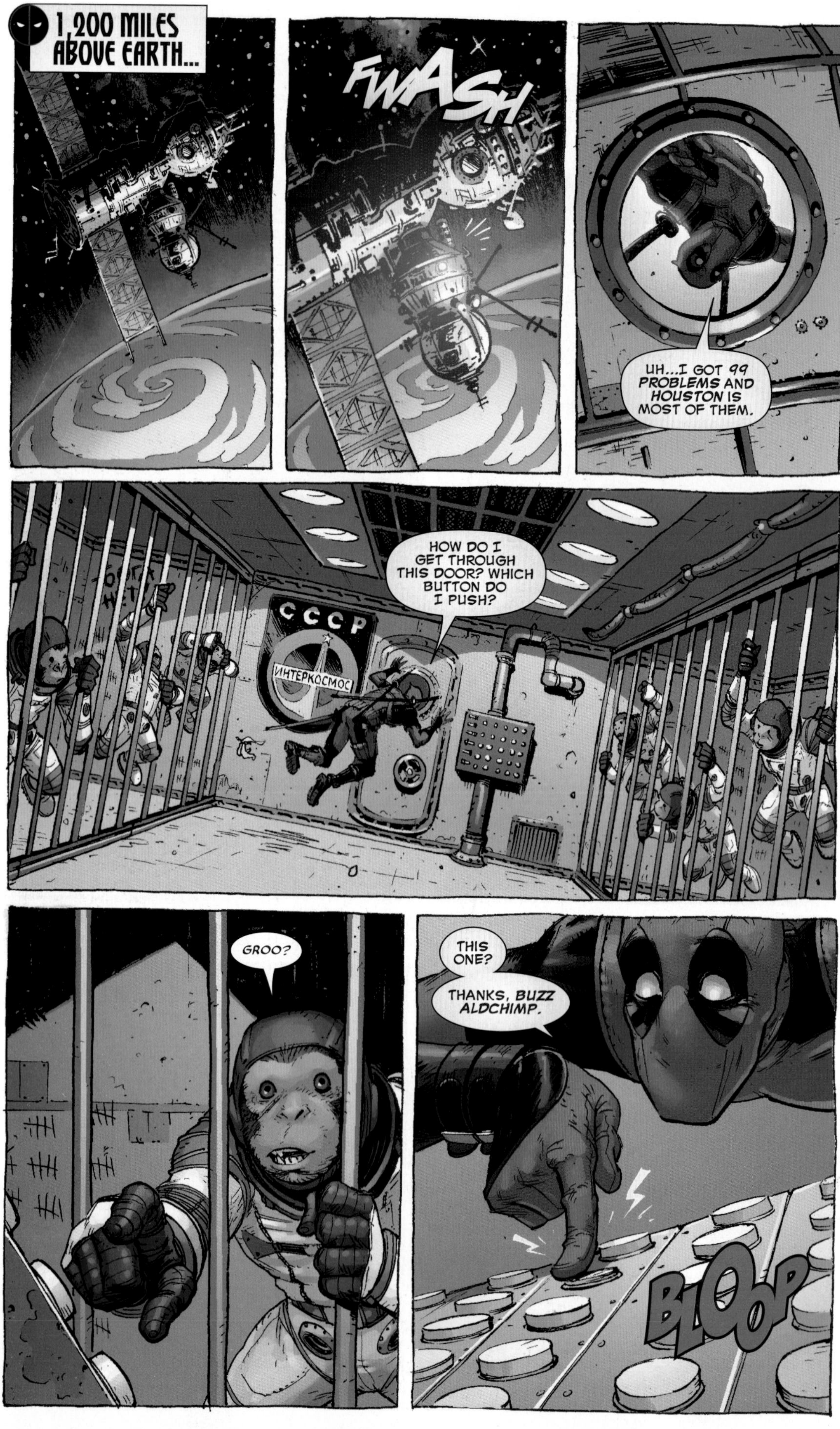
1,200 MILES ABOVE EARTH...
FWASH
UH...I GOT 99 PROBLEMS AND HOUSTON IS MOST OF THEM.
HOW DO I GET THROUGH THIS DOOR? WHICH BUTTON DO I PUSH?
CCCP
ИНТЕРКОСМОС
GROO?
THIS ONE?
THANKS, BUZZ ALDCHIMP.
BLOOP

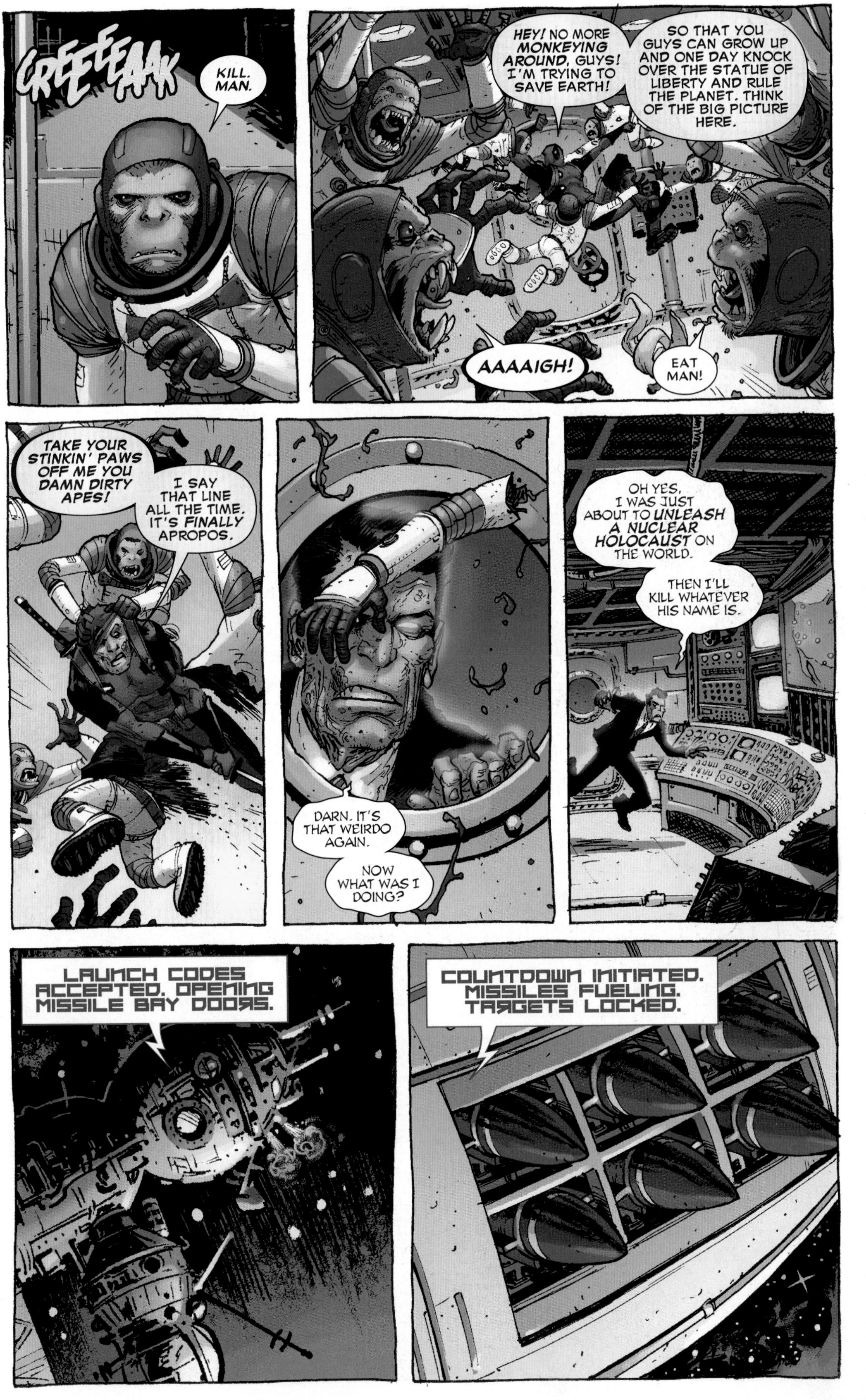
CREEEEAAK
KILL. MAN.
HEY! NO MORE MONKEYING AROUND, GUYS! I'M TRYING TO SAVE EARTH!
SO THAT YOU GUYS CAN GROW UP AND ONE DAY KNOCK OVER THE STATUE OF LIBERTY AND RULE THE PLANET. THINK OF THE BIG PICTURE HERE.
AAAAIGH!
EAT MAN!
TAKE YOUR STINKIN' PAWS OFF ME YOU DAMN DIRTY APES!
I SAY THAT LINE ALL THE TIME. IT'S FINALLY APROPOS.
DARN. IT'S THAT WEIRDO AGAIN.
NOW WHAT WAS I DOING?
OH YES, I WAS JUST ABOUT TO UNLEASH A NUCLEAR HOLOCAUST ON THE WORLD.
THEN I'LL KILL WHATEVER HIS NAME IS.
LAUNCH CODES ACCEPTED. OPENING MISSILE BAY DOORS.
COUNTDOWN INITIATED. MISSILES FUELING. TARGETS LOCKED.

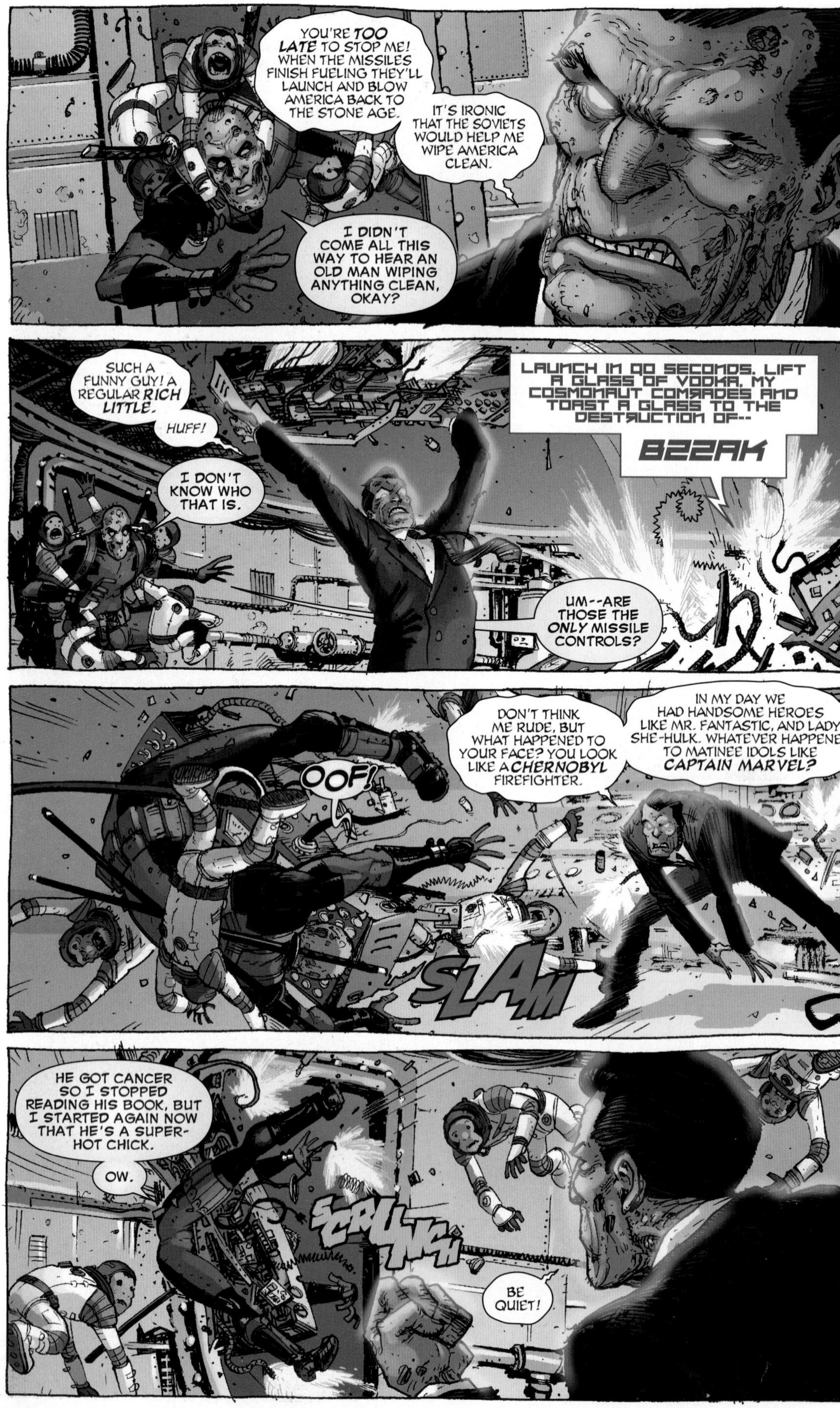
YOU'RE TOO LATE TO STOP ME! WHEN THE MISSILES FINISH FUELING THEY'LL LAUNCH AND BLOW AMERICA BACK TO THE STONE AGE.
IT'S IRONIC THAT THE SOVIETS WOULD HELP ME WIPE AMERICA CLEAN.
I DIDN'T COME ALL THIS WAY TO HEAR AN OLD MAN WIPING ANYTHING CLEAN, OKAY?
SUCH A FUNNY GUY! A REGULAR RICH LITTLE.
HUFF!
I DON'T KNOW WHO THAT IS.
LAUNCH IN 90 SECONDS. LIFT A GLASS OF VODKA, MY COSMONAUT COMRADES AND TOAST A GLASS TO THE DESTRUCTION OF--
BZZAK
UM--ARE THOSE THE ONLY MISSILE CONTROLS?
OOF!
DON'T THINK ME RUDE, BUT WHAT HAPPENED TO YOUR FACE? YOU LOOK LIKE A CHERNOBYL FIREFIGHTER.
IN MY DAY WE HAD HANDSOME HEROES LIKE MR. FANTASTIC, AND LADY SHE-HULK. WHATEVER HAPPENED TO MATINEE IDOLS LIKE CAPTAIN MARVEL?
SLAM
HE GOT CANCER SO I STOPPED READING HIS BOOK, BUT I STARTED AGAIN NOW THAT HE'S A SUPER-HOT CHICK.
OW.
SCRUNCH
BE QUIET!

DO YOU THINK I'LL MAKE THE HISTORY BOOKS FOR RETURNING THE PRESIDENTS TO THE OTHER SIDE? WILL PART OF YOUR STORY BE THAT YOU CAME BACK?

SORRY FOR THE SMALL TALK. I DON'T HAVE ANYONE TO TALK TO, AND THE SILENCES WHEN YOU'RE TRYING TO KILL SOMEONE CAN BE SO AWKWARD.

SHHK

THERE WILL BE NO MORE HISTORY BOOKS. THIS COUNTRY IS OVER.

CAREFUL WITH THE HISTORICAL WEAPON, I'M PUTTING THAT UP FOR AUCTION WHEN THIS IS OVER.

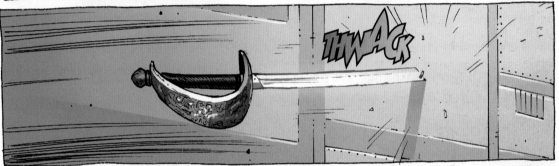

THWACK

I DON'T KNOW WHY YOU GUYS CAME BACK INTENT ON DESTROYING AMERICA. MAYBE YOU WERE GIANT #$%&$ WHEN YOU WERE ALIVE, BUT YOU'RE EVEN WORSE DEAD.

I DON'T GIVE A DAMN EITHER WAY, BUT YOU'RE NOT GOING TO WIN.

AND I DON'T NEED A MAGIC SWORD TO DO MY JOB.

MOMMY, MY TUMMY IS A BOO-BOO!

SPLISH

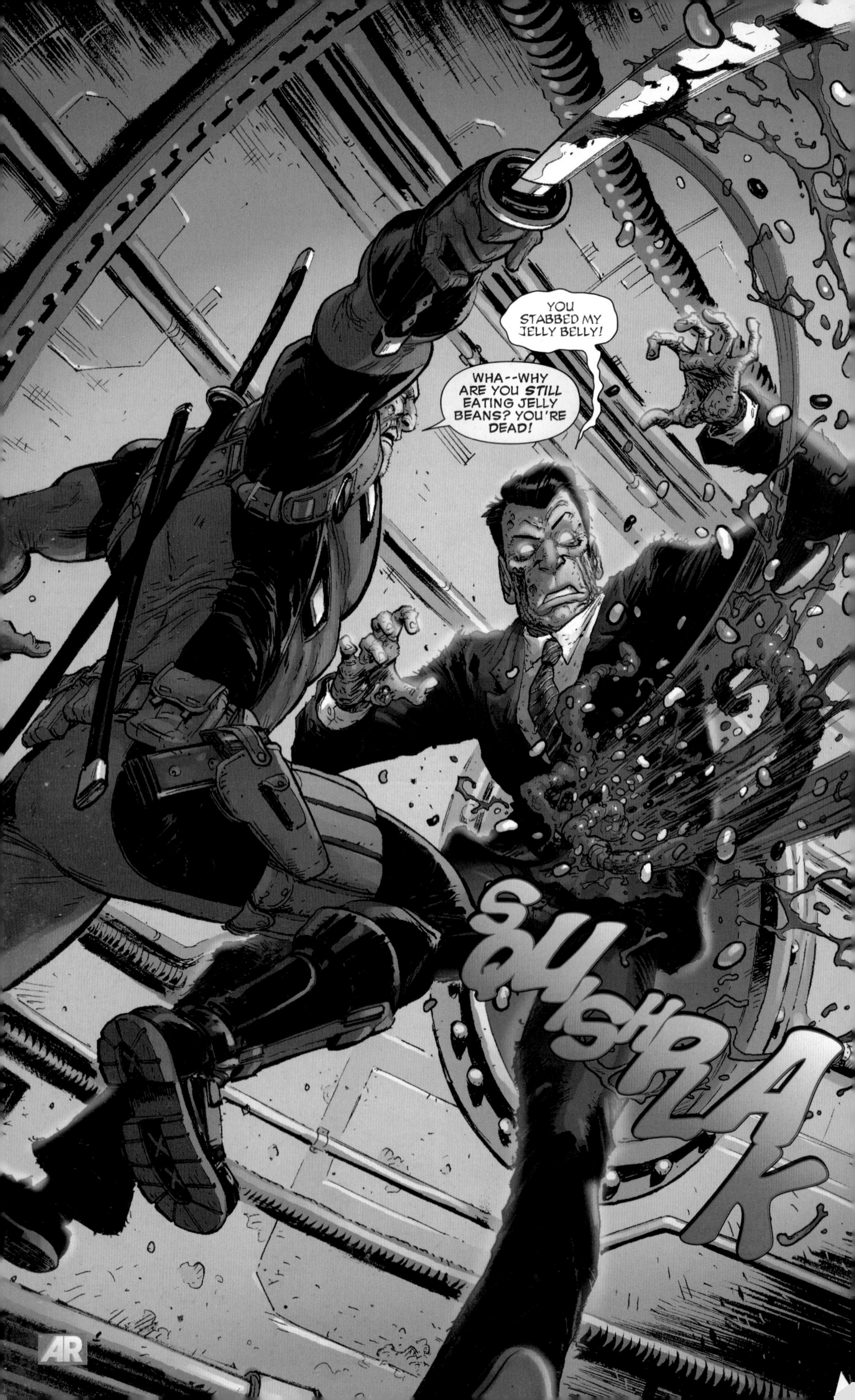
YOU STABBED MY JELLY BELLY!
WHA--WHY ARE YOU *STILL* EATING JELLY BEANS? YOU'RE DEAD!
SQUSHRAK

MY JELLIES! MY PRECIOUS JELLIES!

NOM-NOM-NOM

GAH! LICORICE! GROSS!

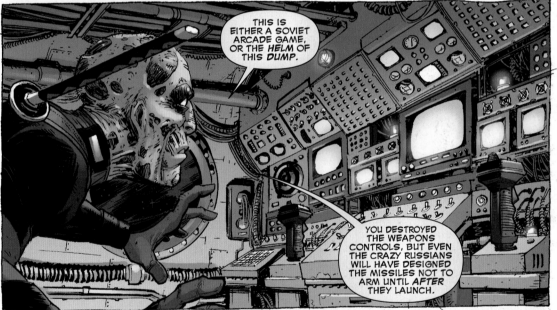

THIS IS EITHER A SOVIET ARCADE GAME, OR THE *HELM* OF THIS *DUMP*.

YOU DESTROYED THE WEAPONS CONTROLS, BUT EVEN THE CRAZY RUSSIANS WILL HAVE DESIGNED THE MISSILES NOT TO ARM UNTIL *AFTER* THEY LAUNCH.

IF THE STATION BURNS UP *BEFORE* THE MISSILES CAN LAUNCH THEN YOU WON'T BE ABLE TO DESTROY AMERICA...WHICH IS TV'S JOB, ANYWAY.

HOLD ON TO YOUR POTATOES, RONNIE. YOU'RE GOING DOWN HARDER THAN ANY PRESIDENT IN HISTORY.

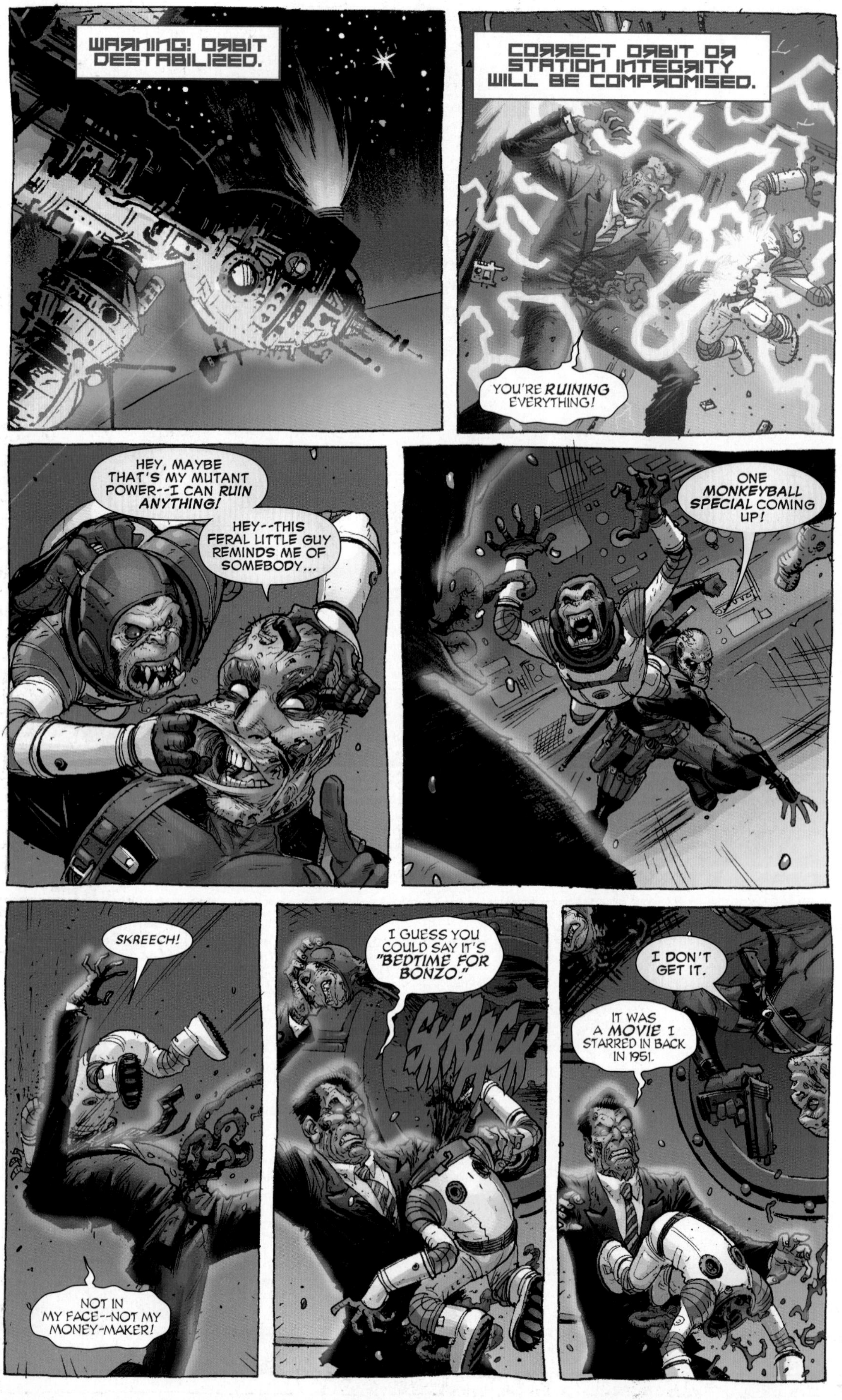
WARNING! ORBIT DESTABILIZED.
CORRECT ORBIT OR STATION INTEGRITY WILL BE COMPROMISED.
YOU'RE *RUINING* EVERYTHING!
HEY, MAYBE THAT'S MY MUTANT POWER--I CAN *RUIN ANYTHING!*
HEY--THIS FERAL LITTLE GUY REMINDS ME OF SOMEBODY...
ONE *MONKEYBALL SPECIAL* COMING UP!
SKREECH!
NOT IN MY FACE--NOT MY MONEY-MAKER!
I GUESS YOU COULD SAY IT'S *"BEDTIME FOR BONZO."*
SKRACK
I DON'T GET IT.
IT WAS A *MOVIE* I STARRED IN BACK IN 1951.

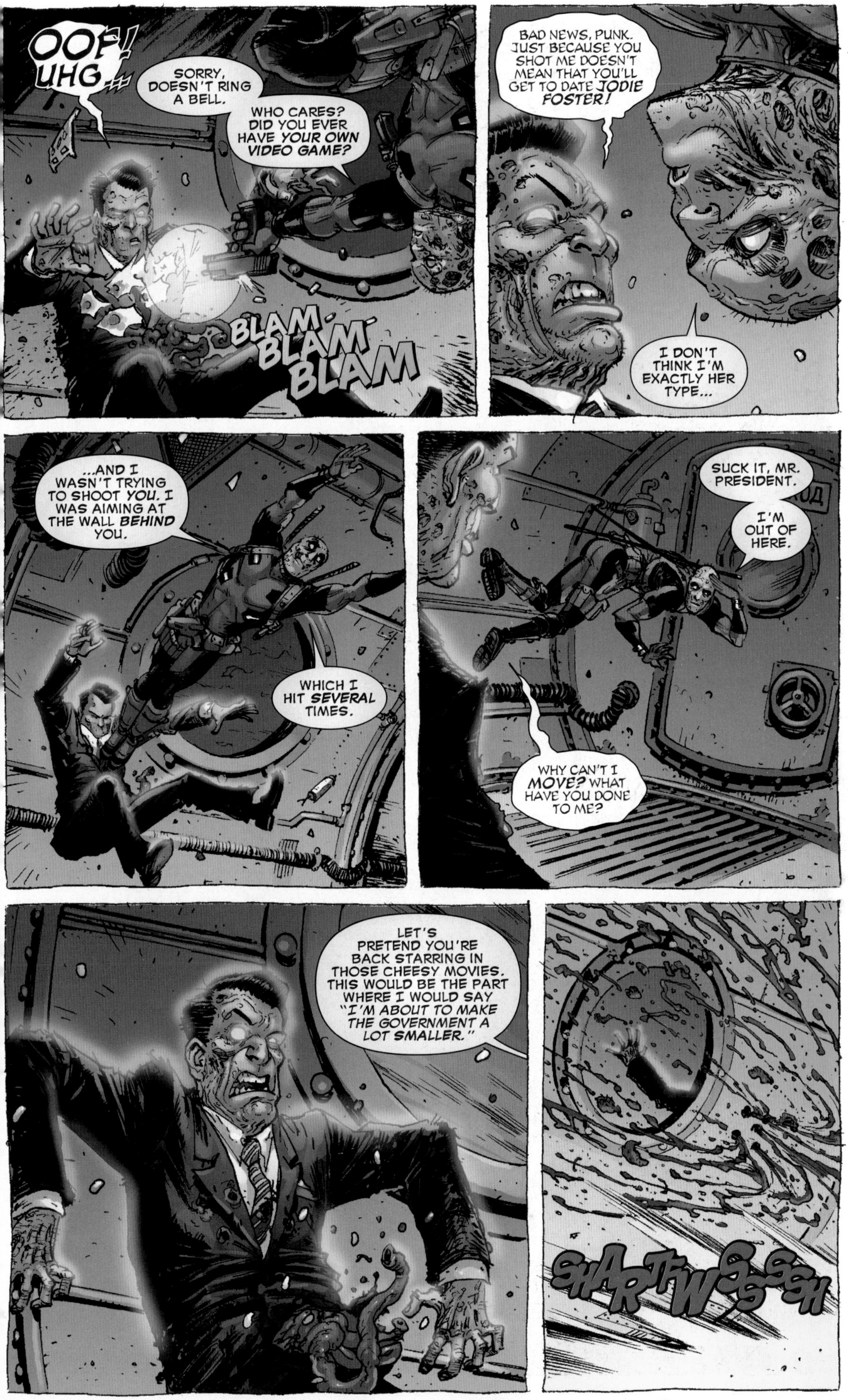
OOF! UHG...!
SORRY, DOESN'T RING A BELL.
WHO CARES? DID YOU EVER HAVE *YOUR OWN VIDEO GAME?*
BLAM BLAM BLAM
BAD NEWS, PUNK. JUST BECAUSE YOU SHOT ME DOESN'T MEAN THAT YOU'LL GET TO DATE *JODIE FOSTER!*
I DON'T THINK I'M EXACTLY HER TYPE...
...AND I WASN'T TRYING TO SHOOT *YOU*. I WAS AIMING AT THE WALL *BEHIND* YOU.
WHICH I HIT *SEVERAL* TIMES.
SUCK IT, MR. PRESIDENT.
I'M OUT OF HERE.
WHY CAN'T I *MOVE?* WHAT HAVE YOU DONE TO ME?
LET'S PRETEND YOU'RE BACK STARRING IN THOSE CHEESY MOVIES. THIS WOULD BE THE PART WHERE I WOULD SAY *"I'M ABOUT TO MAKE THE GOVERNMENT A LOT SMALLER."*
SHARTWSSSSH

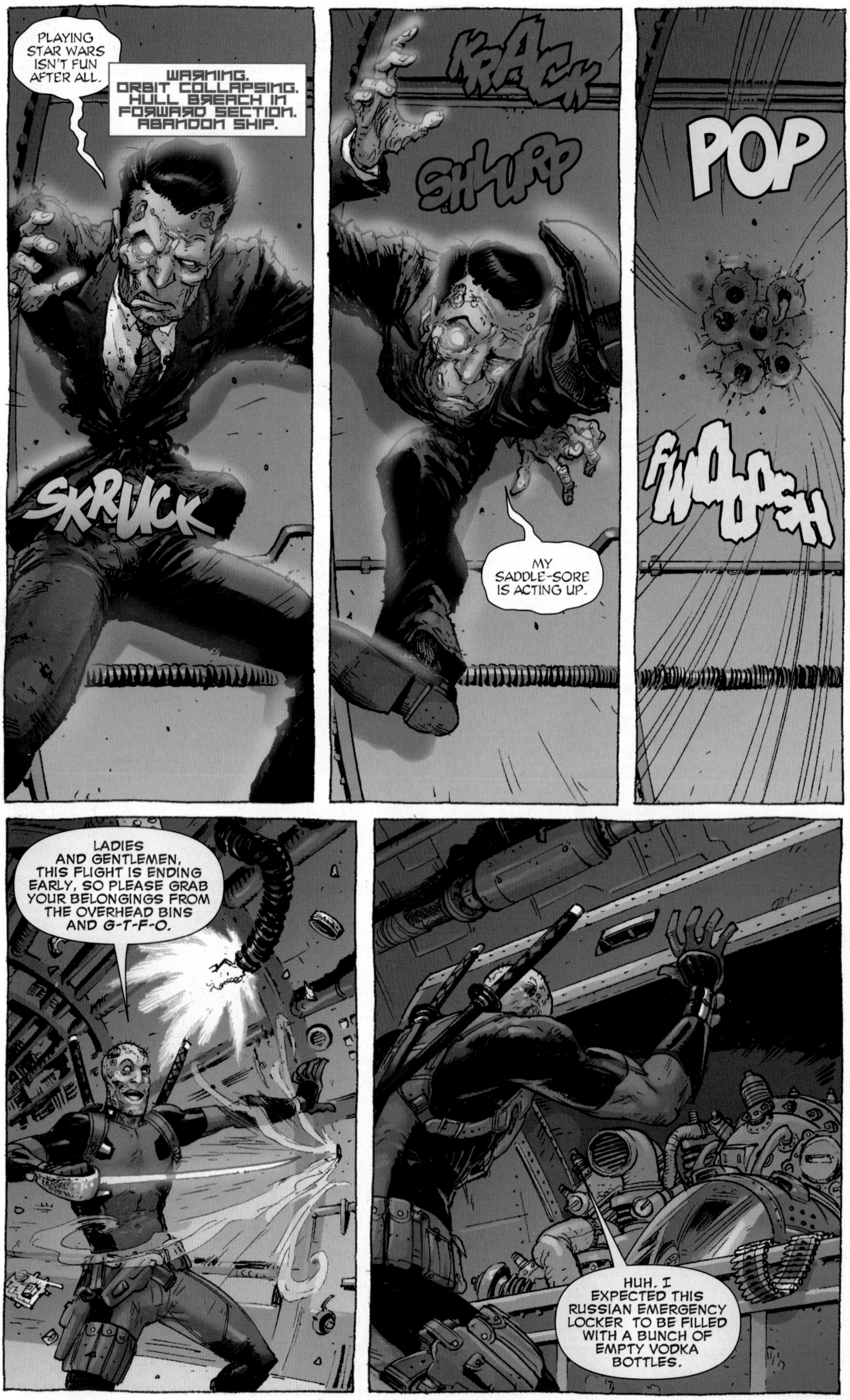

PLAYING STAR WARS ISN'T FUN AFTER ALL.
WARNING. ORBIT COLLAPSING. HULL BREACH IN FORWARD SECTION. ABANDON SHIP.
SKRUCK
KRACK
SHLURP
MY SADDLE-SORE IS ACTING UP.
POP
FWOOOSH
LADIES AND GENTLEMEN, THIS FLIGHT IS ENDING EARLY, SO PLEASE GRAB YOUR BELONGINGS FROM THE OVERHEAD BINS AND G-T-F-O.
HUH. I EXPECTED THIS RUSSIAN EMERGENCY LOCKER TO BE FILLED WITH A BUNCH OF EMPTY VODKA BOTTLES.

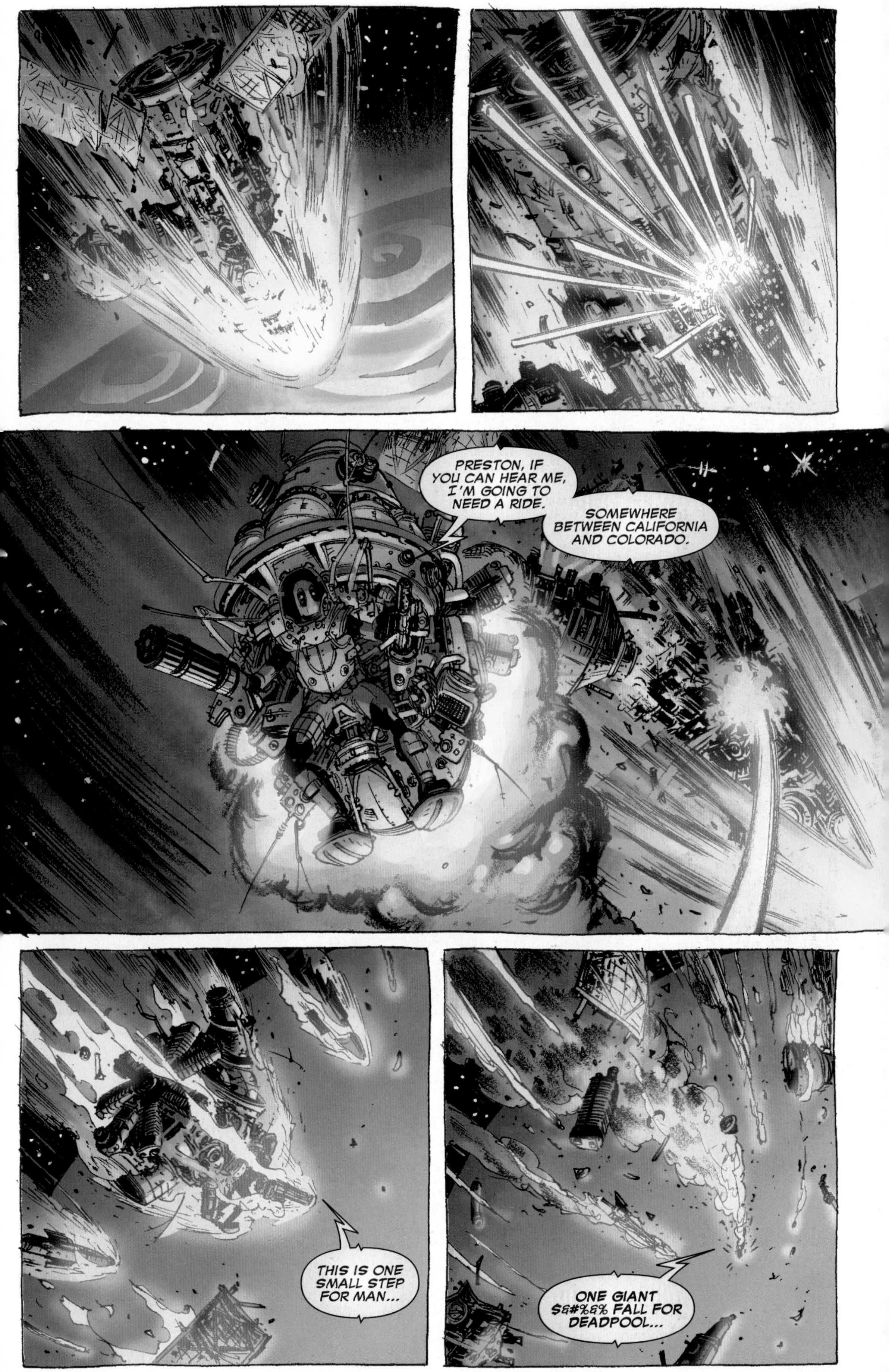
PRESTON, IF YOU CAN HEAR ME, I'M GOING TO NEED A RIDE.
SOMEWHERE BETWEEN CALIFORNIA AND COLORADO.
THIS IS ONE SMALL STEP FOR MAN...
ONE GIANT $&#%&% FALL FOR DEADPOOL...

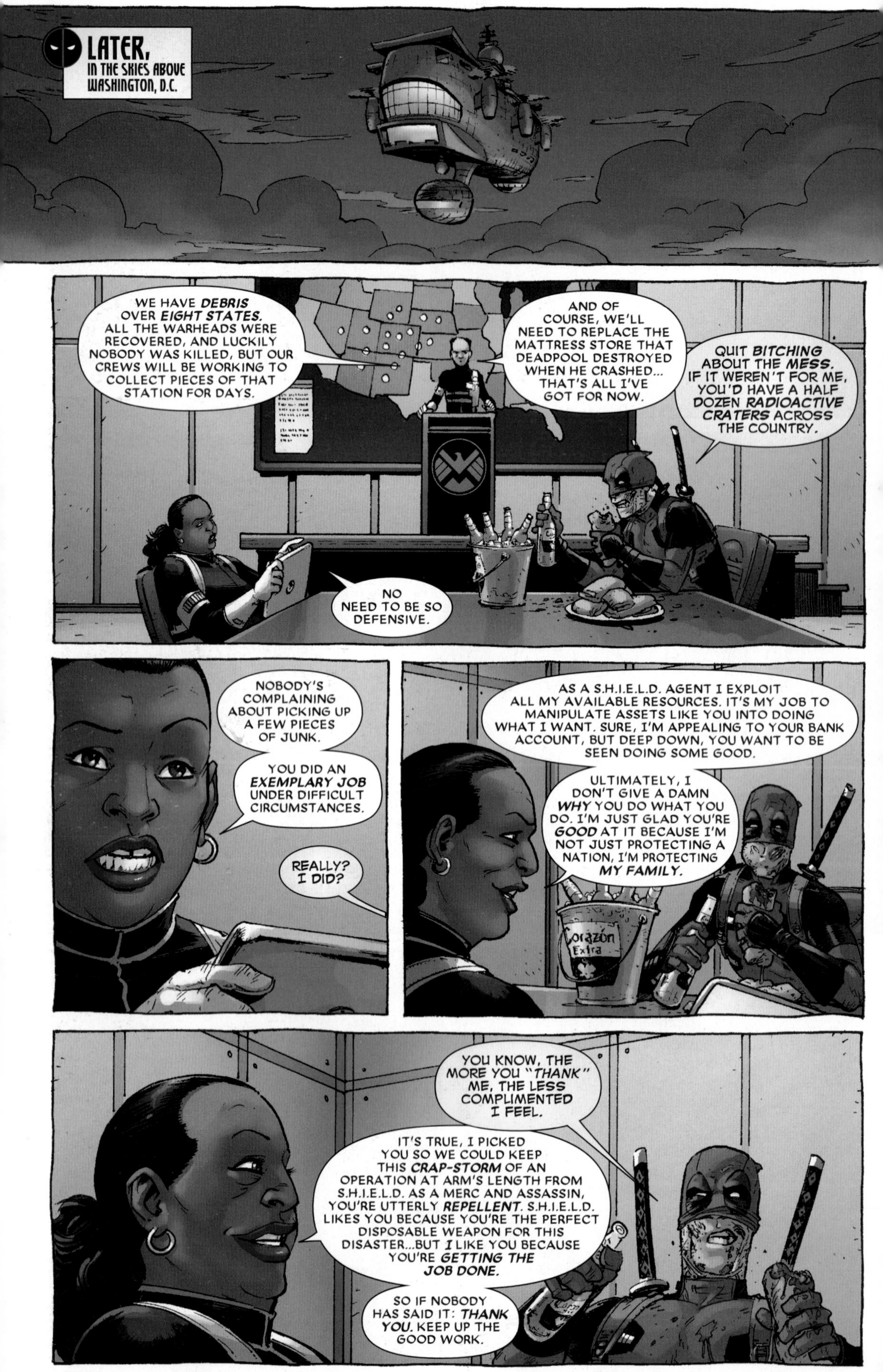
LATER, IN THE SKIES ABOVE WASHINGTON, D.C.
WE HAVE DEBRIS OVER EIGHT STATES. ALL THE WARHEADS WERE RECOVERED, AND LUCKILY NOBODY WAS KILLED, BUT OUR CREWS WILL BE WORKING TO COLLECT PIECES OF THAT STATION FOR DAYS.
AND OF COURSE, WE'LL NEED TO REPLACE THE MATTRESS STORE THAT DEADPOOL DESTROYED WHEN HE CRASHED... THAT'S ALL I'VE GOT FOR NOW.
QUIT BITCHING ABOUT THE MESS. IF IT WEREN'T FOR ME, YOU'D HAVE A HALF DOZEN RADIOACTIVE CRATERS ACROSS THE COUNTRY.
NO NEED TO BE SO DEFENSIVE.
NOBODY'S COMPLAINING ABOUT PICKING UP A FEW PIECES OF JUNK.
YOU DID AN EXEMPLARY JOB UNDER DIFFICULT CIRCUMSTANCES.
REALLY? I DID?
AS A S.H.I.E.L.D. AGENT I EXPLOIT ALL MY AVAILABLE RESOURCES. IT'S MY JOB TO MANIPULATE ASSETS LIKE YOU INTO DOING WHAT I WANT. SURE, I'M APPEALING TO YOUR BANK ACCOUNT, BUT DEEP DOWN, YOU WANT TO BE SEEN DOING SOME GOOD.
ULTIMATELY, I DON'T GIVE A DAMN WHY YOU DO WHAT YOU DO. I'M JUST GLAD YOU'RE GOOD AT IT BECAUSE I'M NOT JUST PROTECTING A NATION, I'M PROTECTING MY FAMILY.
Corazón Extra
YOU KNOW, THE MORE YOU "THANK" ME, THE LESS COMPLIMENTED I FEEL.
IT'S TRUE, I PICKED YOU SO WE COULD KEEP THIS CRAP-STORM OF AN OPERATION AT ARM'S LENGTH FROM S.H.I.E.L.D. AS A MERC AND ASSASSIN, YOU'RE UTTERLY REPELLENT. S.H.I.E.L.D. LIKES YOU BECAUSE YOU'RE THE PERFECT DISPOSABLE WEAPON FOR THIS DISASTER...BUT I LIKE YOU BECAUSE YOU'RE GETTING THE JOB DONE.
SO IF NOBODY HAS SAID IT: THANK YOU. KEEP UP THE GOOD WORK.

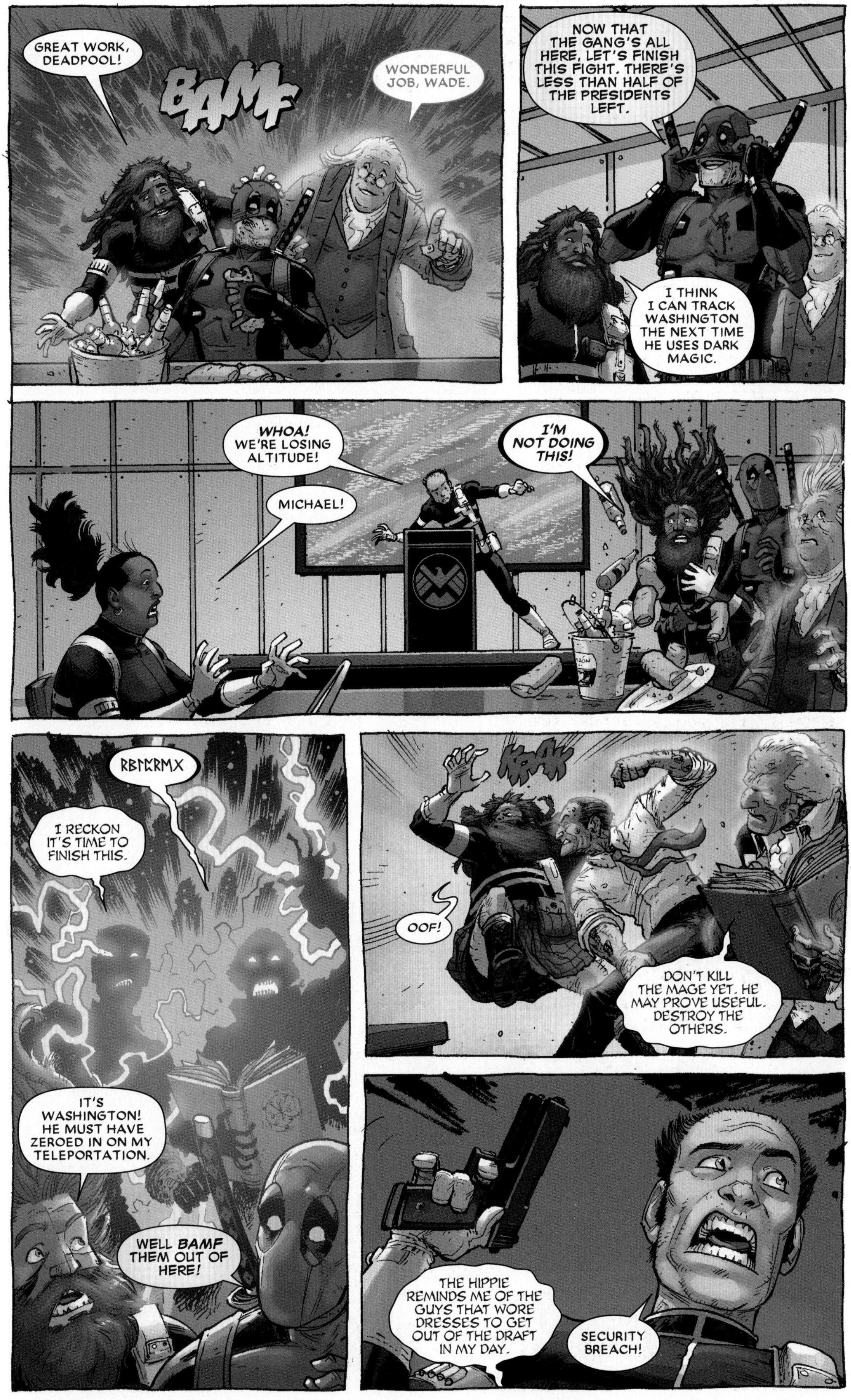
GREAT WORK, DEADPOOL!
BAMF
WONDERFUL JOB, WADE.
NOW THAT THE GANG'S ALL HERE, LET'S FINISH THIS FIGHT. THERE'S LESS THAN HALF OF THE PRESIDENTS LEFT.
I THINK I CAN TRACK WASHINGTON THE NEXT TIME HE USES DARK MAGIC.
WHOA! WE'RE LOSING ALTITUDE!
MICHAEL!
I'M NOT DOING THIS!
I RECKON IT'S TIME TO FINISH THIS.
IT'S WASHINGTON! HE MUST HAVE ZEROED IN ON MY TELEPORTATION.
WELL BAMF THEM OUT OF HERE!
KRAK
OOF!
DON'T KILL THE MAGE YET. HE MAY PROVE USEFUL. DESTROY THE OTHERS.
THE HIPPIE REMINDS ME OF THE GUYS THAT WORE DRESSES TO GET OUT OF THE DRAFT IN MY DAY.
SECURITY BREACH!

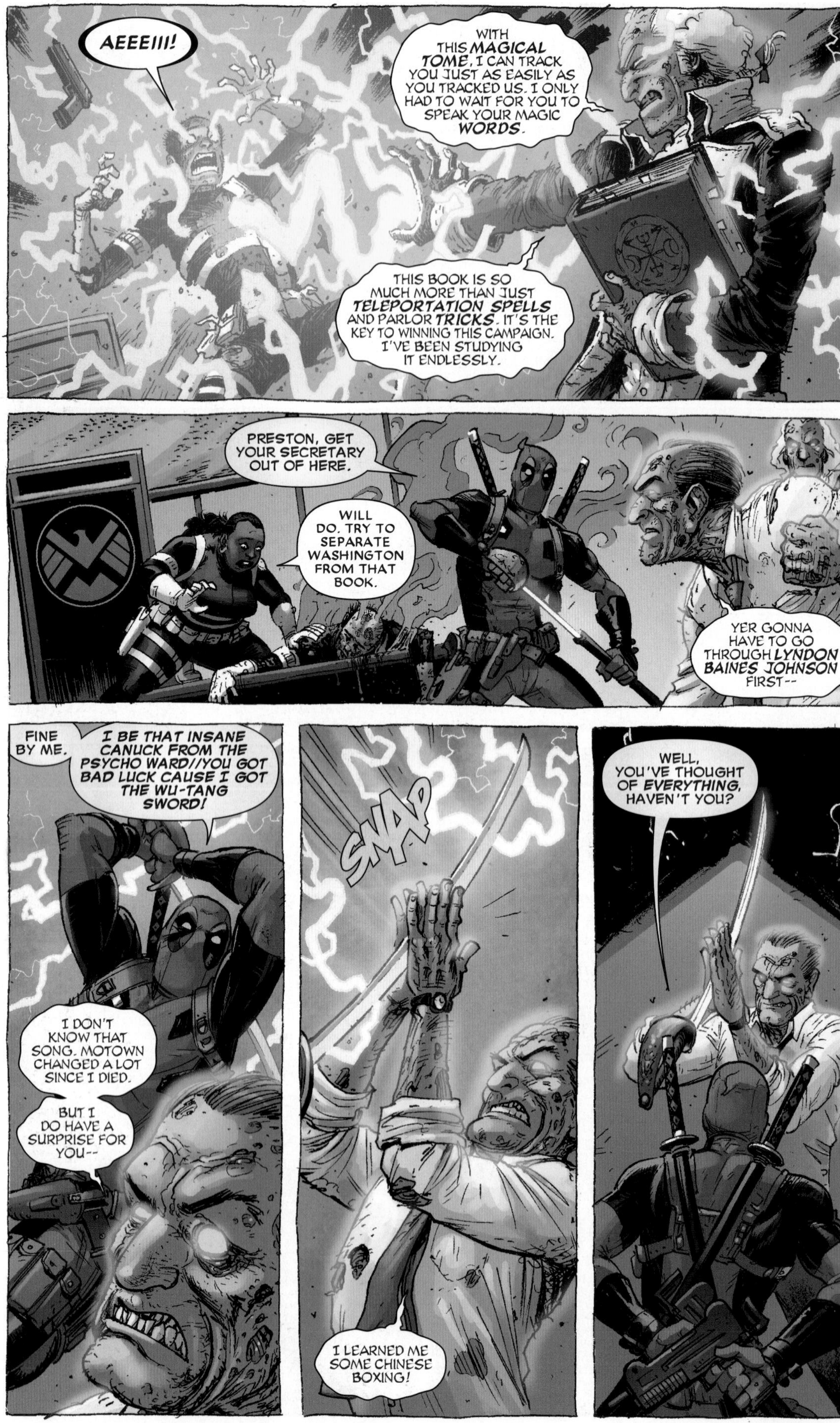
AEEEIII!
WITH THIS MAGICAL TOME, I CAN TRACK YOU JUST AS EASILY AS YOU TRACKED US. I ONLY HAD TO WAIT FOR YOU TO SPEAK YOUR MAGIC WORDS.
THIS BOOK IS SO MUCH MORE THAN JUST TELEPORTATION SPELLS AND PARLOR TRICKS. IT'S THE KEY TO WINNING THIS CAMPAIGN. I'VE BEEN STUDYING IT ENDLESSLY.
PRESTON, GET YOUR SECRETARY OUT OF HERE.
WILL DO. TRY TO SEPARATE WASHINGTON FROM THAT BOOK.
YER GONNA HAVE TO GO THROUGH LYNDON BAINES JOHNSON FIRST--
FINE BY ME.
I BE THAT INSANE CANUCK FROM THE PSYCHO WARD//YOU GOT BAD LUCK CAUSE I GOT THE WU-TANG SWORD!
I DON'T KNOW THAT SONG. MOTOWN CHANGED A LOT SINCE I DIED.
BUT I DO HAVE A SURPRISE FOR YOU--
SNAP
I LEARNED ME SOME CHINESE BOXING!
WELL, YOU'VE THOUGHT OF EVERYTHING, HAVEN'T YOU?

CATCH *THESE.*

BLAM BLAM

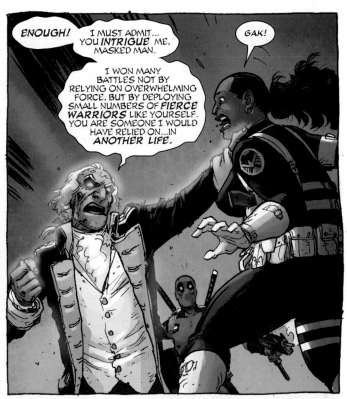

ENOUGH! I MUST ADMIT... YOU *INTRIGUE* ME, MASKED MAN.

GAK!

I WON MANY BATTLES NOT BY RELYING ON OVERWHELMING FORCE, BUT BY DEPLOYING SMALL NUMBERS OF *FIERCE WARRIORS* LIKE YOURSELF. YOU ARE SOMEONE I WOULD HAVE RELIED ON... IN *ANOTHER LIFE.*

YOU ARE *OUTMATCHED* AND OUT-*MANEUVERED.*

SURRENDER. IMMEDIATELY.

OKAY, JUST DON'T *HURT* HER.

NO, DEADPOOL!

÷COUGH÷

OH, I PROMISE... SHE WON'T *FEEL* A THING.

NO.

WADE, FINISH THIS UGLY, UNDEAD, WOODEN-TEETH-HAVING *MOTHER--*

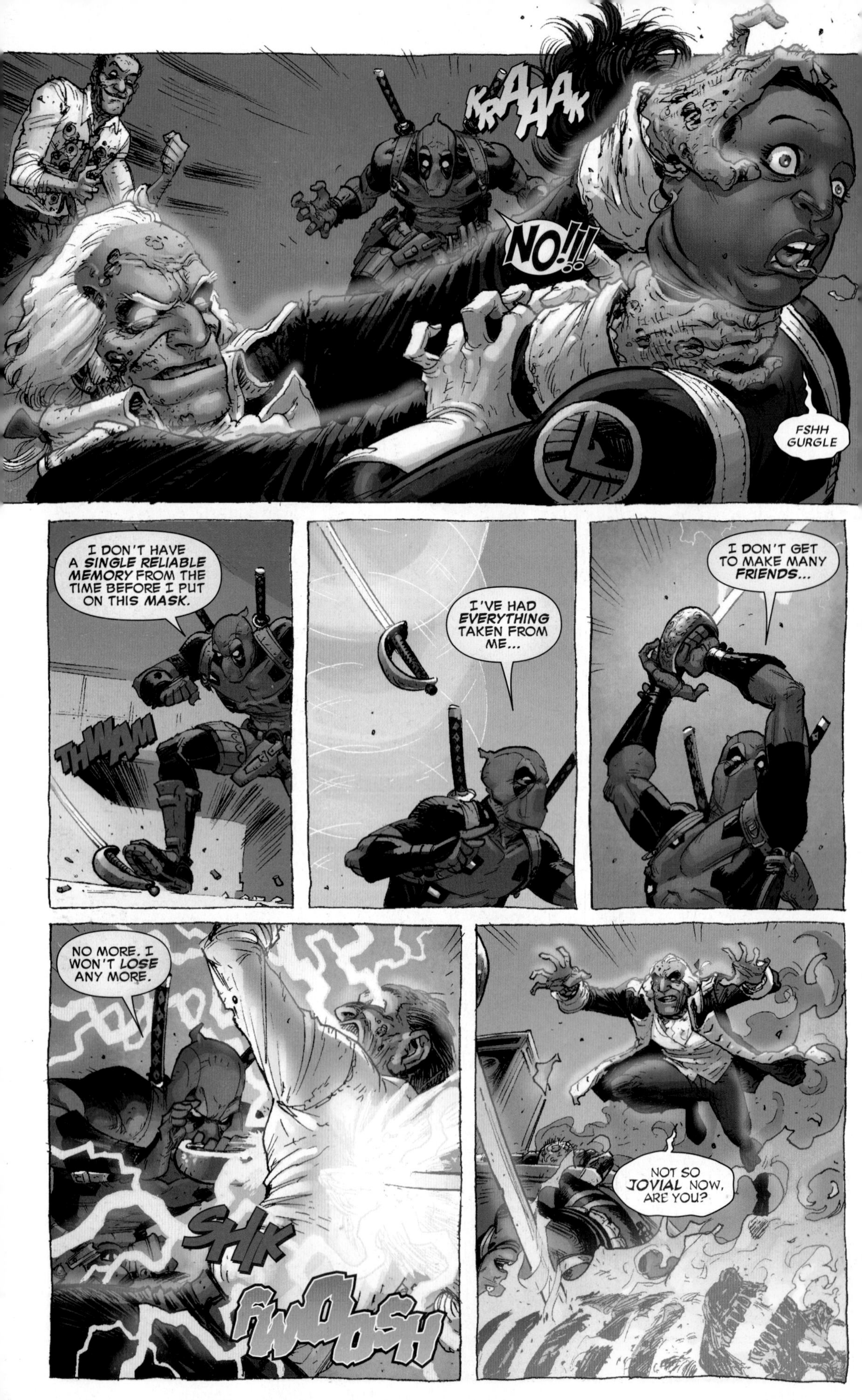
KRAAAK
NO!!!
FSHH GURGLE
I DON'T HAVE A SINGLE RELIABLE MEMORY FROM THE TIME BEFORE I PUT ON THIS MASK.
THWAM
I'VE HAD EVERYTHING TAKEN FROM ME...
I DON'T GET TO MAKE MANY FRIENDS...
NO MORE. I WON'T LOSE ANY MORE.
SHK
FWOOSH
NOT SO JOVIAL NOW, ARE YOU?

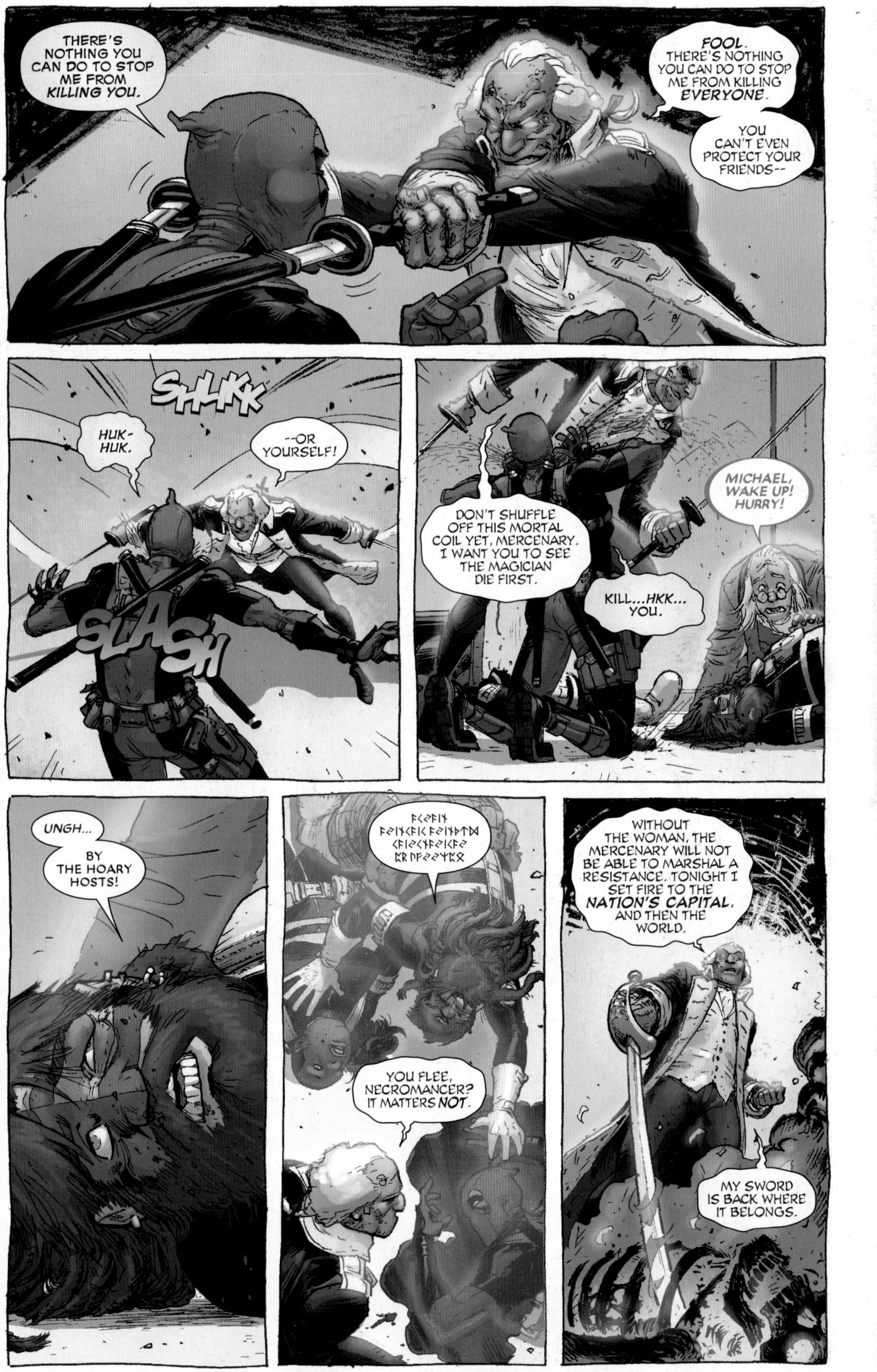
THERE'S NOTHING YOU CAN DO TO STOP ME FROM KILLING YOU.
FOOL. THERE'S NOTHING YOU CAN DO TO STOP ME FROM KILLING EVERYONE.
YOU CAN'T EVEN PROTECT YOUR FRIENDS--
SHLIKK
HUK-HUK.
--OR YOURSELF!
SLASH
DON'T SHUFFLE OFF THIS MORTAL COIL YET, MERCENARY. I WANT YOU TO SEE THE MAGICIAN DIE FIRST.
KILL...HKK... YOU.
MICHAEL, WAKE UP! HURRY!
UNGH...
BY THE HOARY HOSTS!
YOU FLEE, NECROMANCER? IT MATTERS NOT.
WITHOUT THE WOMAN, THE MERCENARY WILL NOT BE ABLE TO MARSHAL A RESISTANCE. TONIGHT I SET FIRE TO THE NATION'S CAPITAL, AND THEN THE WORLD.
MY SWORD IS BACK WHERE IT BELONGS.

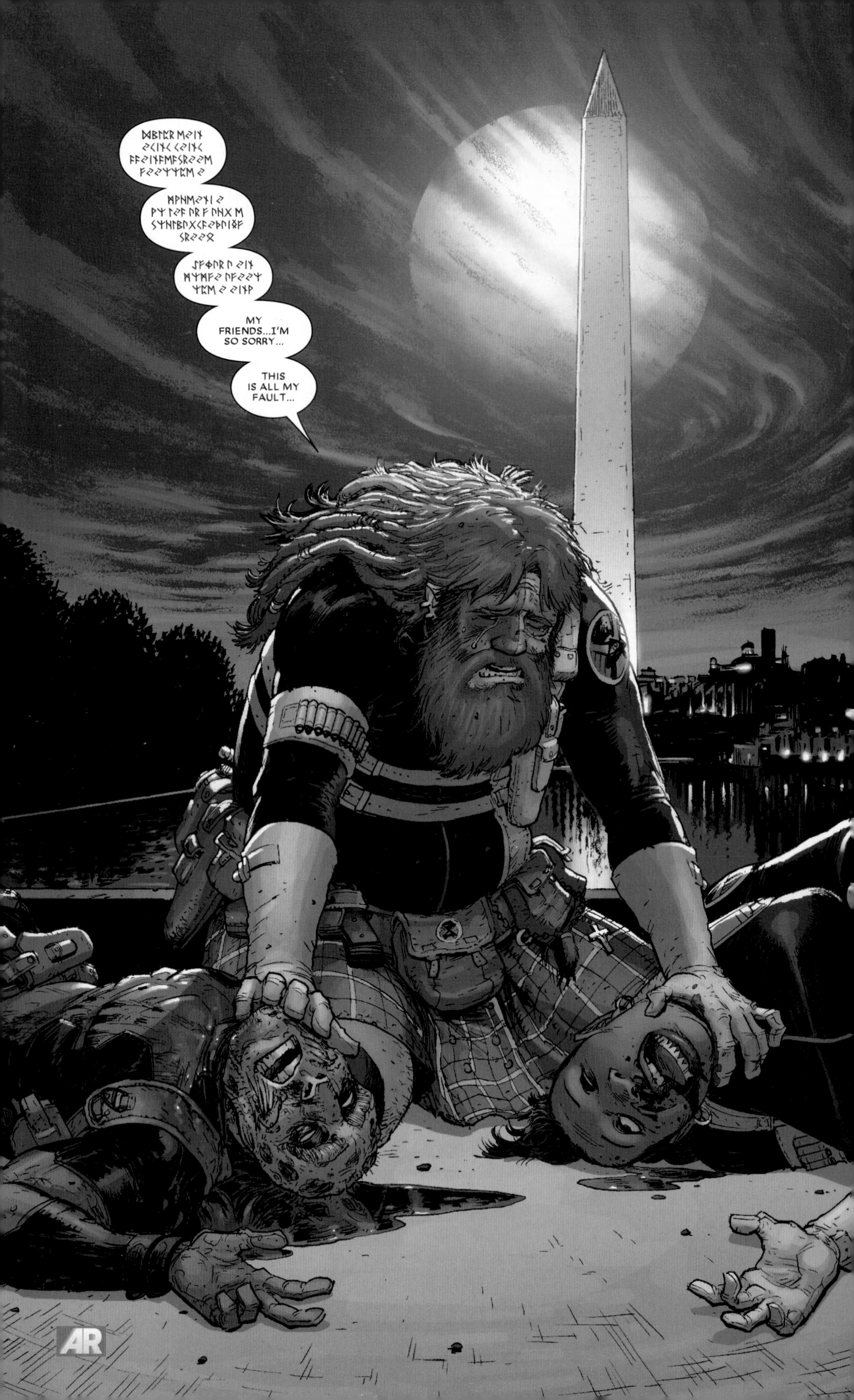
MY FRIENDS...I'M SO SORRY...
THIS IS ALL MY FAULT...

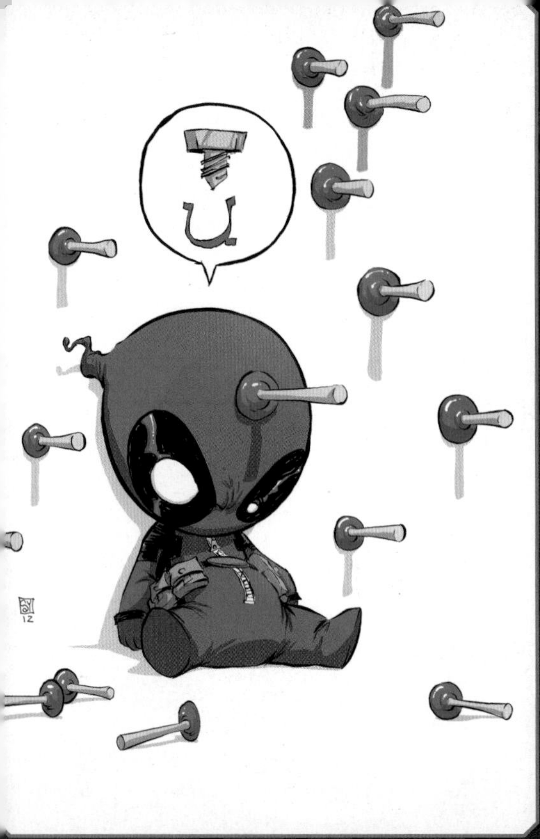

#1 VARIANT
BY SKOTTIE YOUNG

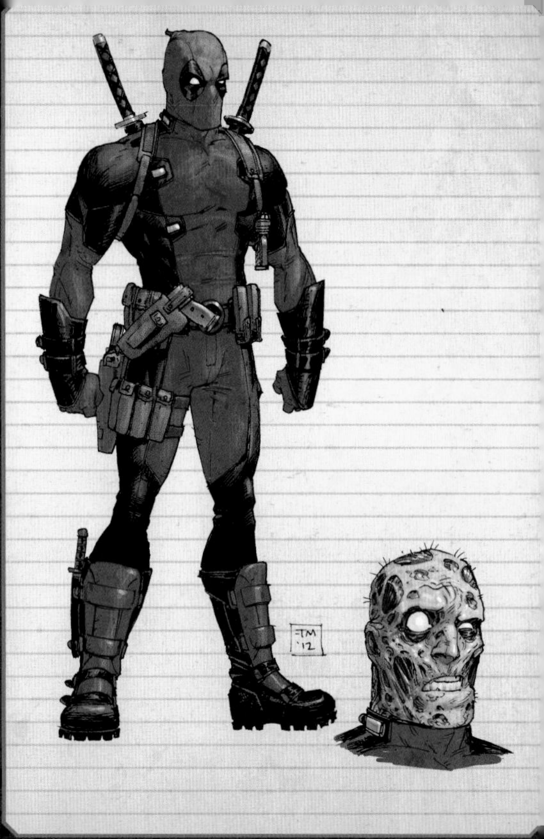

#1 DESIGN VARIANT
BY TONY MOORE

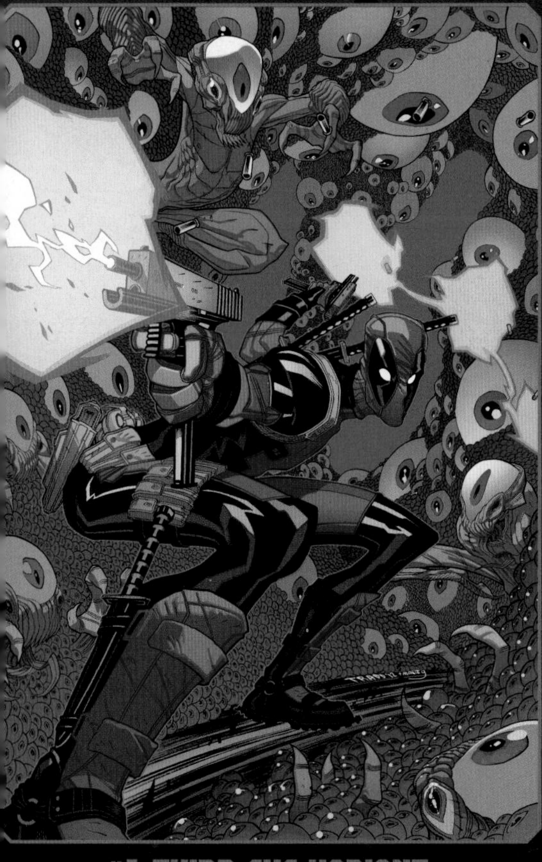

#1 THIRD EYE VARIANT

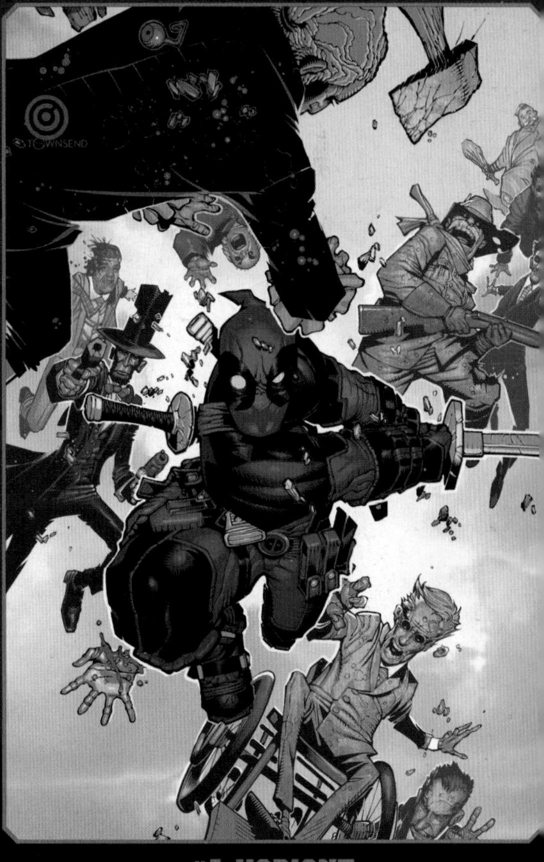

#1 VARIANT

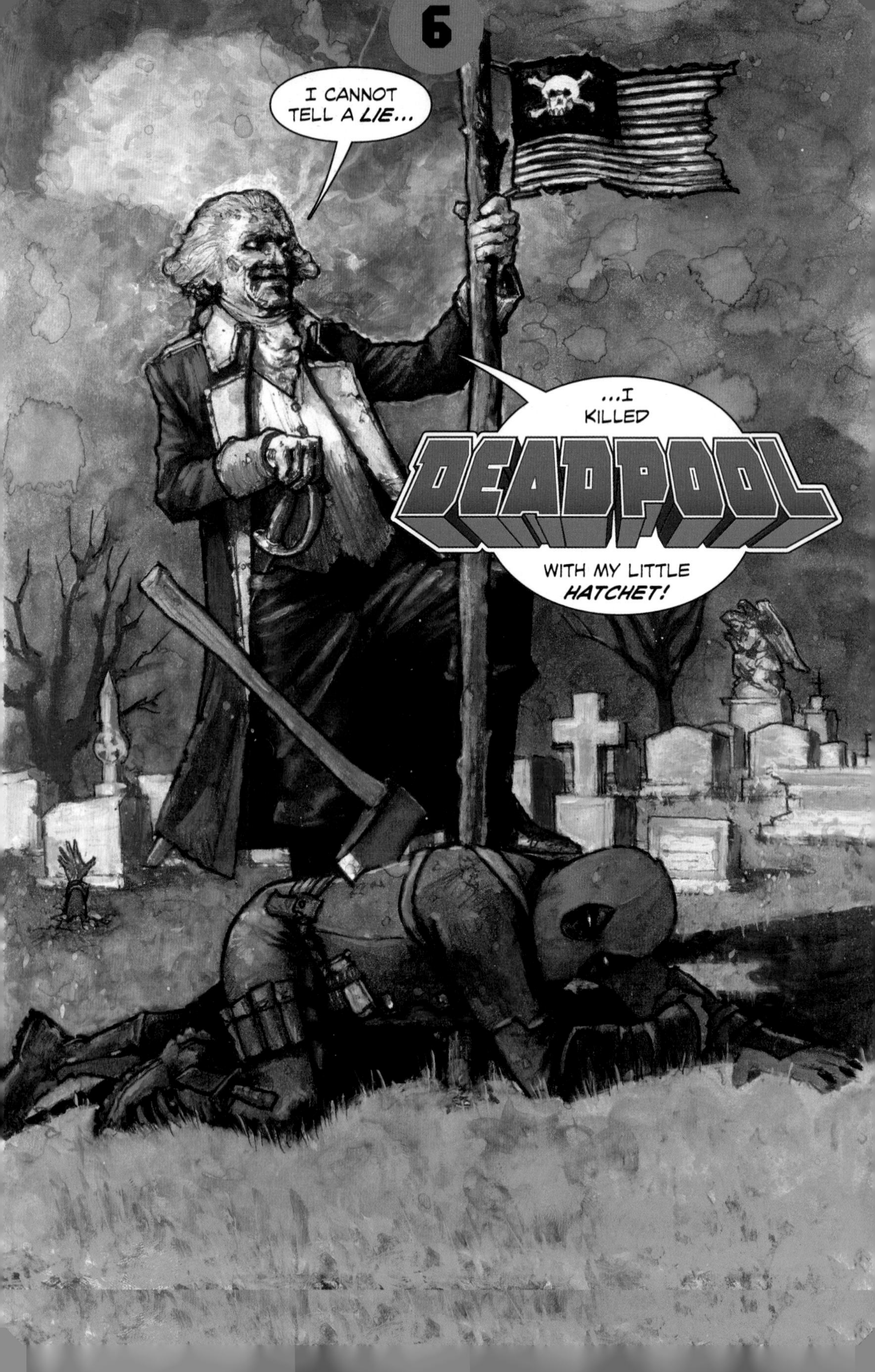
6
I CANNOT TELL A LIE...
...I KILLED DEADPOOL WITH MY LITTLE HATCHET!

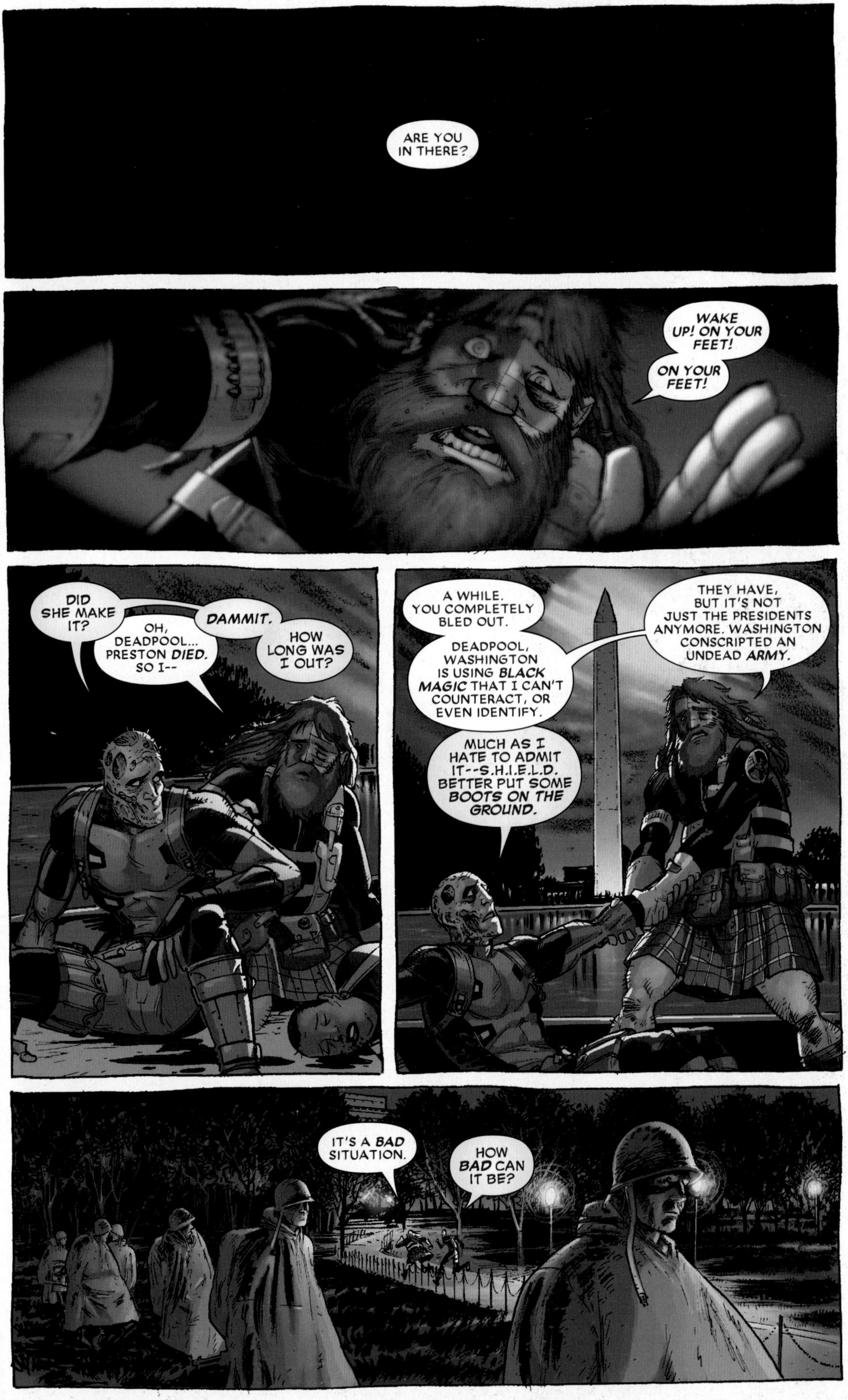
ARE YOU IN THERE?
WAKE UP! ON YOUR FEET!
ON YOUR FEET!
DID SHE MAKE IT?
OH, DEADPOOL... PRESTON DIED. SO I--
DAMMIT.
HOW LONG WAS I OUT?
A WHILE. YOU COMPLETELY BLED OUT.
DEADPOOL, WASHINGTON IS USING BLACK MAGIC THAT I CAN'T COUNTERACT, OR EVEN IDENTIFY.
MUCH AS I HATE TO ADMIT IT--S.H.I.E.L.D. BETTER PUT SOME BOOTS ON THE GROUND.
THEY HAVE, BUT IT'S NOT JUST THE PRESIDENTS ANYMORE. WASHINGTON CONSCRIPTED AN UNDEAD ARMY.
IT'S A BAD SITUATION.
HOW BAD CAN IT BE?

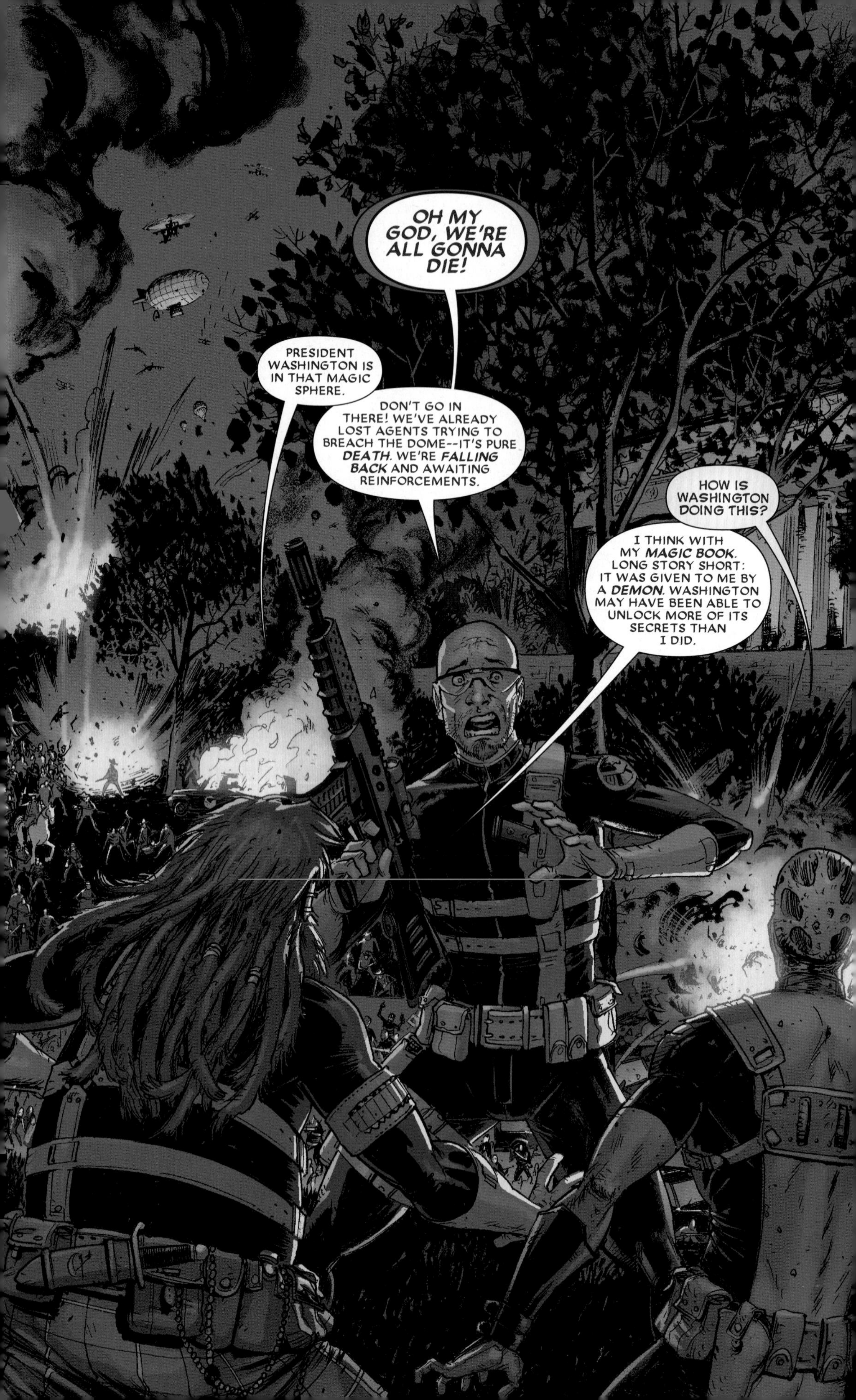
OH MY GOD, WE'RE ALL GONNA DIE!
PRESIDENT WASHINGTON IS IN THAT MAGIC SPHERE.
DON'T GO IN THERE! WE'VE ALREADY LOST AGENTS TRYING TO BREACH THE DOME--IT'S PURE DEATH. WE'RE FALLING BACK AND AWAITING REINFORCEMENTS.
HOW IS WASHINGTON DOING THIS?
I THINK WITH MY MAGIC BOOK. LONG STORY SHORT: IT WAS GIVEN TO ME BY A DEMON. WASHINGTON MAY HAVE BEEN ABLE TO UNLOCK MORE OF ITS SECRETS THAN I DID.

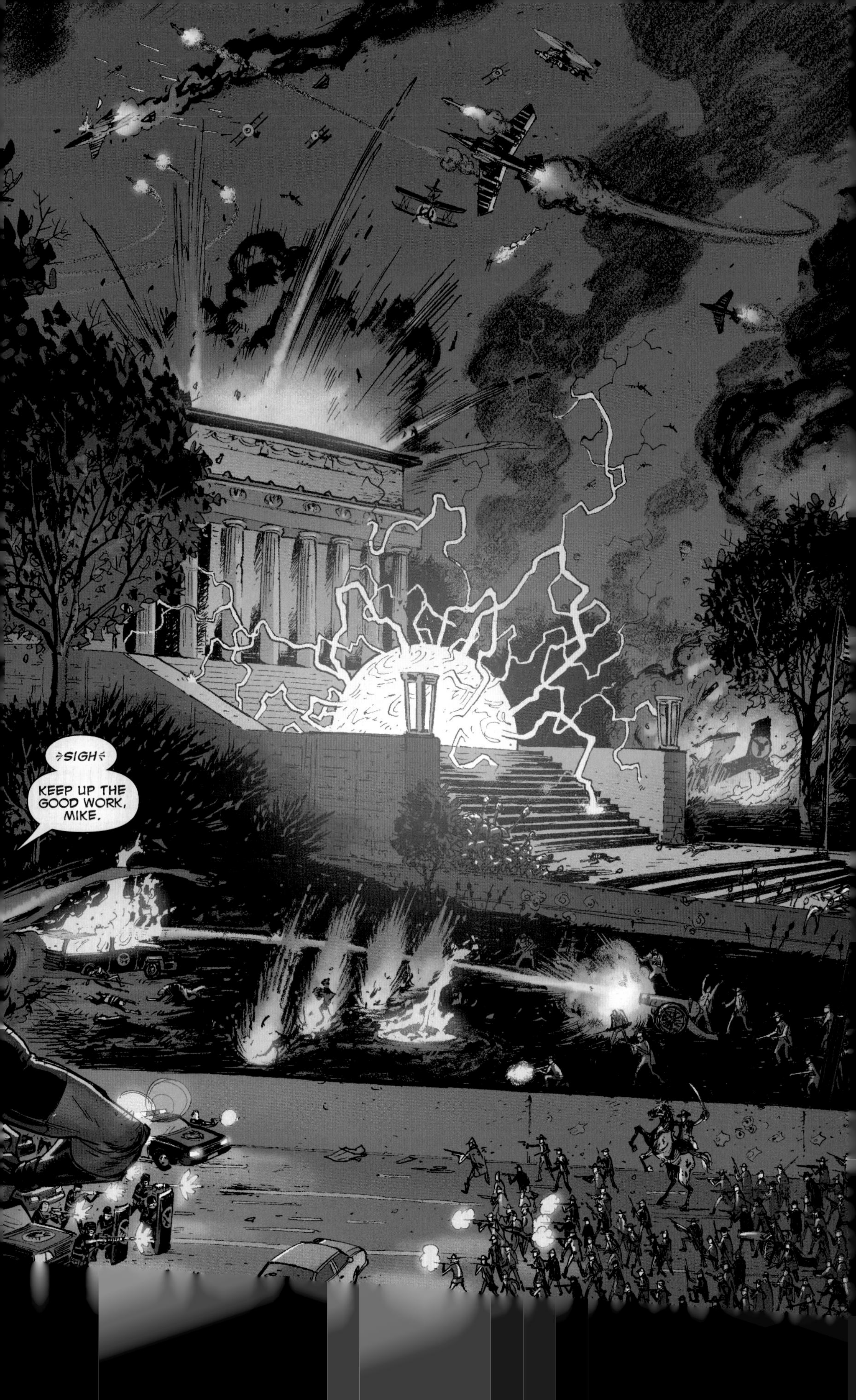
SIGH
KEEP UP THE GOOD WORK, MIKE.

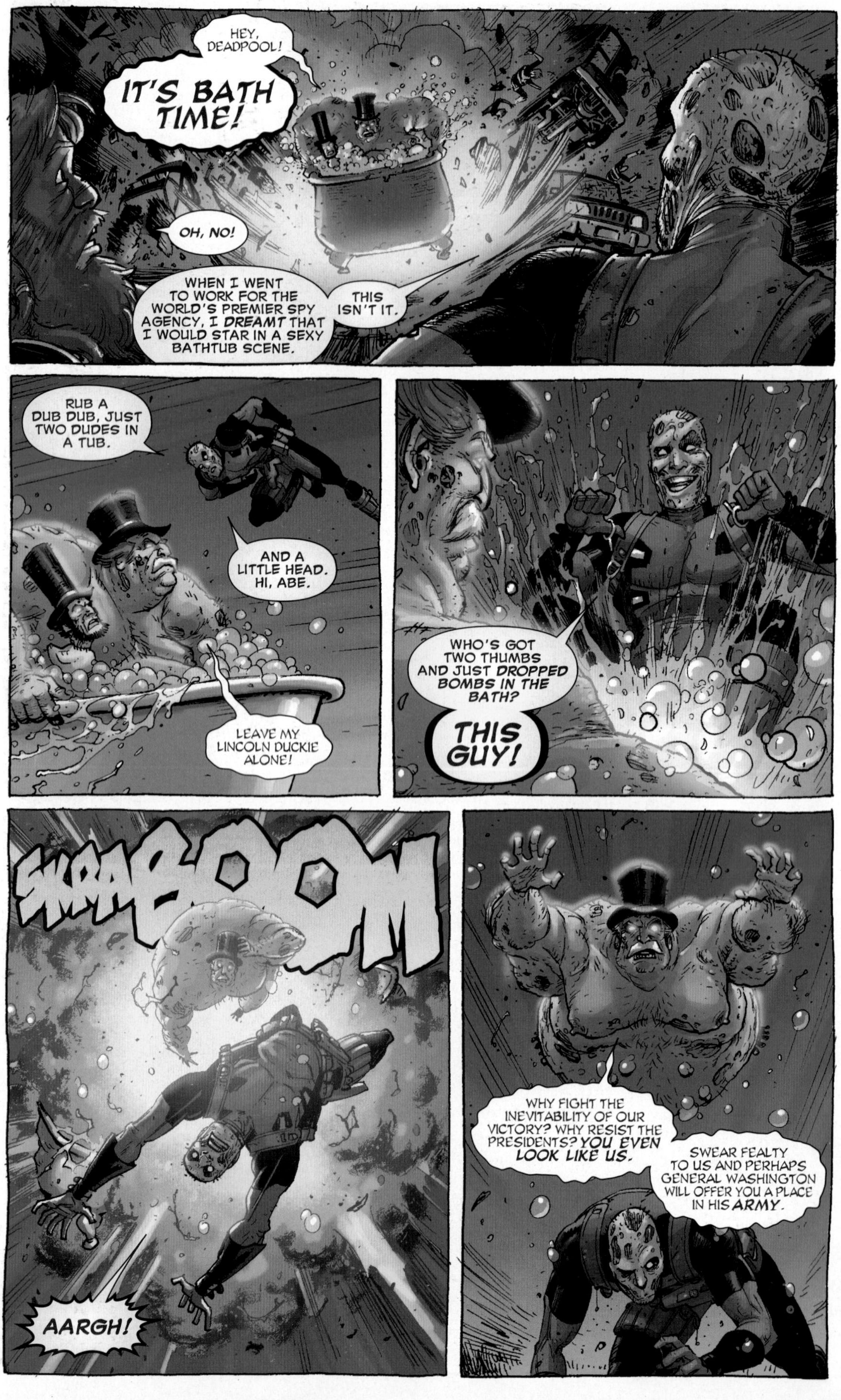
HEY, DEADPOOL!
IT'S BATH TIME!
OH, NO!
WHEN I WENT TO WORK FOR THE WORLD'S PREMIER SPY AGENCY, I DREAMT THAT I WOULD STAR IN A SEXY BATHTUB SCENE.
THIS ISN'T IT.
RUB A DUB DUB, JUST TWO DUDES IN A TUB.
AND A LITTLE HEAD. HI, ABE.
LEAVE MY LINCOLN DUCKIE ALONE!
WHO'S GOT TWO THUMBS AND JUST DROPPED BOMBS IN THE BATH?
THIS GUY!
SKRABOOM
AARGH!
WHY FIGHT THE INEVITABILITY OF OUR VICTORY? WHY RESIST THE PRESIDENTS? YOU EVEN LOOK LIKE US.
SWEAR FEALTY TO US AND PERHAPS GENERAL WASHINGTON WILL OFFER YOU A PLACE IN HIS ARMY.

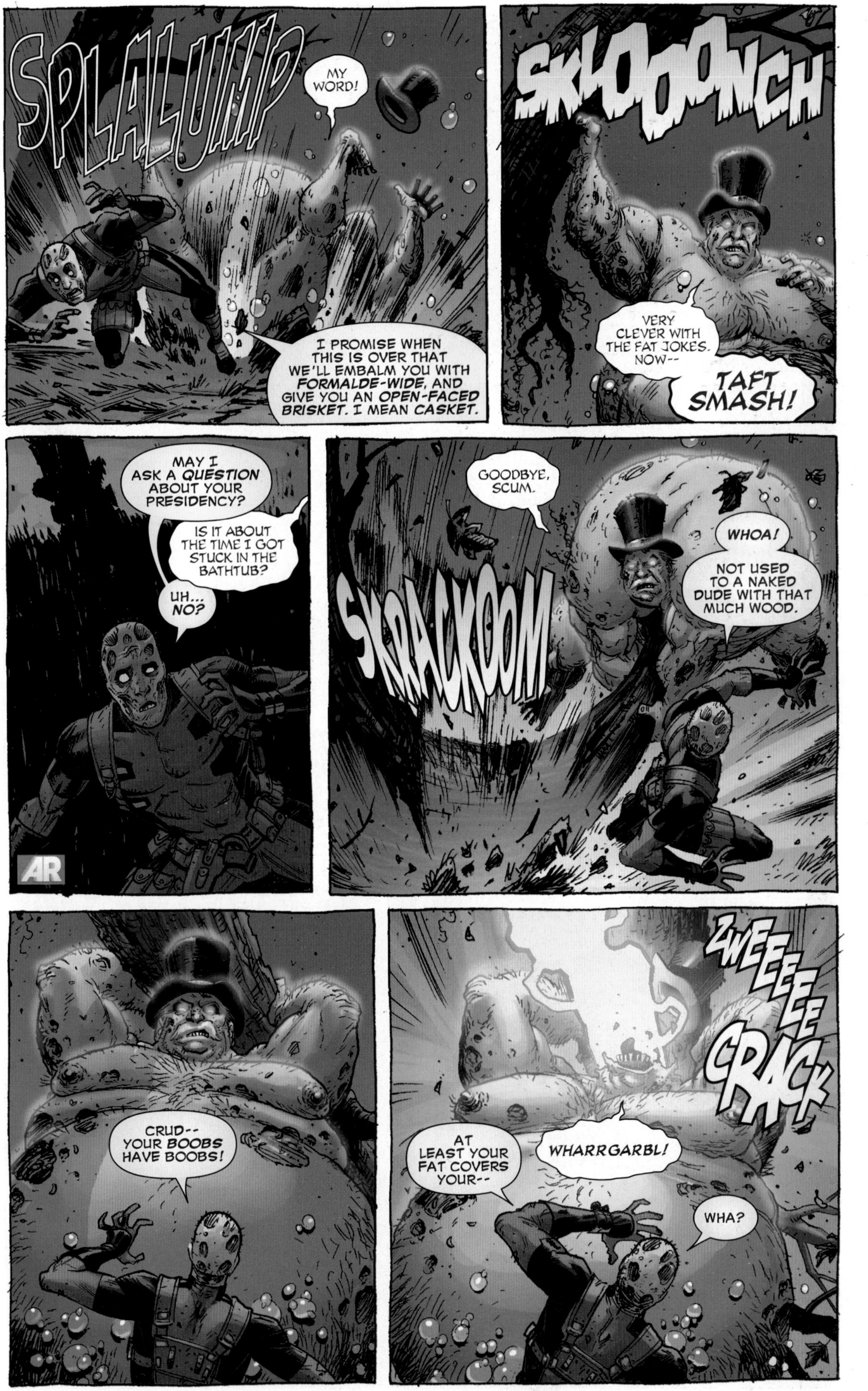
SPLALUMP
MY WORD!
I PROMISE WHEN THIS IS OVER THAT WE'LL EMBALM YOU WITH FORMALDE-WIDE, AND GIVE YOU AN OPEN-FACED BRISKET. I MEAN CASKET.
SKLOOONCH
VERY CLEVER WITH THE FAT JOKES. NOW--
TAFT SMASH!
MAY I ASK A QUESTION ABOUT YOUR PRESIDENCY?
IS IT ABOUT THE TIME I GOT STUCK IN THE BATHTUB?
UH... NO?
GOODBYE, SCUM.
SKRACKOOM
WHOA!
NOT USED TO A NAKED DUDE WITH THAT MUCH WOOD.
CRUD-- YOUR BOOBS HAVE BOOBS!
ZWEEEEEE CRACK
AT LEAST YOUR FAT COVERS YOUR--
WHARRGARBL!
WHA?

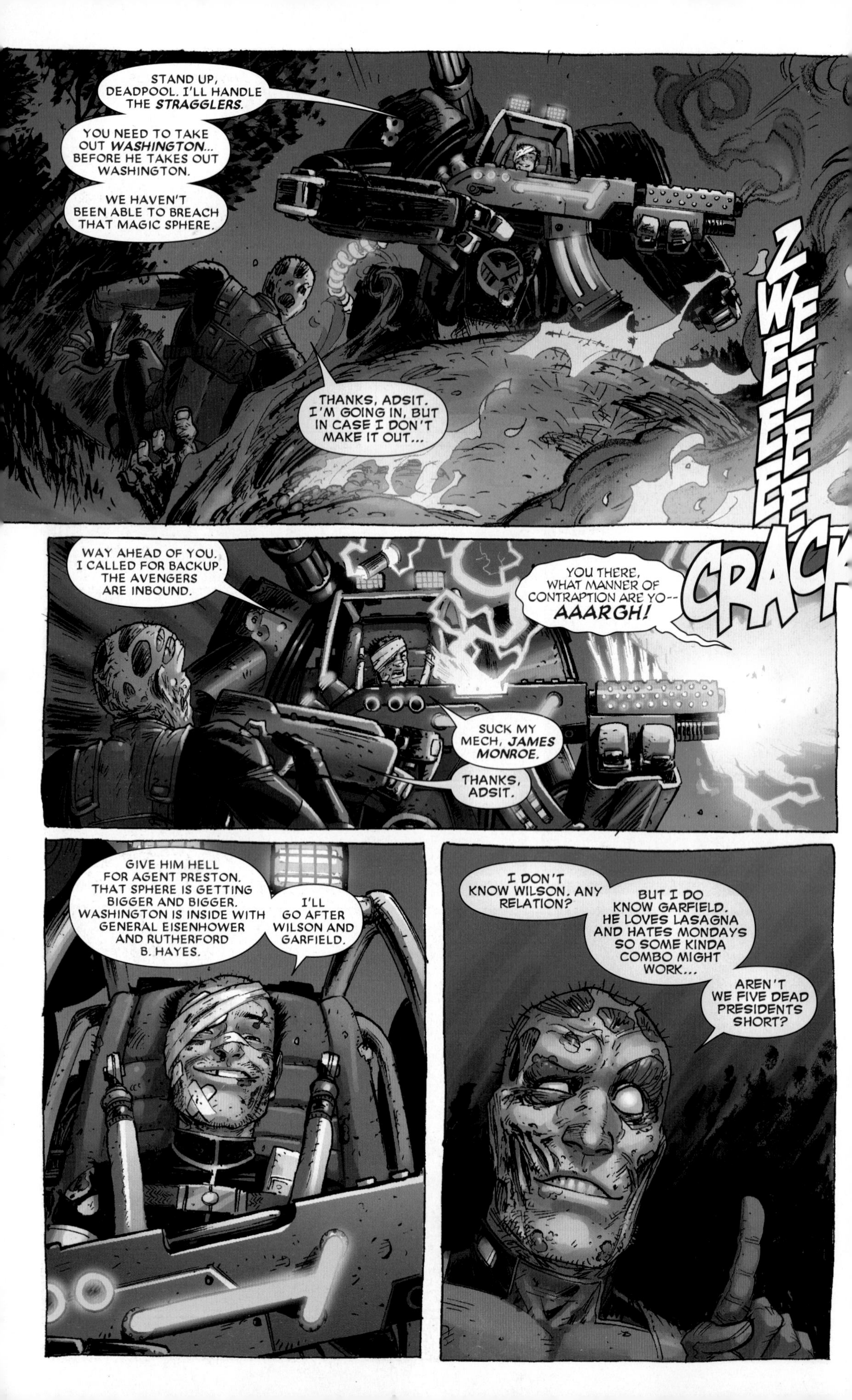

STAND UP, DEADPOOL. I'LL HANDLE THE STRAGGLERS.
YOU NEED TO TAKE OUT WASHINGTON... BEFORE HE TAKES OUT WASHINGTON.
WE HAVEN'T BEEN ABLE TO BREACH THAT MAGIC SPHERE.
THANKS, ADSIT. I'M GOING IN, BUT IN CASE I DON'T MAKE IT OUT...
ZWEEEEEEEEEE
CRACK
WAY AHEAD OF YOU. I CALLED FOR BACKUP. THE AVENGERS ARE INBOUND.
YOU THERE, WHAT MANNER OF CONTRAPTION ARE YO-- AAARGH!
SUCK MY MECH, JAMES MONROE.
THANKS, ADSIT.
GIVE HIM HELL FOR AGENT PRESTON. THAT SPHERE IS GETTING BIGGER AND BIGGER. WASHINGTON IS INSIDE WITH GENERAL EISENHOWER AND RUTHERFORD B. HAYES.
I'LL GO AFTER WILSON AND GARFIELD.
I DON'T KNOW WILSON. ANY RELATION?
BUT I DO KNOW GARFIELD. HE LOVES LASAGNA AND HATES MONDAYS SO SOME KINDA COMBO MIGHT WORK...
AREN'T WE FIVE DEAD PRESIDENTS SHORT?

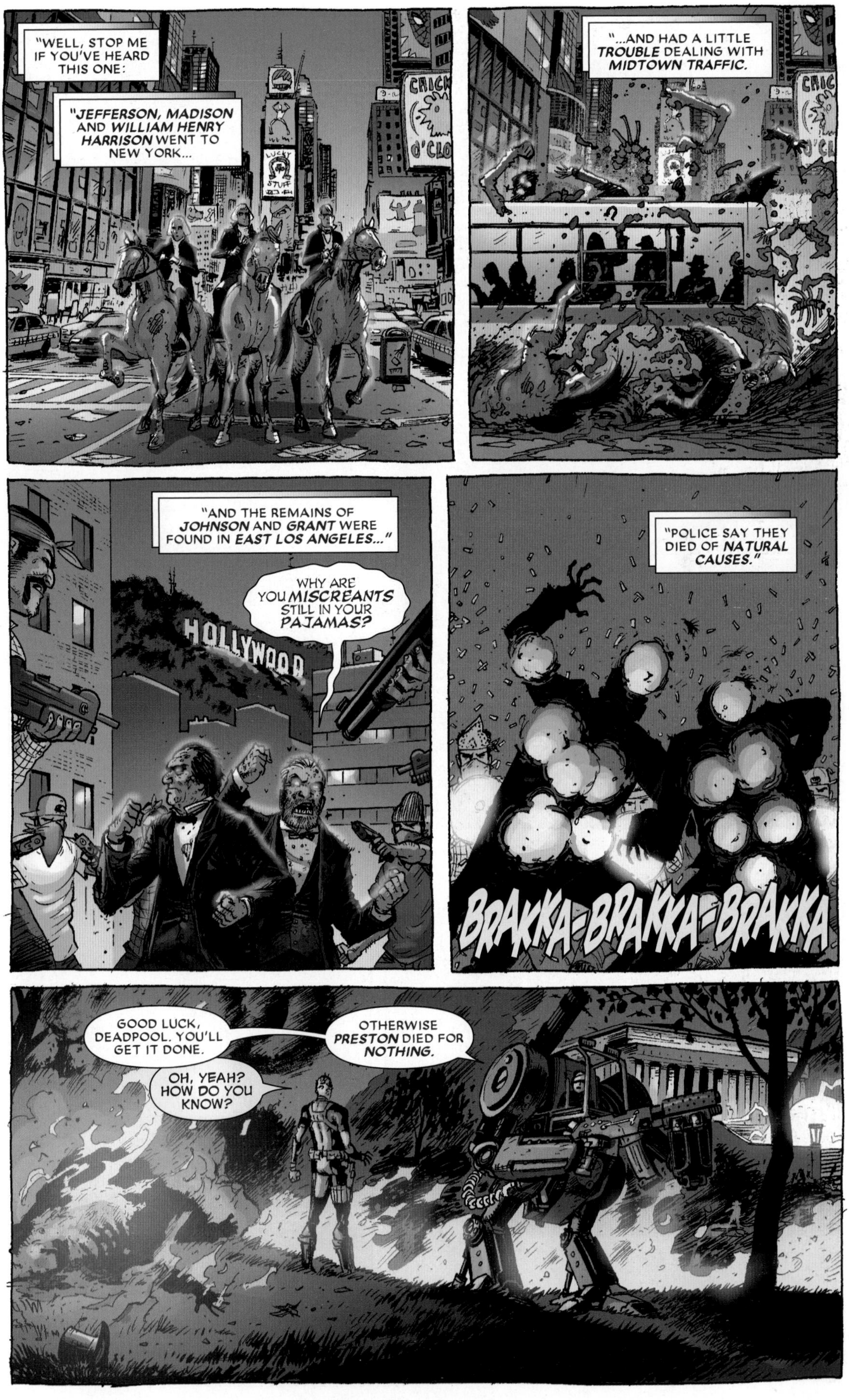
"WELL, STOP ME IF YOU'VE HEARD THIS ONE:
"JEFFERSON, MADISON AND WILLIAM HENRY HARRISON WENT TO NEW YORK...
LUCKY STUFF
"...AND HAD A LITTLE TROUBLE DEALING WITH MIDTOWN TRAFFIC.
"AND THE REMAINS OF JOHNSON AND GRANT WERE FOUND IN EAST LOS ANGELES..."
WHY ARE YOU MISCREANTS STILL IN YOUR PAJAMAS?
HOLLYWOOD
"POLICE SAY THEY DIED OF NATURAL CAUSES."
BRAKKA-BRAKKA-BRAKKA
GOOD LUCK, DEADPOOL. YOU'LL GET IT DONE.
OTHERWISE PRESTON DIED FOR NOTHING.
OH, YEAH? HOW DO YOU KNOW?

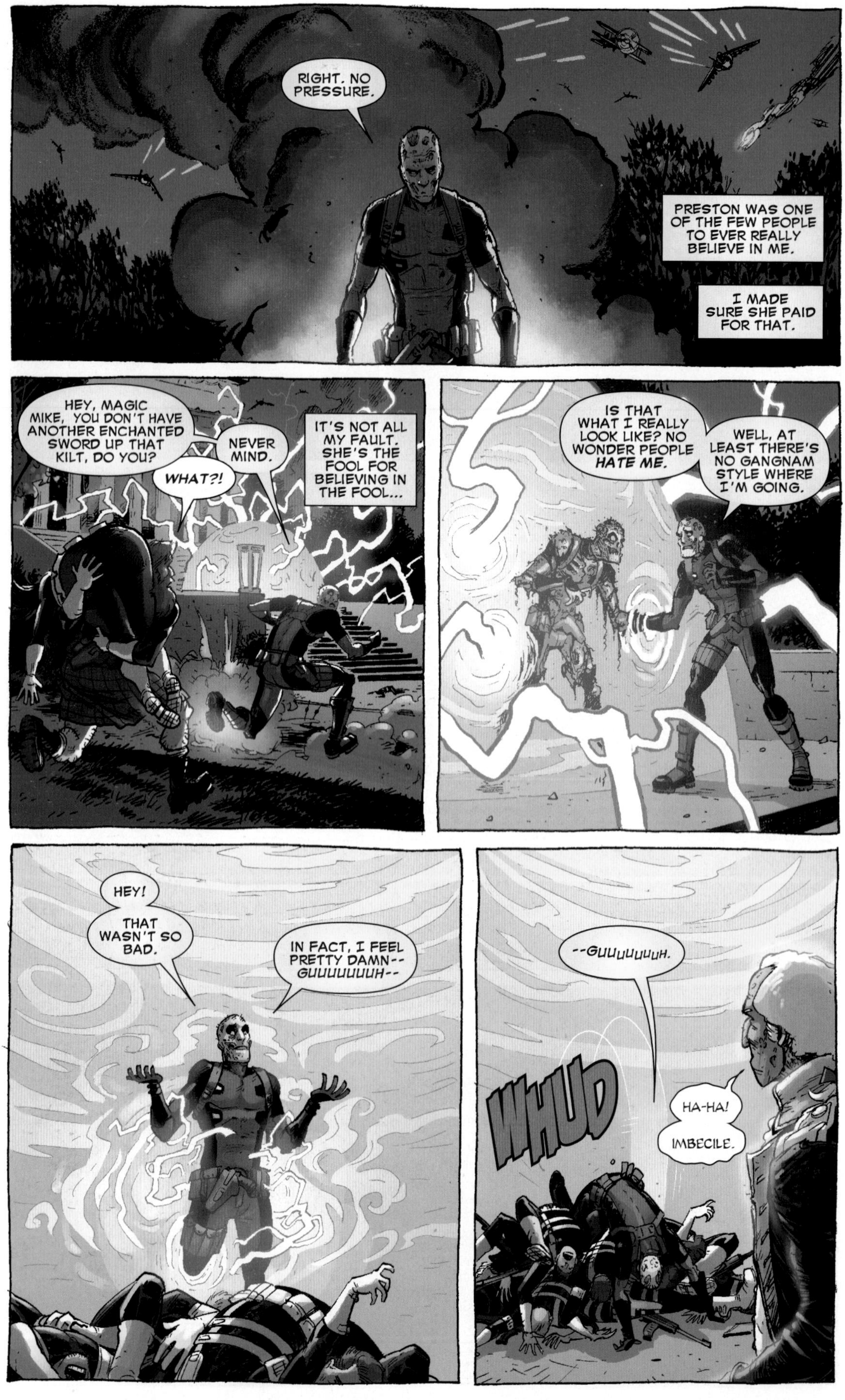
RIGHT. NO PRESSURE.
PRESTON WAS ONE OF THE FEW PEOPLE TO EVER REALLY BELIEVE IN ME.
I MADE SURE SHE PAID FOR THAT.
HEY, MAGIC MIKE, YOU DON'T HAVE ANOTHER ENCHANTED SWORD UP THAT KILT, DO YOU?
WHAT?!
NEVER MIND.
IT'S NOT ALL MY FAULT. SHE'S THE FOOL FOR BELIEVING IN THE FOOL...
IS THAT WHAT I REALLY LOOK LIKE? NO WONDER PEOPLE HATE ME.
WELL, AT LEAST THERE'S NO GANGNAM STYLE WHERE I'M GOING.
HEY!
THAT WASN'T SO BAD.
IN FACT, I FEEL PRETTY DAMN-- GUUUUUUUH--
--GUUuuuuuH.
WHUD
HA-HA!
IMBECILE.

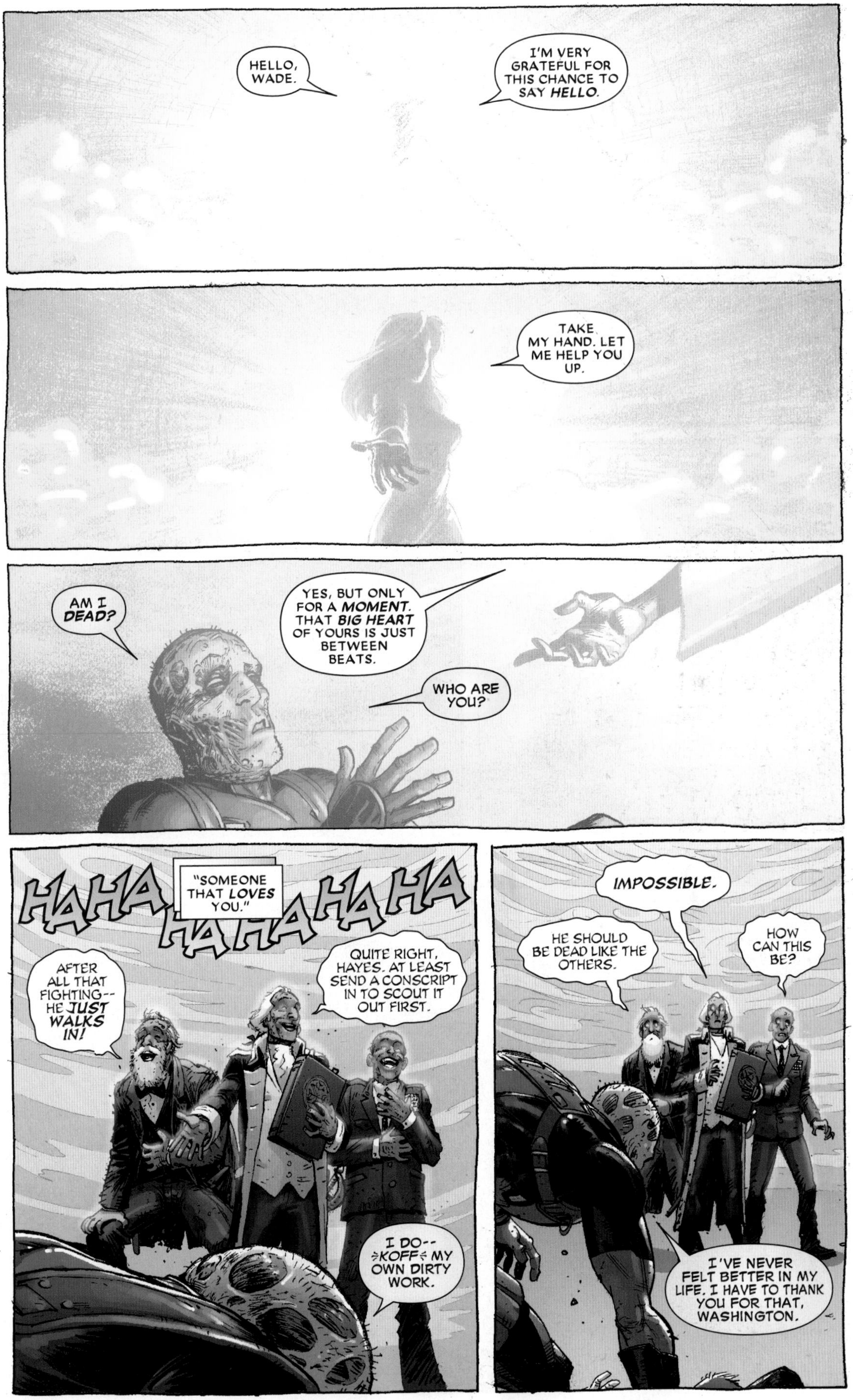
HELLO, WADE.
I'M VERY GRATEFUL FOR THIS CHANCE TO SAY HELLO.
TAKE MY HAND. LET ME HELP YOU UP.
AM I DEAD?
YES, BUT ONLY FOR A MOMENT. THAT BIG HEART OF YOURS IS JUST BETWEEN BEATS.
WHO ARE YOU?
"SOMEONE THAT LOVES YOU."
HAHA HAHAHAHAHA HAHA
AFTER ALL THAT FIGHTING-- HE JUST WALKS IN!
QUITE RIGHT, HAYES. AT LEAST SEND A CONSCRIPT IN TO SCOUT IT OUT FIRST.
I DO-- KOFF MY OWN DIRTY WORK.
IMPOSSIBLE.
HE SHOULD BE DEAD LIKE THE OTHERS.
HOW CAN THIS BE?
I'VE NEVER FELT BETTER IN MY LIFE. I HAVE TO THANK YOU FOR THAT, WASHINGTON.

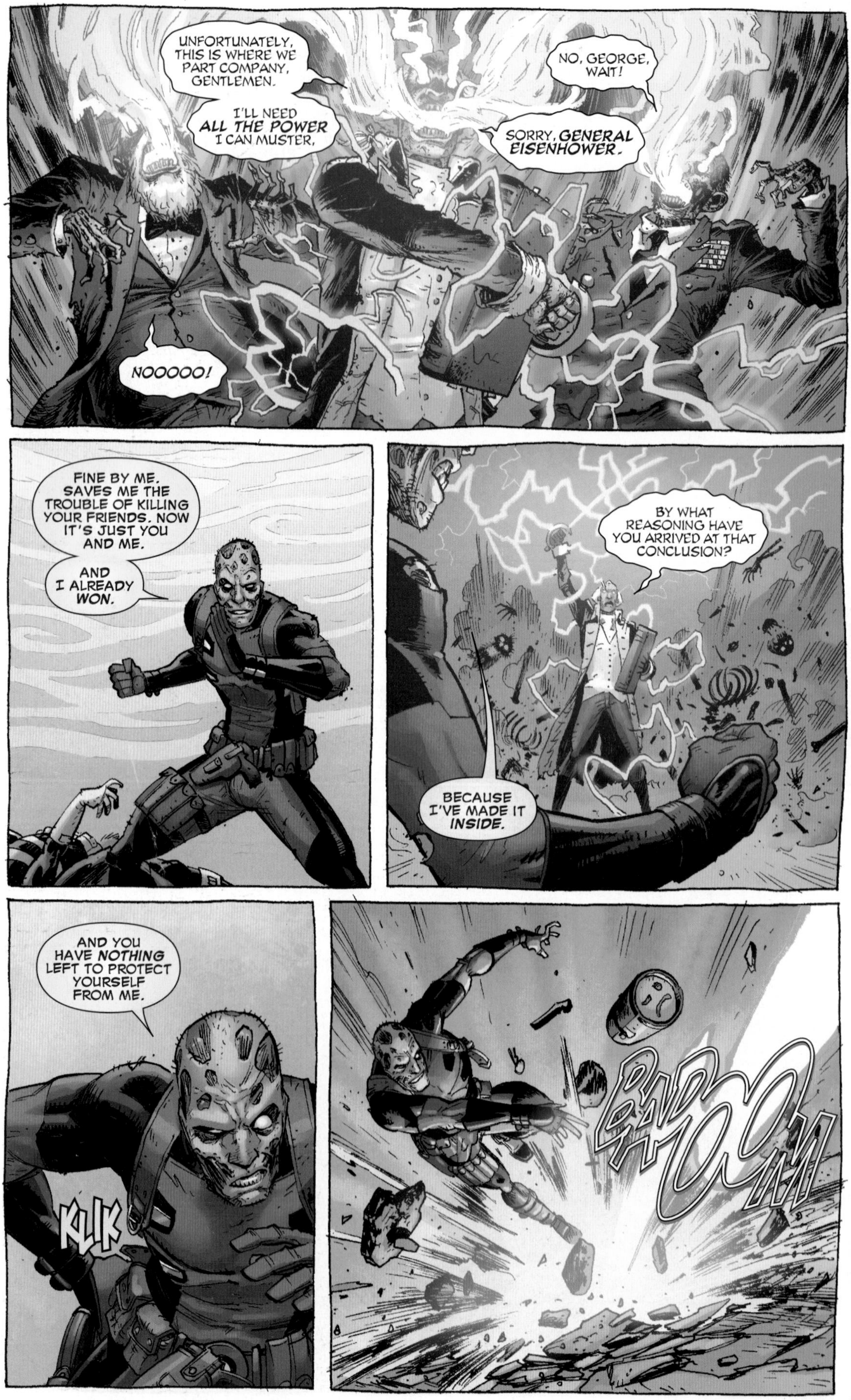
UNFORTUNATELY, THIS IS WHERE WE PART COMPANY, GENTLEMEN.
I'LL NEED ALL THE POWER I CAN MUSTER.
NO, GEORGE, WAIT!
SORRY, GENERAL EISENHOWER.
NOOOOO!
FINE BY ME. SAVES ME THE TROUBLE OF KILLING YOUR FRIENDS. NOW IT'S JUST YOU AND ME.
AND I ALREADY WON.
BY WHAT REASONING HAVE YOU ARRIVED AT THAT CONCLUSION?
BECAUSE I'VE MADE IT INSIDE.
AND YOU HAVE NOTHING LEFT TO PROTECT YOURSELF FROM ME.
KLIK
BADOOOM

I SHALL **BOMBARD** YOU AS I ONCE DID CORNWALLIS.

OH YEAH, DID YOU BORE HIM TO DEATH, TOO?

ᚾ ᚠ ᛋ ᛒᚱᚨᚠᚾᛖᚲ ᛗᛈᚱ ᛗᛋᚱᛖᛦ ᛗᚤᛗ

THERE IS SUCH A THING AS A FATE WORSE THAN DEATH. YOU WILL HAVE NOWHERE TO GO WHEN I KILL YOU ONCE AND FOR ALL. THE ONLY REASON YOU MADE IT INTO THE SPHERE AT ALL IS BECAUSE YOU'RE **DEAD INSIDE.**

THERE IS NOTHING FOR A MAN LIKE YOU. NOWHERE THAT YOU BELONG.

ACTUALLY, I USED TO BELIEVE EVERY WORD YOU JUST SAID. BUT **NOT ANYMORE**--

SHWIK

DAMN YOU!

THIS COUNTRY MADE ITSELF IN YOUR IMAGE--BIG AND TOUGH.

TOUGH ENOUGH TO HANDLE EVEN YOUR RETURN.

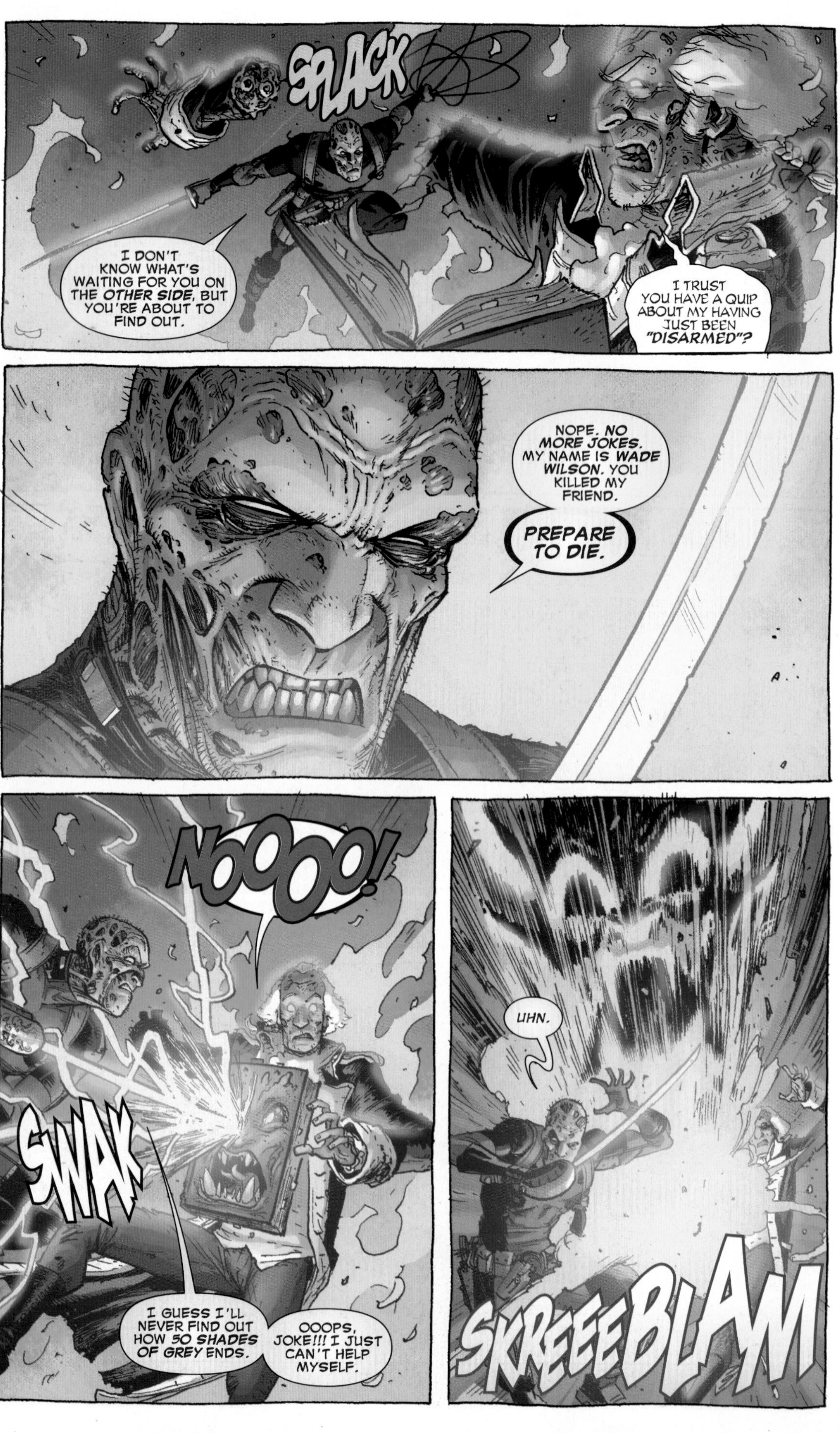
SPLACK
I DON'T KNOW WHAT'S WAITING FOR YOU ON THE OTHER SIDE, BUT YOU'RE ABOUT TO FIND OUT.
I TRUST YOU HAVE A QUIP ABOUT MY HAVING JUST BEEN "DISARMED"?
NOPE. NO MORE JOKES. MY NAME IS WADE WILSON. YOU KILLED MY FRIEND.
PREPARE TO DIE.
NOOOO!
SWAK
I GUESS I'LL NEVER FIND OUT HOW 50 SHADES OF GREY ENDS.
OOOPS, JOKE!!! I JUST CAN'T HELP MYSELF.
UHN.
SKREEEBLAM

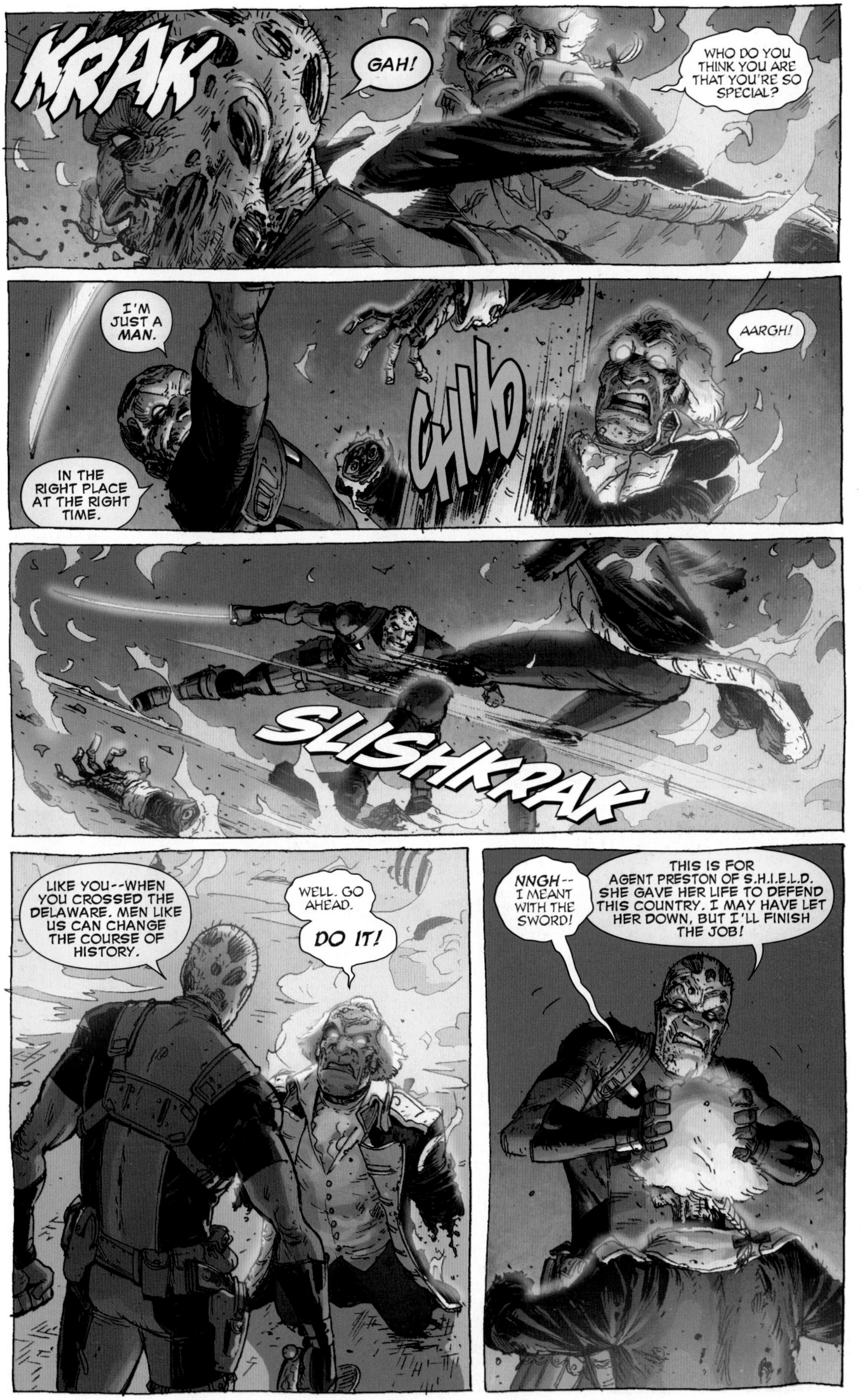
KRAK
GAH!
WHO DO YOU THINK YOU ARE THAT YOU'RE SO SPECIAL?
I'M JUST A MAN.
AARGH!
CHUD
IN THE RIGHT PLACE AT THE RIGHT TIME.
SLISHKRAK
LIKE YOU--WHEN YOU CROSSED THE DELAWARE. MEN LIKE US CAN CHANGE THE COURSE OF HISTORY.
WELL. GO AHEAD.
DO IT!
NNGH--I MEANT WITH THE SWORD!
THIS IS FOR AGENT PRESTON OF S.H.I.E.L.D. SHE GAVE HER LIFE TO DEFEND THIS COUNTRY. I MAY HAVE LET HER DOWN, BUT I'LL FINISH THE JOB!

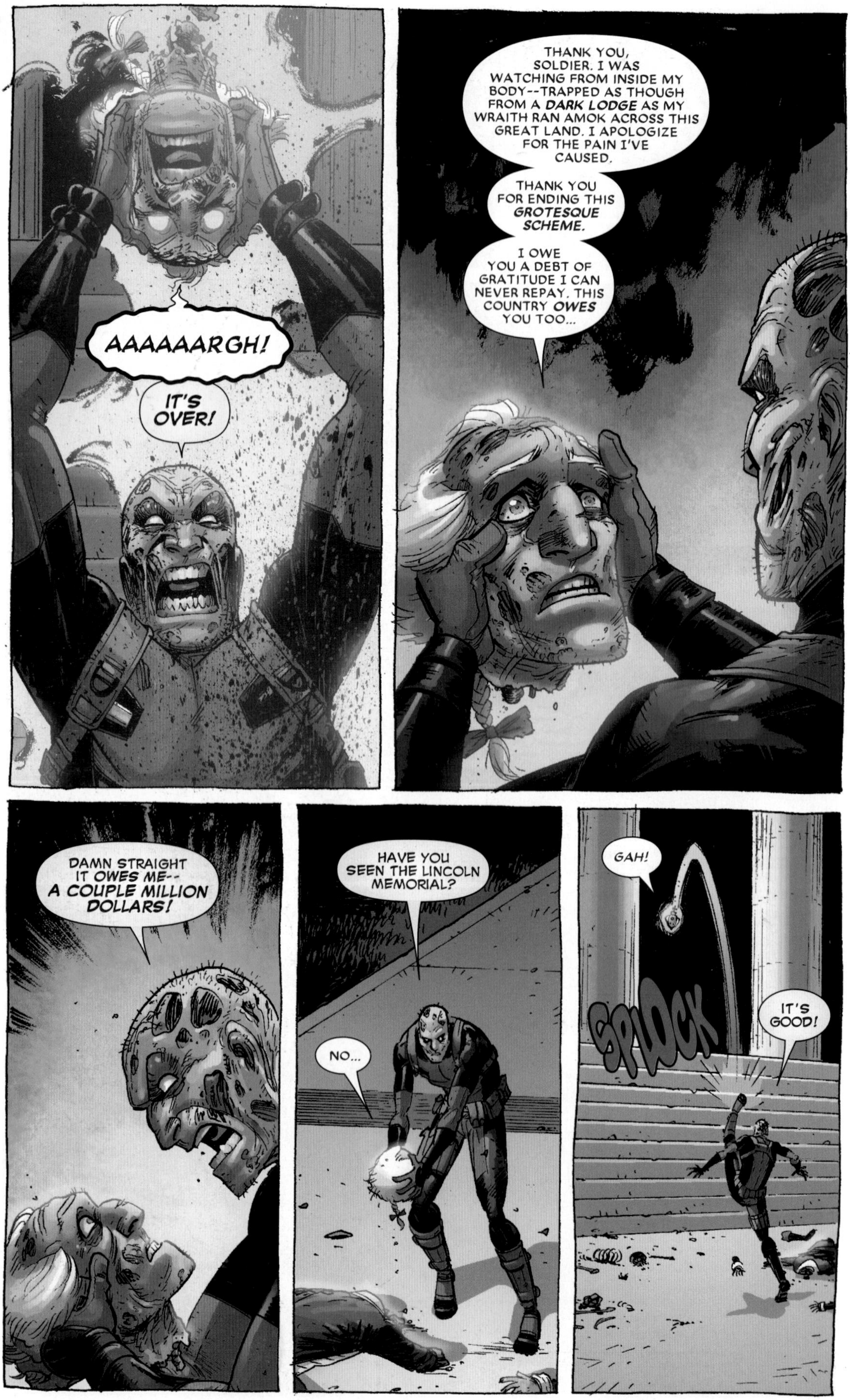
AAAAAAARGH!
IT'S OVER!
THANK YOU, SOLDIER. I WAS WATCHING FROM INSIDE MY BODY--TRAPPED AS THOUGH FROM A DARK LODGE AS MY WRAITH RAN AMOK ACROSS THIS GREAT LAND. I APOLOGIZE FOR THE PAIN I'VE CAUSED.
THANK YOU FOR ENDING THIS GROTESQUE SCHEME.
I OWE YOU A DEBT OF GRATITUDE I CAN NEVER REPAY. THIS COUNTRY OWES YOU TOO...
DAMN STRAIGHT IT OWES ME-- A COUPLE MILLION DOLLARS!
HAVE YOU SEEN THE LINCOLN MEMORIAL?
NO...
GAH!
SPLOCK
IT'S GOOD!

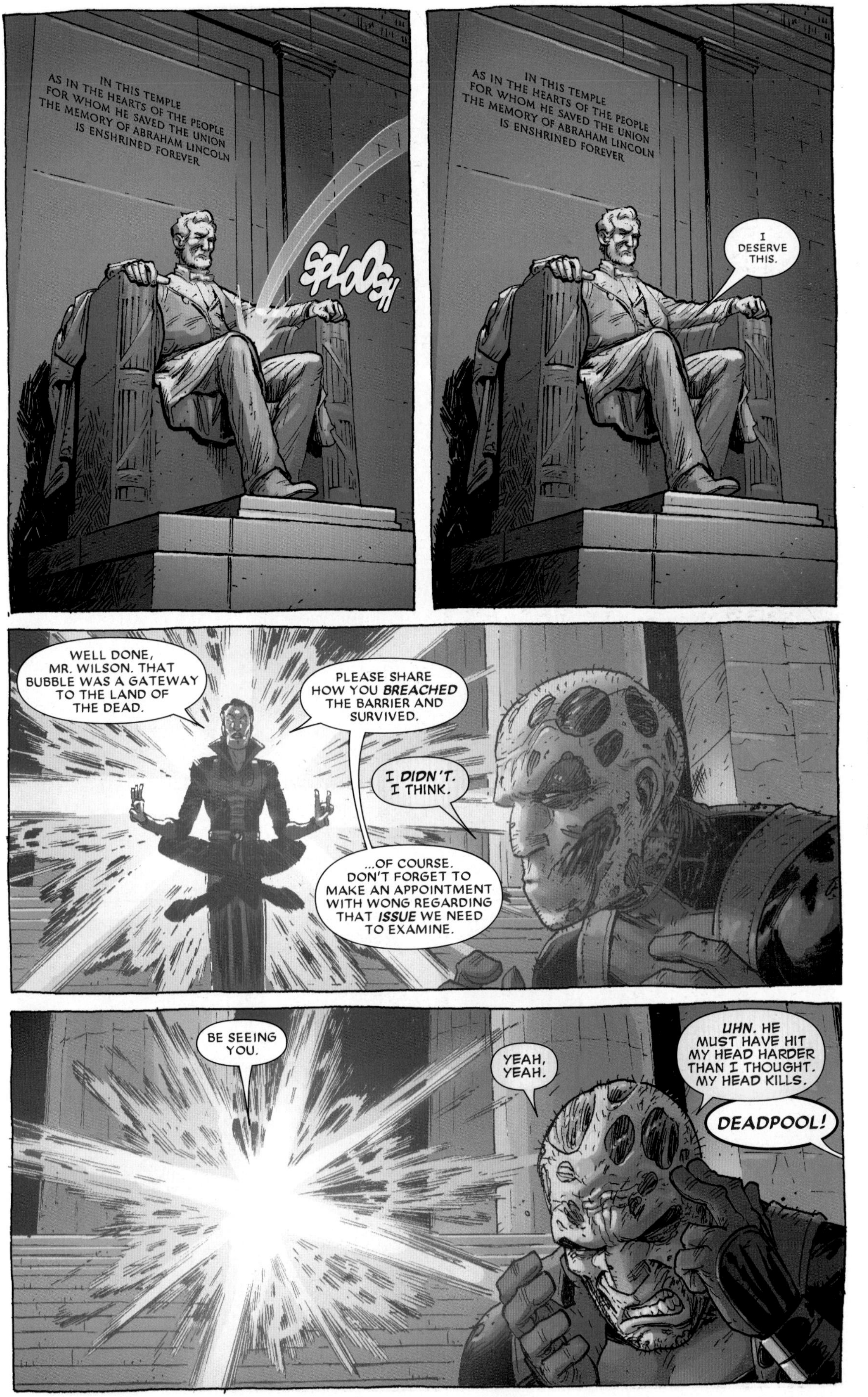
IN THIS TEMPLE
AS IN THE HEARTS OF THE PEOPLE
FOR WHOM HE SAVED THE UNION
THE MEMORY OF ABRAHAM LINCOLN
IS ENSHRINED FOREVER
SPLOOSH
IN THIS TEMPLE
AS IN THE HEARTS OF THE PEOPLE
FOR WHOM HE SAVED THE UNION
THE MEMORY OF ABRAHAM LINCOLN
IS ENSHRINED FOREVER
I DESERVE THIS.
WELL DONE, MR. WILSON. THAT BUBBLE WAS A GATEWAY TO THE LAND OF THE DEAD.
PLEASE SHARE HOW YOU BREACHED THE BARRIER AND SURVIVED.
I DIDN'T. I THINK.
...OF COURSE. DON'T FORGET TO MAKE AN APPOINTMENT WITH WONG REGARDING THAT ISSUE WE NEED TO EXAMINE.
BE SEEING YOU.
YEAH, YEAH.
UHN. HE MUST HAVE HIT MY HEAD HARDER THAN I THOUGHT. MY HEAD KILLS.
DEADPOOL!

THIS WHOLE OP TURNED INTO A COMPLETE AND UTTER CRAP-SHOW WHEN YOU SHOWED UP!

GO TO HELL, GORMAN.

AGENT PRESTON WAS AN *IDIOT* FOR TRUSTING YOU!

THAT'S NOT FAIR, SIR.

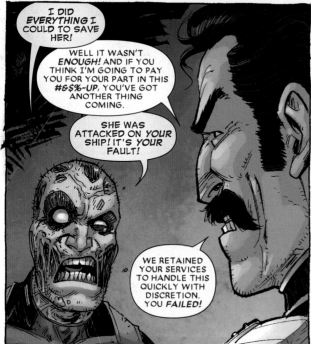

I DID *EVERYTHING* I COULD TO SAVE HER!

WELL IT WASN'T *ENOUGH!* AND IF YOU THINK I'M GOING TO PAY YOU FOR YOUR PART IN THIS #&$%-UP, YOU'VE GOT ANOTHER THING COMING.

SHE WAS ATTACKED ON *YOUR* SHIP! IT'S *YOUR* FAULT!

WE RETAINED YOUR SERVICES TO HANDLE THIS QUICKLY WITH DISCRETION. YOU *FAILED!*

I MUST-ACHE YOU A QUESTION: DO YOU THINK IT'S GOOD FOR YOUR LONG-TERM HEALTH TO MAKE ME AN ENEMY?

PAY ME MY MONEY.

OR YOU'LL WHAT?

I'LL KILL *YOU!* STARTING WITH YOUR DUMB 'STACHE!

YAAAARGH!

YOU'VE MADE A VERY POWERFUL ENEMY, DEADPOOL. YOU THINK S.H.I.E.L.D. IS SOME MICKEY MOUSE OPERATION?

YOU HAVE *NO* IDEA--

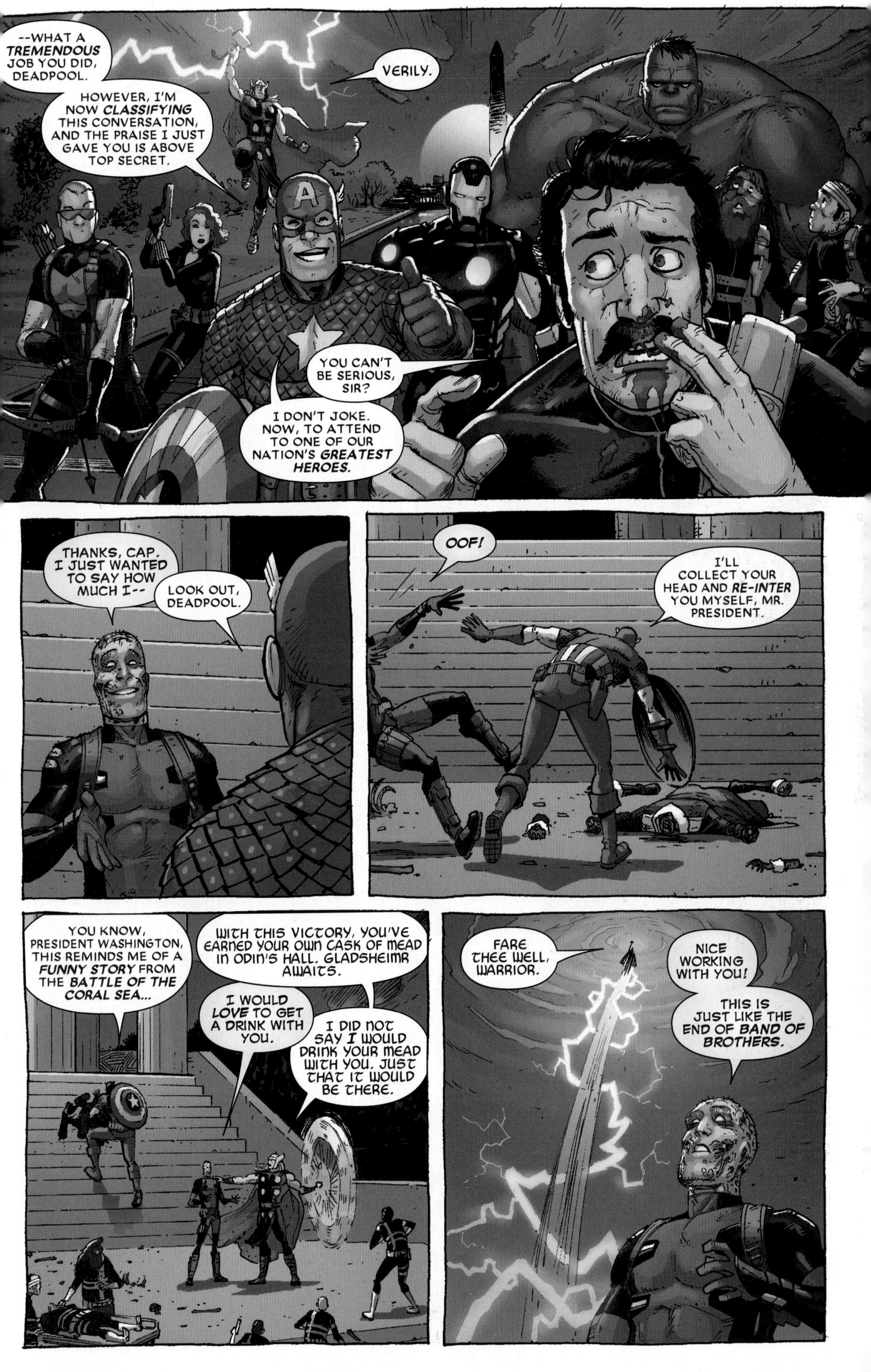
--WHAT A TREMENDOUS JOB YOU DID, DEADPOOL.
HOWEVER, I'M NOW CLASSIFYING THIS CONVERSATION, AND THE PRAISE I JUST GAVE YOU IS ABOVE TOP SECRET.
VERILY.
YOU CAN'T BE SERIOUS, SIR?
I DON'T JOKE. NOW, TO ATTEND TO ONE OF OUR NATION'S GREATEST HEROES.
THANKS, CAP. I JUST WANTED TO SAY HOW MUCH I--
LOOK OUT, DEADPOOL.
OOF!
I'LL COLLECT YOUR HEAD AND RE-INTER YOU MYSELF, MR. PRESIDENT.
YOU KNOW, PRESIDENT WASHINGTON, THIS REMINDS ME OF A FUNNY STORY FROM THE BATTLE OF THE CORAL SEA...
WITH THIS VICTORY, YOU'VE EARNED YOUR OWN CASK OF MEAD IN ODIN'S HALL. GLADSHEIMR AWAITS.
I WOULD LOVE TO GET A DRINK WITH YOU.
I DID NOT SAY I WOULD DRINK YOUR MEAD WITH YOU. JUST THAT IT WOULD BE THERE.
FARE THEE WELL, WARRIOR.
NICE WORKING WITH YOU!
THIS IS JUST LIKE THE END OF BAND OF BROTHERS.

YOU THINK YOUR FREAK-SHOW FRIENDS WILL KEEP ME FROM *DESTROYING* YOU?

UNFORTUNATELY, THEY'RE *NOT MY* FRIENDS, GORMAN. IF THEY WERE, THEY COULD SOMEHOW KEEP ME FROM *KILLING* YOU.

KEEP LOOKING OVER YOUR SHOULDER. BEFORE I'M DONE WITH YOU--YOU'RE GOING TO *BEG* TO PAY ME.

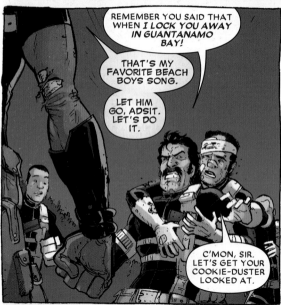

REMEMBER YOU SAID THAT WHEN *I LOCK YOU AWAY* IN GUANTANAMO BAY!

THAT'S MY FAVORITE BEACH BOYS SONG.

LET HIM GO, ADSIT. LET'S DO IT.

C'MON, SIR. LET'S GET YOUR COOKIE-DUSTER LOOKED AT.

THERE'S SOMETHING I *HAVE* TO TELL YOU.

YOU *LOVE* ME. I KNOW, MICHAEL.

NO! THANK ODIN.

BUT THIS IS SERIOUS. I TRIED TO SAVE PRESTON AND--

YOU *DID* WHAT YOU COULD.

NOW PLEASE STOP TALKING. MY HEAD KILLS.

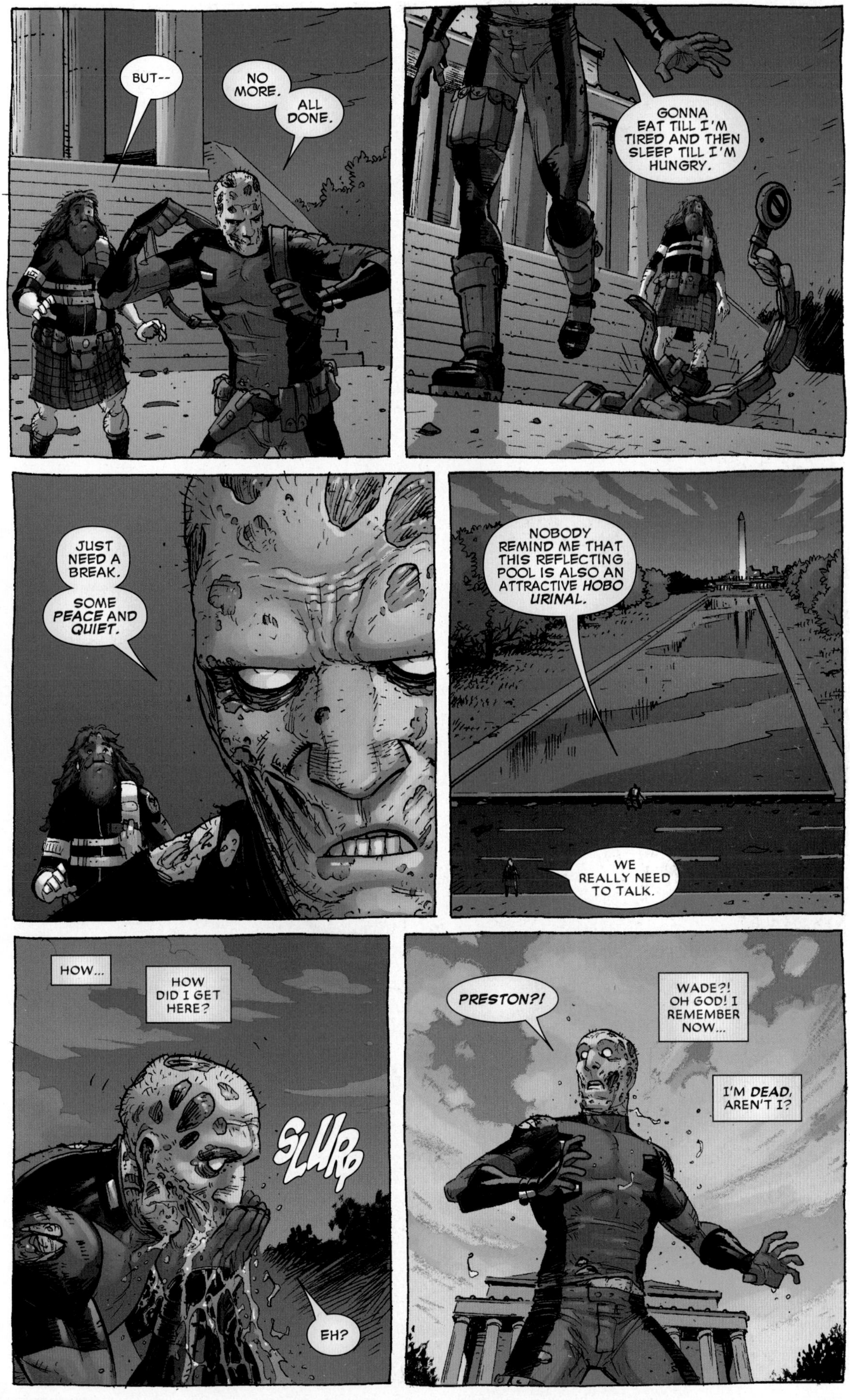
BUT--
NO MORE.
ALL DONE.
GONNA EAT TILL I'M TIRED AND THEN SLEEP TILL I'M HUNGRY.
JUST NEED A BREAK.
SOME *PEACE* AND *QUIET*.
NOBODY REMIND ME THAT THIS REFLECTING POOL IS ALSO AN ATTRACTIVE *HOBO URINAL*.
WE REALLY NEED TO TALK.
HOW...
HOW DID I GET HERE?
SLURP
EH?
PRESTON?!
WADE?! OH GOD! I REMEMBER NOW...
I'M *DEAD*, AREN'T I?

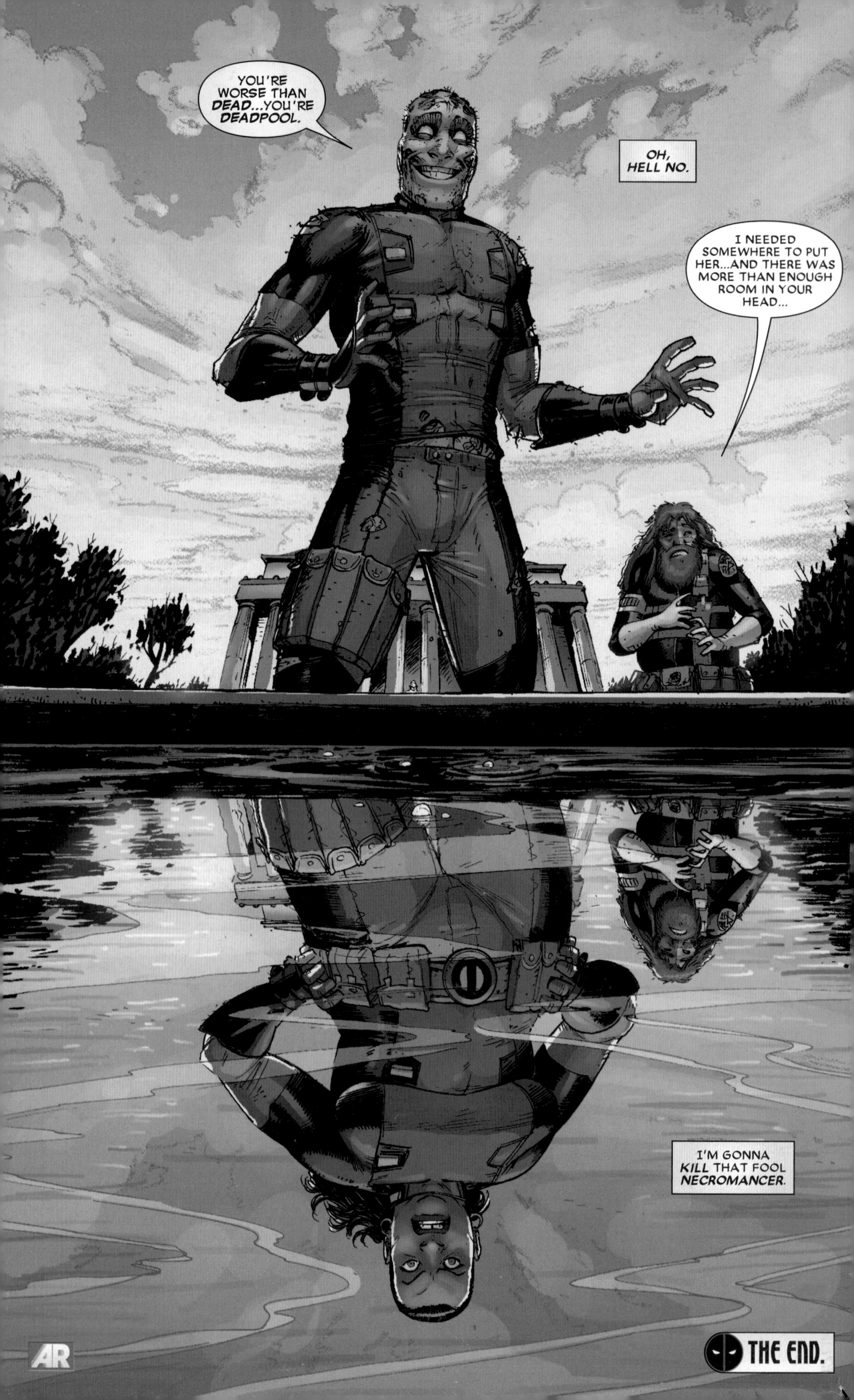
YOU'RE WORSE THAN DEAD...YOU'RE DEADPOOL.
OH, HELL NO.
I NEEDED SOMEWHERE TO PUT HER...AND THERE WAS MORE THAN ENOUGH ROOM IN YOUR HEAD...
I'M GONNA KILL THAT FOOL NECROMANCER.
THE END.

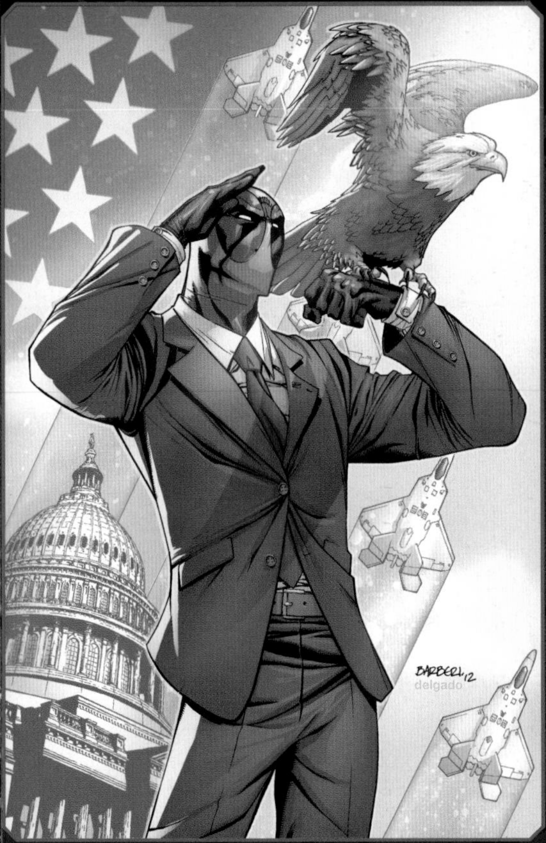
BARBERI '12
delgado

#1 HASTINGS VARIANT
BY **CARLO BARBERI & EDGAR DELGADO**

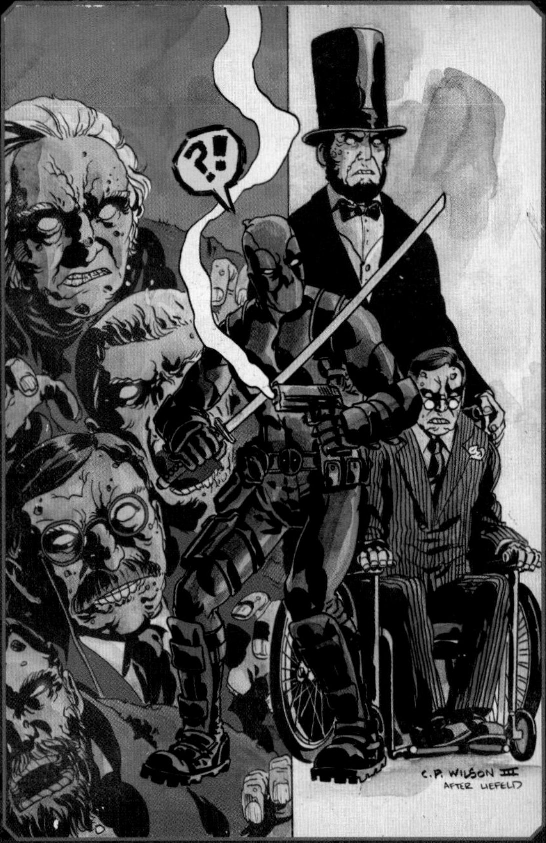
?!
C.P. WILSON III
AFTER LIEFELD

#1 LARRY´S COMICS VARIANT
BY **C.P.WILSON III**

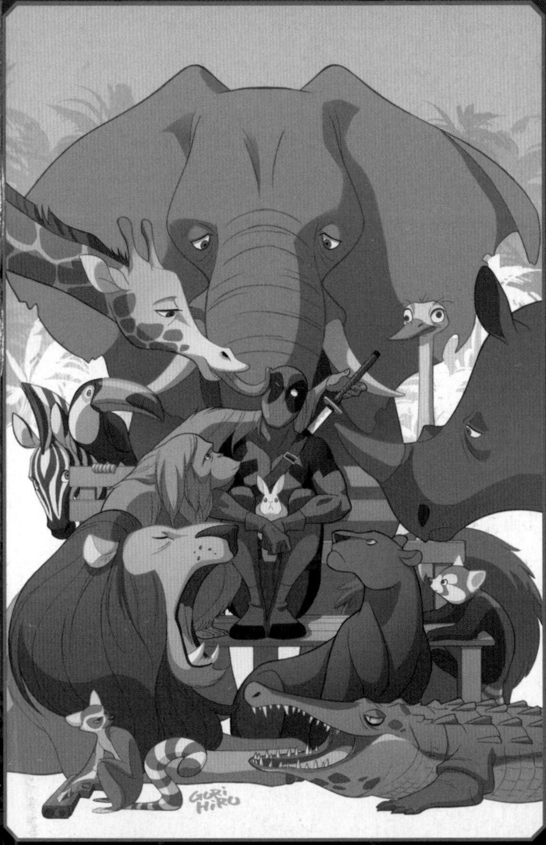
GURIHIRU

#2 VARIANT
BY **GURIHIRU**

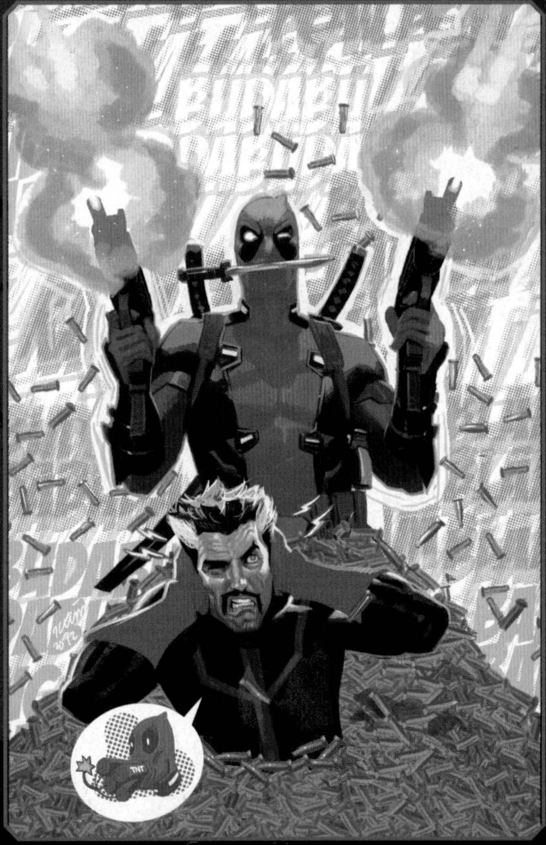
TNT

#3 VARIANT
BY **DANIAL ACUÑA**

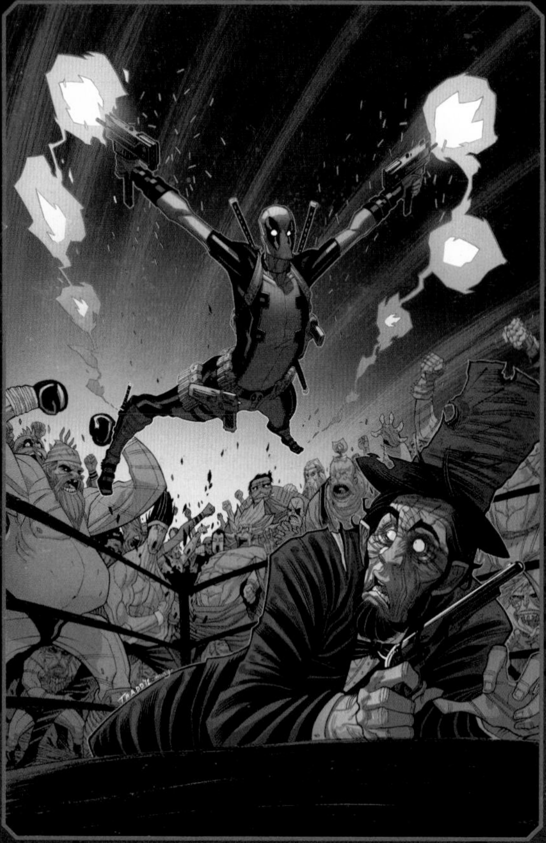

#4 VARIANT
BY **TRADD MOORE & MARTE GRACIA**

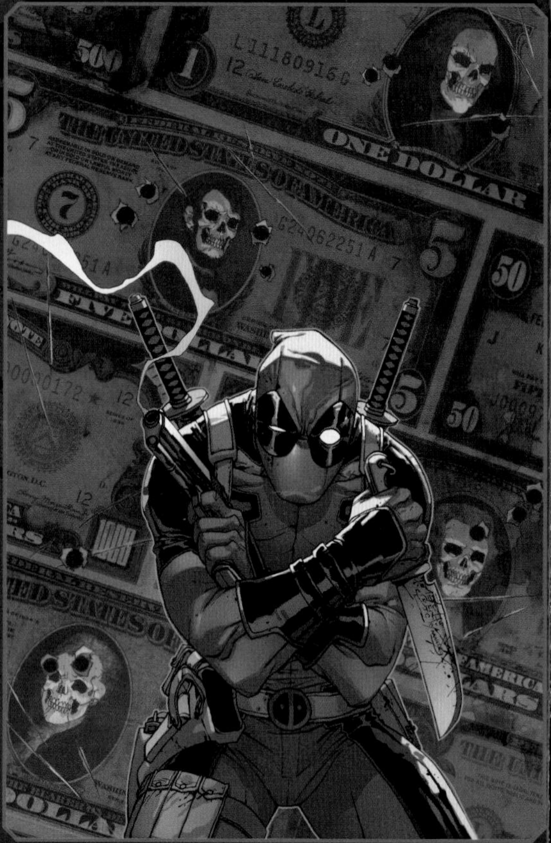
ONE DOLLAR

#5 VARIANT
BY **GIUSEPPE CAMUNCOLI & MARTE GRACIA**

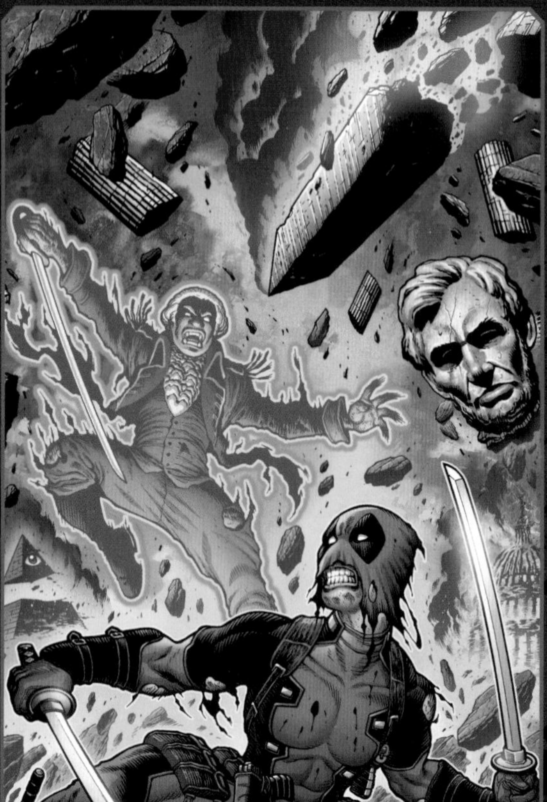

#6 VARIANT
BY **ADAM WARREN & GURU-EFX**

DEAR DEADPOOL

WRITE IN TO US AT OFFICEX@MARVEL.COM

DON'T FORGET TO MARK "OK TO PRINT"!

Welcome to the first issue of what is soon to be the top-selling letters page (that comes with a free comic book attached) published by Marvel Letters Pages. I know all you PoolHeads out there are just champing at the bit to write me, but... my first issue isn't even on sale yet! So, I had some of the slack-jaws over at Marvel send me some letters, just to bring you readers that awesome letter answering goodness right away!

Hi Pooly!
I have two very important questions to ask you! Where were you while the Avengers fought the X-Men? And do you miss taking care of a baby Nathan-Dayspring-Askani'son-Christopher-Summers-Soldier-X-Cable? Thank you so much for trying to save the world from evil zombie presidents!

Your buddy in the Bullpen,
Irene Lee

Hi Irene,
I spent AvX drinking beers and laughing with Uatu. That pituitary giant can hold his liquor.
As for babysitting, I don't miss it. When you're holding a baby, you always need a second or third hand. To reload a gun, or to stab away. It's especially tough to babysit for any kids after Cable. He was such a cute, durable baby. Human babies are so badly made. One drop and the panel fills with siren sound effects and screaming. No, thank you!! Unless you need me in a pinch to fill in, in which case my standard hourly rates apply.

-D

Dear Deadpool,
You've got plenty of muscles that you're always showing off to the ladies. I'd like to know what your daily workout routine is like? We have a Marvel push-up club here at the office and we can really use some inspiring words from the regenerating degenerate playboy!

Sincerely,
The Marvel Push-Up Club President and best looking guy in the Bullpen! Manny!

Manny, push-ups are for losers like Wolverine. Luckily, trimming the fat has always been easy for me. I use a sharp knife and usually prune back my spare tire a couple of times a year.

-D-Pooly

Dear Deadpool,
Deadpool, did you enjoy dressing up as Marvel Girl to distract Cable that one time? (It was a little weird, since she's his mom. Sort of.) Are there any other superheroine costumes you're dying to try on?

Jennifer Smith

Thanks for your thoughtful question. I have no problem slipping into women's clothes. In fact, keep your eyes peeled for me to use a cunning disguise to get within stabbing distance to the reanimated JFK.

-Dead

Dear Mr. Deadpool,
I hope this missive finds you well, I am the wraith of Franklin Pierce, the fourteenth president of these United States. I understand that we are to face one another in combat and I am writing to discuss a few ideas I had. History seems to have forgotten me, and I wanted to let you know that I'm open to be a recurring villain. Please don't hesitate to contact me for any reason.

Warmest regards,
Franklin Pierce

Your "missive" reads like a Nigerian scam letter.
No. Just no. I'm sending you back to hell, and it will probably be off-panel.
Oh, Spoiler!
That's it for this month, but...like my comic? Wanna tell me how great I am? Need advice on ladies? Write in to me! I'll set you straight.

-Deadpool

Hey, it's only the second time we've done our letters column and I'm already thinking it's a bad idea. Scratch that, horrible idea. Like it would be a horrible idea to let a bunch of bears loose on the deck of the Titanic and make everyone wear honey suits... Actually that Titanic bear thing sounds kind of fun, if you're gonna die anyway, might as well let bears eat you. I'm bad at analogies and things. Let's get started with this train-wreck.

Dear Mr. Pool,
The football soccer team my dad supports is Everton. They are from the British city of Liverpool. I think of this city, and I am fond of it. Therefore, even before I ever read any of your thrilling sequential narratives, I was disposed to like you. Or at least like 50% of you, which is about 47% more than I like most people. Actually, no. Rewind. I also think of Blackpool, which is basically Britain's answer to Vegas. By which I mean "It's British, therefore a bit rubbish." And that reminds me of a day out to Blackpool when I was a kid, when I spent the time walking down the beach, trying to catch fish with a plastic crisp packet. My dad made me go there, now I think about it, which makes me instantly less fond of him, so that "50% liking you" thing gets downgraded both from a falling in my regard for my parent and reminding me of bloody Blackpool.
What I'm dancing around saying is that me loving your adventures has several black marks against it before I even start reading. So me liking it as much as I do is a minor miracle, a triumph against adversity and AN ADVENTURE IN THE MIGHTY MARVEL MANNER in and of itself.
So well done, you. Hugs, but only hugs in a full-body condom suit, you sticky little thing, you.

Kieron Gillen

P.S. Wait--Pool also reminds me of the popular bar-room game pool, which I'm crap at, and suffer immense social shame when I'm forced to play. So I dislike you again. Sorry.

Dear English named person,
I only read part of your letter, basically the part where you liked our book. The other part made me fall asleep and wake up hating you. Thanks for liking our book and no thanks for the other stuff. Go sweep a chimney.

Love, Deadpool

Idiots,
You guys are idiots and you're going to get us all fired.
Matt Fraction
OK TO PRINT ON COVER ONLY

Fraction, I used to hate fractions, but you're the good kind. No argument about your letter. But you better hope I don't get fired because otherwise I think I'll hang out in your FF book.

DEADPOOL #1 is the answer to every prayer I didn't know I had in comics. Not only is the action well paced and incredibly well drawn, but I guess the writers(?) (Gerry Duggan and Brian Posehn) did an OK job too. I think deep down, we always knew that one day FDR would come back in his wheelchair and threaten to wipe out New York. And lucky for us Deadpool is the only one that can (wants) to take care of it. From the first page to the last page, DEADPOOL #1 has everything I ever wanted to see, including a pun regarding the aforementioned wheelchair. Stop reading this letter and order the damn book already.

Matt Mira

Matt,
Your letter confused me. And that's easy because I'm dumb. At first it's a complimentary note to the "creative" "team" involved and then it ends by telling me to stop reading the letter. Glad I didn't stop reading then because the next thing you do is tell me to order the book. Smarty-face, I don't have to order the book; I am the book. The book is me. Maybe you're the one that should order the book.

Love, the Deadpool

To Whom It May Concern,
I know Brian and Gerry personally and can't stress enough what a horrible idea it was to hire them to write for this book. You're turning over this great franchise to a character actor and his best friend. It's like giving X-Men to Jerry O'Connell and, well, some dude he hangs out with. Wait. That actually sounds pretty good. Could you kick off Brian and Gerry and get Jerry O'Connell and his friend to do Deadpool? Not only would you get a superior book, but also

a handsome face to show to fans.
I also wanted to say I love Tony Moore's work so far on the series.

Mike Drucker

Dearest Mike (rhymes with Frucker),
This letter made me so &*#@%$ mad. Can you believe the fat kid from 'Stand By Me' got to lie on top of Rebecca Romijn and put a baby inside her? Where is your god now? Any god?

Yours, Dead to the Pool

Dear Deadpool,
I have had the privilege of reading an advance copy of your new #1 (for free, sorry). I'll be honest, I came for my love of stocky, be-facial-haired creative teams (Duggan, Posehn, Moore & White = Grand Slam in that respect). But in the end – you won me over with bi-partisan willingness to re-kill our dead presidents from any side of the aisle*.
QUESTION TIME!
1) What does Taft smell like?
A tub of sadness and ham.
2) Did you ask any of them to sign your money? And if so – do you think that makes it increase in value?
This is a good idea. Where were you when this series was "written"? If I kill Duggan & Posehn do you want the job?
3) Have you considered gaining a few pounds and growing some sort of facial hair? I'd be really, really into that.
I could be into that. But be gentle, I don't want to find out the hard way that my healing factor can't mend a broken heart.
4) Would you be willing to appear on a variant cover for Gambit so that we can sell crazy Uncanny Avengers numbers, too?
Why do I get the sense that you're only interested in me for my huge numbers?

Love,
James "Bear-chaser" Asmus
LOL- Ass-mus!!

PS - Buy Gambit.
Real subtle.

*Note: I didn't say "either" side of the aisle because we've had presidents from more than our two, contemporary political parties. And I wanted to show off that knowledge, casually.
You know more than the idiots writing this slop. Now you're just running up the score.

Dear Deadpool,
Your mom.

Love,
Shumphries

My mom. She's so fat she ate the rest of your letter.
Yours, Deadpoolingly

Dear Editor,
I'm really excited about the relaunch of Deadpool, unfortunately I don't read. So my question is simply, how long do I have to wait until this is turned into a movie? And once it is, will I hate the lead actor?

Paul Scheer

Paul, here's what I know about the Deadpool movie: ███████ and it probably won't star ██████████ but if I had my way, they'd ███████████

DP

Wow, I have the best fans.
Suck it,
Deadpool

Dear Posehn,
Yes...%&$# YES!!
That is all.

Love,
James
South Gate, CA

P.S. Don't %&$# this up. We will come for your ass.
P.P.S You can definitely print this.

Thanks…%&$# Thanks!!!

Love,
Posehn

P.S. I'll %&$#ing try not to.
P.P.S We definitely won't.

So yeah, this new Deadpool series I can accept nothing but awesome things in future issues. You know the typical crazy run of the mill shenanigans our favorite merc with a mouth Wade Wilson does like highjacking old ladies cars, pantsing Wolverine, or staying up late and eating lots of candy. Pretty much you big wigs at Marvel just keep doing what you do best and make our good old friend Deadpool the same jerk that annoys every member of the Marvel Universe that they cannot stand him. By doing this I will continue to buy his comics!

Sincerely Yours,
Mark Anonia

Mark,
That's the plan. High-jacking candy, pantsing old ladies and eating Wolverine. Same old Deadpool. We can't wait to continue to take your money.

Sincerely,
Marvel big wigs

Dear Deadpool,
My teacher says being an awesome chimichanga-eating, regenerative ninja assassin is not a stable career. Can you please back me up?

Sincerely,
Nick

P.S. if you ever need a sidekick I am available, how does Deadkiddypool sound?

Dear Nick, your teacher would know a lot about career choices.
I'm sure you've heard that those that can't eat chimichangas and be a regenerative ninja assassin teach.

Deadpool

P.S. If it ever gets that bad, I'll let you know. Your name sounds horrible. Deadpocketpool isn't taken.

Hey, Deadpool how's it going?
I thought I'd write in to you because I figured it would be my best chance to get a letter printed. I mean thousands of people must write in to cool characters like Captain America and Spider-Man (oh ps Spidey called he wants his mask back). You however must get what, like one letter bi-monthly, so I figured "Hey," I'll write to you.
These guys you have writing your book seem to know what they're doing and the art is awesome. Enjoy it while it lasts 'cause they'll be given an A-level book when the big-wigs at Marvel catch on.
So, I know you're gonna print this letter cause you're gonna have to fill your letter page with something and I'll keep buying your book till I see it, then I'll take my money and start buying The Savage Wolverine (ouch). Don't take it personal though, bud, it was fun while it lasted.
If you make it back up to Canada again sometime stop by for a visit. I live in the third igloo on the left.

Luciano Marrai

Luciano,
Not sure we're gonna print your letter.

Kisses,
Deadpool

Dear Deadpool and/or Deadpool team,
My twin sister and I are huge fans. Like stupid killer huge in our fandom. Being Canadian, yeah, there's Wolverine, but there's something inherently sexy and exciting about having a Canadian hero like Deadpool. When we heard about the November new DPoodle team, we thought that this would be the best thing ever, but you never know. It's like taking a supermodel home, on the surface you think you're making a good decision and then ten minutes later, you're making up reasons why you have to be up early. We just read DEADPOOL #1 and loved it. Absolutely adored it. Now that's a Deadpool we would never kick out of bed. Seriously, please continue the amazing work and thank you for the panel with Wade's bum.

Sincerely,
Sylv & Jen

Dear Sylv and/or Jen,
Glad you loved it. Did you guys write this letter together? Are you joined at the head or a place that's less horrifying?

Sincerely,
DPoodle…Wait, DPoodle?!?

Dear Deadpool,
Longtime fan, lapsed reader. Thought I'd give the newest volume a shot, but was severely disappointed. Your jokes were ill timed and fell flat all throughout the first issue. It's almost as if you're being written by a moderately funny one-note comedian who played second fiddle to David Spade in a crappy 90's sitcom, you know? But it's like that guy couldn't even finish writing you the whole way through, so he got some other guy no one's heard of to help him, but that guy didn't really do anything to help, you know? Point being, Deadpool, you were way better when you were drawn without feet. And although your feet looked decent in this issue, I doubt Alan Moore will draw more than three issues. Too bad, an all too common misfire for you, Wade. Hopefully you kept all these guys away from your video game.

Best,
Jake Kolenberg
Buffalo, New York

Jake?
Moderately funny? One-note? Second fiddle? Why the personal attacks? Brian Posehn wants to know if you're really David Spade. Rick Remender? Bendis? That Fraction guy? Are you Brian's agent? His manager? His wife? Are you Brian? Are you a guy who can't draw feet? Anyway, glad you don't like the book.

Won't miss you,
Deadpool

Dear Deadpool,
Is that who's answering this letter? If this is Deadpool, I just wanted to let you know that while you do make me laugh, you are kind of a scumbag. A likeable scumbag, but a scumbag nonetheless. Your past volume was totally awesome and gave me something to look forward to every few weeks. My hat's off to Daniel Way, who stayed me throughout those years. I hope Brian and Gerry get out of this alive, and if that completely awesome, off the wall, mind-blowing, laugh-inducing first issue is any indicator, they won't. Not with their sanity intact at least. And don't think I'm getting soft on you, 'cause I'm not, you'll just take it all in and your ego will get even bigger, if that's possible. If you keep up the crazy antics and witty comments, who knows, you might actually become a good guy. But right now it's all about the dough, and I respect that, a man's gotta have priorities. How are you supposed to enjoy chimichangas and hot babes without money to earn by lying, cheating, killing, and wisecracking your way through the Marvel Universe?
And if it's Brian and Gerry reading this, I just wanted to let you guys know that that first issue was better than ever expected, and a great introduction to MARVEL NOW!. Please keep up the awesome work, it's great to have you guys on the Deadpool team! Shout outs to Tony Moore for the awesome art, can't get enough of it. As a huge Deadpool fan (and comic book nerd), thank you so much! Sorry for the lengthy message. See you in a few weeks!

Jake A Molz
Future employee of MARVEL Comics (hopefully)

P.S. Deadpool, would you like to explain how you and Thor got in that giant monster? Apparently something went down, cause Mjolnir totally wants to kiss you, I heard. Thor's probably jealous that's why he's all pissed at you and stuff.
P.S.S. You're still a scumbag.
P.S.S.S. Also, your mom's fat.

Jake,
Yes, it's me reading this, your unfriendly neighborhood Deadpool. I don't know who Brian and Gerry are. This is my real life. These things happen to me and some chimp writes them down and another more talented chimp draws them. Thanks for reading.

P.S. Ask Thor.
P.S.S. I'll take it.
P.S.S.S. Um, not cool. My mom is dead. She died of cake.

Mr. Deadpool,
Thank you for re-killing these evil presidents for us. Just so you know, James Madison was the President when the United States invaded Canada in 1812, if you want to get even.

All the best,
Chip Snyder
Bruce, Mississippi

Chip,
You're welcome. Stick around, Madison will get his. I'm gonna invade his ass Canadian style. Um… yuck.

DP

Helloooo Deadpool!
I heard you really, really care what I think about your new book so here it is:
You should really see a dermatologist. I think you have a small mole above your eye that should be checked out. Anywho, nice job taking down Stephen Hawking. That guy really deserved it. Oh, and be careful around those undead ex-presidents, they have diseases even you haven't heard of. Besides that, I really respect the way you take care of situations. You have a certain eloquence to your fighting, it's all like "AHHHH DIE!!!! I'LL KILL YOU ALL!!!". Subtle, ye effective. Keep up the good work!!!

-Connor Bir

Connor,
You're not good at compliments.

D to the P

Dear Deadpool,
When it comes to stewed prunes, are 3 enough? Are 4 too many?

Yur Buddie
DiRT

DiRT,
Nice names, were your parents annoying actresses or in a horrible band? How can you even ask me that? I've been on record. There are never enough prunes.

Dead "Never Enough Prunes" Pool

Dear Deadpool,
Boy, have I mentioned that you have got one/foine/badonk-a-donk. Oh, anywho, back to the point, congrats or the new series! I am so proud of you! Any chance you'll be getting another hero in the comic any time soon for a little team-up steam-up action?

- Sarah

Sarah,
Thanks for the nice words about my bottom. You should see it naked. On second thought…
You ask when I'm gonna team up with other heroes. There's talk of me and Spider-Man teaming up, I can't wait to get it on with him… I mean, nothing weird, just Spidey and I getting all sweaty, rolling around with some bad men Like, I said, nothing weird. I'd also like to team up with Iron Man. I'd love to get in his pants. I mean, wear his costume. I feel weird now.

Bye
Deadpool

Dearest Deadpool,
I've seen so much of your intestines these last few issues, I feel like I can just call you Wade. Wade, what was up with you almost putting the moves on She-Hulk?!? She's my babe!! Stay away!!
I tried to dress up like you for Halloween, but everyone thought I was just in a cheaply made Spidey suit? Have any quips I can use next time someone calls me "Second Rate Spider-Man?"

Stay Away From She-Hulk,
Daniel Bellay

Daniel, don't worry about She-Hulk and I. It will never work out with us. She just wants to do dirty stuff to my body and I want to talk about books and things and cuddle. As far as next time someone calls you a second-rate Spider-Man, maybe you should tell them to "shut up" or call them a "second-rate turd"… And then stab them in the face or chop up their guts with your katana. That should work.

Good luck,
Deadpool.

Dearest Deadpool,
It is with a warm feeling in my heart that I write this letter to you. I wish to inform you that by far is your book the best of Marvel Now! (is one exclamation point enough?!) Thor is a long haired roustabout compared to such a potent warrior as you. Agent Hulk? Why if someone is looking for power they need look no further then Deadpool!! However, I have a few missives after reading your debut issues:

1. Why aren't you on the Uncanny Avengers team? I bet someone as worldly as you could teach everyone a thing or two about human/mutant relations.
2. What's with all the dead presidents? I'm Canadian, you're Canadian, why don't you throw in some dead prime ministers for hijinks?
3. How'd you get Tony Moore to illustrate your exciting monthly adventures? You know what it takes for him to "relax" at night?
4. I see you're taking pity on Doctor Strange and giving him some work in the coming months; can we look forward to you helping any other similarly down on their luck heroes?

XOXO,
Matt Ferguson

Matt, thanks. Your words gave me a warm feeling. Warm feelings make me uncomfortable. Now I'll answer your questions.
1. I don't think I'll be joining the Uncanny Avengers while Rick Remender is writing them. Last time I worked with Rick he touched my bottom. He's a bad person. Good writer. Bad person.
2. I respect my prime ministers too much to kill them. And who would ever bring our dead prime-ministers back

to life to save Canada? Canada doesn't need to be saved, it's perfect. Especially now that America has the Bieb and Carly Rae Jepson.

3. Easy--I asked him. Relax? He's a hill-person so he probably hunts and eats stuff off his land.

4. Down on their luck? They're heroes, not hobos. I will be teaming up with a couple of hobos later today, we're fighting a can of pork and beans.

You can keep your Xs and Os,
Deadpool

Sup D-Dawg,
Couldn't help but notice you kinda KILLED an elephant in issue 2, having any troubles from PETA? 'Cause killing an elephant is kind of a big deal (and an awkward one at that). Also, the speedos are a good look! Have you ever thought of becoming a Calvin Klein model? That way you are sure to get some action from Sue and Emma.

Sincerely,
Your fan (an elephant loving fan also...)
William Gordon

William,
I don't remember killing an elephant. The way I remember it is he kinda got in the way of Teddy Roosevelt and I, collateral damage. Two tons of stinky collateral damage. And please quit thinking about me in speedos. Model? Is that a joke about my face? Do you want to get stabbed a bunch?

DP

Dear Deadpool,
I must admit that your intestines are my favorite intestines in the whole world. Just the thought of them makes me smile. But since they're outside your body so often do they ever dry out?

Kathryn Jones

Kathryn,
My intestines are real jerks lately--every time I get into a little scuffle they want to climb out of my body and run away. Where is the loyalty?

Deadpool

Dear Mr. Pool,
Candied yams. Chimichangas. Lube. Diet soda. Just needed a place to write my shopping list.

Love,
Hugs and kisses,
Eddie Dugan

P.S. Where do you find the time to star in a comic, work on a video game and still respond to fans?

Mr. Dugan,
That sounds like my grocery list except for one item, diet soda? Uchh!!

Deadpool

P.S. I don't have time to respond to fans. I let the writers pretend to be me, they've got nothing going on.

Dear Deadpool,
Hello to you from a big fan. My name's Vicky. And let me tell you, you are one gorgeous mercenary. You also must get a lot of flattery, but that's besides the point. Anyways, I'd like to bring up a certain masked vigilante many people seem to be so fond of, and I'm sure you are too. Spider-Man. Tell me, what do you think of this relationship between the two of you and how do you feel about Spideypool? (If a definition is needed, Spideypool = Spider-Man x Deadpool. You and Spidey together.)

Did you know people write stories about you two? You should read one sometimes. They are fascinating. I am also a big fan of this pairing. And a big fan of you and Spider-Man in general. On a scale of one to ten, one being the lowest and ten being the highest, you are a number eleven. You are in my top five list, for sure. But there I go again with the flattery. I can't help it. You are amazing. I believe it's time for me to finish this letter up. I hope you have a fantastic day.

Sincerely yours,
One of your many number one fans that go by the name of Vicky

Vicky, you are a bad person. You're up there with Rick Remender and Pol Pot. I looked up images for spideypool on the internet. I have been throwing up ever since. I threw up on three different computers looking at drawings of Spidey and I doing unnatural things. I have to wrap up this letter so I can go back to throwing up at pictures of us.

Deadypool

Dear Deadpool, Pooly, Wadey, Baby!
Will you marry me?

lots of love,
Keeping my fingers crossed ;)
Jane Kasteelen xxx
Sunderland - England :)

P.S. Please??

Jane,
I'm not the marrying type. That said, send me pics. Of you. No spideypool pics, please. I'm out of throw up.

Deadpool

I liked DEADPOOL part 3. I liked the helicopter cutting the zombie up and also when Deadpool punched the other zombie. Deadpool has a mask like Spider-Man and swords. My favorite characters are Wolverine, Deadpool, Transporter 2 and the black man in MATRIX. Also Carly Rae Jepson is hot. If there are Deadpool stickers can you please send me one thank you.

Patton Oswalt

Parton, thanks, buddy. I'm a fan of you too. I like when you make faces and yell stuff. You're funny when you yell stuff. I also like how tiny you are. You're like a tiny taquito I could put in my pocket to nibble on and laugh at any time I want. I'll trade you stickers when you make Parton Osweird stickers.

Deadpool

Hey Team Deadpool!
I just started to read issue three. I got as far as the start of the recap page. Your General Hospital reference and the suggestion that Carly needs a smack down has earned you a full calendar year of my purchasing this book regardless of content. I am going to read the comic now.

Martin Kinney

Martin, glad you liked the reference and happy you'll read the book now. We'll have to thank the old lady at Marvel that writes the recap pages.

Team Deadpool

Dear Deadpool,
Have you ever been so mad you've fired lasers outta your eyes and then punched Hulk, in his Hulky junk? Also, lasers.

Sincerely,
Jack W.

Jack,
Maybe I did. And maybe Hulk smashed my genitals into paste. A lot of paste. Maybe. Not the lasers though.

Deadpool

Hey, Deadpool, astig ka 'pre! (It's Tagalog for, "You're bad-ass, man!").
This is my first time picking up a Deadpool comic because in the 90s when I was in elementary school, I saw Deadpool for the first time, and asked my comic savvy friend who you were, and he just said, "Oh, that guy dies then comes back to life." So, it didn't really make me follow you then. (Shame on me, sorry Deads!) But anyway, I'm a soon to be doctor now, and with Marvel Now!, this is my chance for a fresh start to know you, and you're pretty cool.

There's just something about the way you project yourself and your antics that makes me see beneath all the insanity and humor, and appreciate the hardworking character. That just makes me want to support you as a character. (Pretty weird because this is the first time, as I have always supported writers or artists, and actually writing directly to a character is also a first and is pretty weird too, haha!) Anyway, to the creative team behind you, KUDOS, you guys have made another fan who will stick with your comic! :) Props to Tony Moore for being nice at the 2012 NYCC! So there-- more power Deads! And let's thank my Brod Carl Uy for suggesting Marvel Now! and making me a reignited Marvelite! So until Deadpool runs out of words to say, MAKE MINE MARVEL! :D

'Topher Constantino
Philippines

Topher, you too are bad-ass, man. I'm glad your friend suggested you check out Marvel Now! As far as your friend in the '90s, I'm glad you ditched that guy. Stick around, Doc, because things are about to really go insane in this book. At least that's what the creative team that writes my words told me. MAKE MINE 'TOPHER!

Deadpool,
Seriously, get this out of your system and hand it on to a more competent team. This just isn't entertaining in any way, shape or form.
Safe to print, safe to print off and give yourself a vicious paper-cut and safe to use to write your letter of resignation on the reverse.

Droo

Droo, I'm sorry you don't find it entertaining. Is that at all like the word "entertaining"? Thanks for your mean-spirited letter. I'm glad you hate our book enough to spend several minutes of your life writing and sending it to us. I spent less time writing this.
If you are reading this, please give yourself a vicious wrap-the-page around-your-fist-and-punch-yourself-in-the-face and write a formal apology on the reverse.

Love, Team Deadpool

Dear Deadpool,
I've been a fan of yours for a few years now, and I love the new comic. Daniel Way was good, these new guys are better. I really think they've tapped into the you from the 90's. I actually understand all the references! I'm super-psyched to be a part of the Deadpool Nation, and I am really looking forward to the game and movie. MERC WITH A MOUTH 4LIFE!

Regards,
Cody Kovach

Cody, you rule!! Thanks for the nice words, brother. If I gave you Droo's address (see above) would you deliver him a katana enema?

Your buddy, DP

Dear Deadpool,
May I please have your arm? I mean, it will just grow right back. So, really, it would be like nothing happened. Except I would have a dismembered arm. Your arm. So, wanna go for it?

David Norton

David, it's yours. Unfortunately, you didn't give a return address. So I just left it in a paper bag at the Marvel offices. I hope it's still there.

Your one-armed buddy,
Deadpool

Dearest Deadpool,
Thanks for speaking to me during issue # 3 and letting me know about the necromancer's misguided sense of patriotism. I guess even Ben Franklin can't hear me. But you can, so I want you to answer my question. Where was checkers (*nixon's dog)? Im a big history buff and I saw the cover for issue #3 but checkers wasn't even in the story. What gives, are you afraid that PETA would come after you for killing a dead dog?

Thank you kindly,
Mudit Sharma

Dear Mudit,
Checkers didn't make the book. We have a lot of dead presidents to kill in six books so their pets didn't make the cut. Deadpool isn't afraid of PETA, wait til you read what I do to a bunch of... Hold on, are PETA reading this?

Deadpool

Dear Mr. Deadpool,
I can honestly say that I haven't really been a fan of comic books, but upon picking up the first issue of Deadpool and seeing you electrocute FDR after jumping out of the large Godzilla-esque monster, I purchased the subsequent issues without a second thought. Your quest to re-kill the zombified ex-presidents is one that I support 100 percent. There need to be more heroes like you willing to save the country by tarnishing the images of the historical figures who brought it to "greatness" (for lack of a better word). Also, if Jimmy Carter had been dead at the time that this was published, it would be great if there were somehow a rabbit involved in his re-killing.

Best Regards,
Matthew Tetska

Matthew, thanks. Can I ask what you were dong in a comic book shop if you're not a fan of comical books? The hot ladies? The scintillating conversation? The hot ladies?

Kisses,
Deadpool

Dear Deadpool,
I love you as much as I love my Sundays. Come spend one Sunday with me, and I'll cook for you.

Much love,
Anne

Anne, a hot lady reading my book? What are you cooking and where do you live? I love free food as much as I love disemboweling someone. Man, now I'm really hungry.

Yours truly,
Deadpool

Dear Deadpool,
Having loved your recent team-up with Doctor Strange, I was wondering if a team-up with the the Defenders is on the cards? I think you and Namor would get along swimmingly.

Keep up the good work,
Rhona Hamilton

Rhona, another lady? Yay me!! I'm glad you enjoyed my adventures with the good Doctor. I'm always down for a good team-up. I've been bugging Namor for months but he doesn't follow me on Twitter so I can't direct message him. Wait, swimmingly? BOO!!!

Keep up the wordplay,
Deadpool

To Whom It May Concern,
Will Deadpool also be fighting zombie Confederate President Jefferson Davis, or are Gerry & Brian intent on ignoring one of the greatest tragedies our nation ever faced? Please let me know before I buy this book.

Mike Drucker

Mike, sadly no. He didn't make the cut. I asked Brian and Gerry and they said our greatest tragedy is Hostess Cakes closing. Buy the book anyway.

Deadpool

Mr. Deadpool,
I am so glad that you gave President Lincoln the bashing he desired. I mean, he did shoot you in the head twice. What an &%$#*%! Did you have cool fantasies about She-Hulk again after the second time that was shown in the comic? I did have a question about your wrestling match with Abe though, how did Lincoln's hat stay on during the entire fight? Your mask came off but his hat didn't? It doesn't make very much sense. Anyway, keep up the good work and happy hunting!

Yours Truly,
John Ray Roberts

John, doesn't everybody have "cool" fantasies about She-Hulk? Our book isn't MAX, so Gerry and Brian actually pulled back a little. The stuff in their head would make Larry Flint throw up. As far as Lincoln's hat, it stayed on because we wanted it to. Let's say all the zombie goo on Lincoln's head kept his hat glued to it. Does that make sense? Who cares?

Love,
Mr. Deadpool

Hey Private Wilson!
I'm an Air Force Cadet and I'm trying to work hard at my physical exams. I am currently good enough to pass, but I want to build more muscle so I can get a better grade and have a nice, toned-looking body likes yours. What is your daily workout routine? How about your diet, does it match your work out? Do you suggest a work out partner or should I go solo? I'm glad to hear from you.

Your Favorite Cadet,
Jon

Jon, glad you asked me about workout routines and not the writers. Those guys haven't seen a gym since they barely made it out of high school. As for me, I do P90X for two hours when I wake up, then I eat thirty raw eggs. After that I do Insanity for three hours and I eat four chickens and a fetal pig for lunch. Protein, protein, protein. I end my day with a six hour run, Tae Bo, Zumba and Sweating to the Oldies. Then I murder and eat a cow. If you can find a partner that can hang with that, marry them.

Kisses, Deadsy.

P.S. Don't you owe me some money? What ever happened to that?

After that advice, you owe me money.

Dearest Deadpool,
I recently wrote a term paper about you for my English class. The topic was "Southern Literature" and I figured that you're from Canada and that is south of the North Pole, so it's fair game, right? Wrong. At least that's what my professor said. He also said comics are not a proper form of literature and that your comics sound particularly awful.

Needless to say, I failed that class and will have to take it again next semester. Do you have any tips on how I can pass next time?

Regards,
James Johnson

James, don't sweat English class, my writers didn't. How to pass? Start bringing a katana to class and make sketchy faces at your professor. That should work. If it

doesn't swing the katana around your head and scream "don't fail me" when the class is really quiet. Good luck!

Love,
Dead to the Pool

Dear Deadpool,
Do you ever do birthday parties? Cause if you did, the white dress Monroe act would be a hit.

KEEP IT METAL,
Isaac

It's not white anymore. It's got JFK all over it.

P.S. Ever tried reheating chimichangas with that magic sword, you know, just to get that ZAAAAP flavor?

I lost the sword before I could shove it in anything that I put in my mouth, but it was on my mind.
Dear Deadpool,
For some reason, you were extremely attractive as Marilyn Monroe. Not gonna lie to myself. In fact, if I dry clean your dress, will you go to prom with me as Marilyn? I know it's sudden but think about it.

Best wishes,
Joseph Munguia
Rancho Cucamonga, California

I wish I could, but I'm getting that dress dry cleaned for a hot date that night with your dad.

XO
DP

P.S. I promise not to hold you too tight.

Is that a Bieber song?

Deadpool?

Yes?

Could I have your babies? They'd be useful assets to my army.

No?

Forever a fanboy,
Luke Molloy

Wait, you're a dude? How would we have babies? Well, I guess we could try if you're game.

P.S Keep the Marylin Munroe dress. It's a good look.

Have you met Joseph Munguia, of Rancho Cucamonga?

Dearest Deadpool,
Your stories are giving me hives. Does that outfit of yours ever get washed? I know you'd like me to comment on the recent occurrences of your action adventures, but I simply cannot get over how absolutely disgusting and dreadful it must be for Agent Preston to smell you on a consistent basis. May I suggest some body soaps or perhaps a gentle detergent?

Daniel Bellay

Well, now Agent Preston gets to ride inside now. Anything to add, Preston?
Leave me out of this nonsense.

Dear Deadpool,
That was an awesome montage with u killing dead presidents, and I used ur advice to listen to Pantera 5 Minutes Alone, great idea. Plz have more badass killing montages and plz kill hydrabob for me.

Love ur Fan,
Raed

Raed, if I ever did kill Hydra Bob I'd recommend "Let's Hear it for the Boy" from the Footloose soundtrack for the montage.

Yours, Deadpool

Croeso (Hello) Team DP,
I just want to thank you guys. Not only are you providing gorgeous art, killer action and all the funnies - you're also providing quality AR content. For £2.10 of my British money not only do I get a great comic, but I also get to see Posehn's sweaty naked body, hear Deadpool's voicemail and get the history of Wade from a small cat. Keep it comin'!

Hwyl am nawr (bye for now)
Jack Cooper, Wales

Jack,
Brian has a favor to ask -- tell the wig-wearing ponces in your government to let him back into your country. Brian

didn't know you could get banned for nuding up in the Marvel Universe.

Dear Spider-Man,
Your swords and guns are cool and all, but why don't you use your web sling abilities and wall climbing to catch the bad guys anymore? Also what happened to your skin?

Your friendly neighborhood fan,
Chad Ehrhardt

Chad, I'm not Spider-Man, so that kills your questions. Thanks for taking the time from your busy schedule of not reading the covers of your comical books.
Ehrhardt? Any relation to Steve Ernhardt, from my high school?

P.S. how did you survive two gun shots to the head from Lincoln??

He's a &#$$% with a clown gun.

Dear Deadpool,
What is a Deadpool? What does that even mean? Seriously you have a horrible name, bro. I can't believe you have a monthly publication with such a ridiculous name. You might want to get that fixed. To that end I suggest the following replacement names:
1. The Ugly Death
2. Senior Repulsive
3. Bad Odor-man
4. The Rambler
5. Deadnizzle

Those bozos you have locked in a cage working on your book are doing a sufficiently adequate job of keeping me entertained. Do not replace them for at least another issue.

Regards,
Amin Mossavat
Toronto, ON, Canada

Thanks for writing in and for your constructive criticism about my name, Amin Mossavat. That really rolls off the tongue.

P.S. Congratulations on overcoming your numerous mental disabilities to achieve some small success.

Like Patton Oswalt!

P.P.S. Do you even lift bro? Because you look like you don't. Just saying.

Bro, don't even. Don't. Bro.

Hey you with the face,
I am a long time DP fan (I enjoy Deadpool as well). I had serious doubts about the new men behind the man behind the mask behind the uh... shaddup. I can proudly say that any doubts were shoved hastily up my [explicit deleted] as this issue delivered on all accounts. I love what Way did with the book (for the most part) and was skeptical about a comedian writing the book. Of course Posehn does have a morbid sense of humor that fits perfectly with the material. Long story short. I apologize and am ready for this new (improved?) Deadpool. I do miss the multiple thought balloons... oh well. Half damp kitten socks.

Sincerely,
David C. Molle

David, half damp kitten socks? Sorry you had a stroke at the end of your letter. Maybe a healing factor would come in handy. Oh well, Martian sandwich monkey foot.

Sincerely, Pooly

Dear DEADPOOL writers --
I liked the last issue with the monkey and space and the President fight. Deadpool is awesome. There should be a story where he's fighting a guy with a chain and then he whips the chain at the guy and says back on the chain gang lol. Do you have Deadpool temp tattoos I would like some.

Signed,
Patton Oswalt

P.S. I saw the Iron Man Three preview it has Gandhi in it.

Oh, hey, Patton! We were just talking about you. Haven't you sent us a letter before? Aren't you an actor? Don't you have a show to ruin? Glad you like the book. We don't know who Gandhi is. Is he one of the Guardians Of The Galaxy?

Love, your friends,
the Deadpool writers

DEADPOOL

AR INDEX